the Unofficial Guide® to Starting a Business Online

Second Edition

Jason R. Rich

WILEY

Wiley Publishing, Inc.

For general information on our other products and services or to obtain technical sup-port please contact our Customer Care Department within the U.S. at (800) 762-2974, outside the U.S. at (317) 572-3993 or fax (317) 572-4002.

Wiley also publishes its books in a variety of electronic formats. Some content that appears in print may not be available in electronic books. For more information about Wiley products, please visit our web site at www.wiley.com.

Library of Congress Control Number: 2005936654

ISBN-13: 978-0-471-74838-0
ISBN-10: 0-471-74838-2

Manufactured in the United States of America

10 9 8 7 6 5 4

Second Edition

Book design by Melissa Auciello-Brogan
Page creation by Wiley Publishing, Inc. Composition Services

Acknowledgments

I'd like to thank Pam Mourouzis and Donna Wright at Wiley for making the second edition of this book possible and for offering me guidance as the manuscript was created.

I'd also like to thank all of the people who agreed to be interviewed for this book and who provided me with valuable information to pass on to you.

Some of the companies that were instrumental in providing information for this book include: Yahoo!, Google, ClickIncome.com, Galaxy Internet Services, Louisdog.com, SimplyCheap.com, JOriginals.com, AnglersVice.com, OnlyOneCreations.com, Fridgedoor.com, eBay.com, Adobe, Macromedia, and Microsoft Corporation.

Finally, thanks to you, the reader, for picking up this book. It's my greatest hope that the information you're about to read will be useful in pursuing your own goals and objectives for launching an online-based business venture or e-commerce website.

See you in cyberspace!

Contents

J ason R. Rich (jr7777@aol.com, www.jasonrich.com) is the bestselling author of more than 30 books, as well as a freelance writer and newspaper/magazine columnist.

Rich has written a number of books on business-related issues, including: *Make Your Paycheck Last, Brain Storm: Tap Into Your Creativity to Generate Awesome Ideas and Remarkable Results, The Unofficial Guide to Earning What You Deserve, The Unofficial Guide to Marketing Your Business Online, Job Hunting For the Utterly Confused* and *First Job, Great Job: America's Hottest Business Leaders Share Their Secrets.*

Rich has also written a series of popular, family-oriented travel guides for Adams Media's *Everything* series and is the author of *American Idol Season 3—All Access* (Prima/Random House) and *American Idol Season 4—The Official Behind-The-Scenes Fan Book* (Prima/Random House), the official books about America's hottest televised talent competition, *American Idol.* During Season 4 of *American Idol,* Rich served as the senior editor of *American Idol: The Magazine.*

Two of his most recently published books are *The Bachelor's Guide to Life* (iUniverse) and *2002 High Paying Jobs You Can Get Without a 4-Year Degree* (Entrepreneur Press).

Rich lives just outside of Boston, Massachusetts, with his new puppy Rusty (www.MyPalRusty.com) and also works as a public relations and marketing consultant to companies in a wide range of industries.

S o, you're interested in starting an online-based business or creating an online presence for your established brick-and-mortar business? As you're about to discover, there's no better time to get started!

When the first edition of this book was published in 1999, the first sentence of the Introduction read, "According to *Internet Computing*, 'Consumer shopping over the Web will be a $6 to $8 billion dollar business by the year 2000.'"

Let's jump forward to the present. As of June 2005, the U.S. Census Bureau of the Department of Commerce announced that the estimate of U.S. retail e-commerce sales for the *first quarter* of 2005 was $19.8 billion, an increase of 6.4 percent from the fourth quarter of 2004. (Traditional retail sales grew only 1.5 percent for the same period.) During the first quarter of 2005, e-commerce–based retail sales represented 2.2 percent of all retail sales in the U.S.

Internetnews.com estimated that in 2005 alone more than 202.1 million new personal computers will be sold. In 2004, an estimated 187 million personal computers were sold. Many of these computers will ultimately be connected to the Internet, with users eager to surf and shop online.

Furthermore, sales of Smartphone devices (wireless devices capable of surfing the Internet, from companies such as Nokia, PalmOne, and RIM) also continued to surge in 2005. The latest figures from Canalys (a leading provider of consulting and market analysis, www.canalys. com) show that more than 10 million smart mobile devices were shipped globally during the first quarter of 2005.

With so many new online shoppers, are you wondering what they're actually buying online these days? According to ClickZ (www.clickz.com) and Neilsen/NetRatings, as of February 2005, the top 15 online retail categories, based on average order size, were the following:

1. Computer hardware
2. Event and movie tickets
3. Automotive
4. Office supplies
5. Consumer electronics
6. Child/baby care products
7. Sporting goods and outdoor activity items
8. Home and garden supplies
9. Shoes and athletic footwear
10. Flowers, greetings, and specialty gifts
11. Computer software
12. Jewelry and watches
13. Health, wellness, and beauty supplies
14. Apparel (clothing) and accessories
15. Toys, games, and hobby supplies

These days, there are hundreds of thousands (perhaps more) e-commerce websites and online-based businesses in existence. Some are run by multibillion-dollar corporations, but many are operated by people just like you, who have created an online business as a hobby, as a part-time job, or as a full-time career.

As a soon-to-be online business operator, it's important to understand that you'll be facing a lot of competition in cyber-space. However, there's still an incredible opportunity for you to earn profits, especially if your online business offers something that's new, unique, and not readily available at your local mass-market retailer or superstore. You'll soon discover that your best chance for success is to target a very specific niche market with your online business.

After all, when you launch your online business, you'll be competing with traditional retailers such as Wal-Mart and the stores at your local mall, plus all of the other well-established online retailers. Finding items or services to sell online that are unique, customized, one-of-a-kind, hand-crafted, collectible and/ or that target a niche market may seem like a challenge at first, but you'll discover this type of product offers the best profit potential in cyberspace. Of course, people also continue to make money selling books, CDs, and consumer electronics, for example, but they face a much higher level of competition.

On Thanksgiving Day 2004 (the busiest shopping day of the year in cyberspace), Hitwise, Inc. reported that on the Web, the 10 busiest online shopping-related sites included the following:

1. eBay.com
2. Amazon.com
3. Wal-Mart.com
4. BestBuy.com
5. Target.com
6. Dell.com
7. CircuitCity.com
8. Sears.com
9. Yahoo! Shopping (http://shopping.yahoo.com)
10. BizRate.com

If you're enticed by all of these statistics, you believe cyber-space offers viable business opportunities for you, and you're someone with an entrepreneurial spirit looking to capitalize on this fast-growing marketplace, you're reading the right book!

Okay, enough with the boring (albeit impressive) stats. The rest of this book will get down to business and help you design, launch, and manage your online venture.

Beware of online scams

As a Web surfer, your e-mail inbox probably gets bombarded by a constant inflow of offers from companies doing business on the Web. Aside from the countless invitations to visit the newest porn websites, you've probably also received dozens of business opportunity offers via e-mail, explaining how you, too, can become rich using your computer to sell products or services on the Internet.

Yes, there are many business-opportunity scams being hyped in cyberspace. The truth is, however, that if you're careful and make well-educated decisions, the World Wide Web offers an incredible chance for virtually anyone to establish a successful online business. For a far lower investment than starting most other types of companies, such as a retail store or traditional mail-order business, you can establish an online business (or e-commerce website) and begin selling products or services on the Internet.

The Unofficial Guide to Starting a Business Online, 2nd Edition, was written for the average computer owner who is interested in setting up a small-business or e-commerce site on the Internet. This book will guide you through the entire process of planning your online-based business venture, creating your website, promoting and marketing your business, and managing the day-to-day operations of your business. If you already operate an established traditional business, this book will help you expand into cyberspace by helping you create an online presence.

If you're interested in starting an online-based business or e-commerce site (which involves actually selling goods or services online), you'll need to make many choices when it comes to actually planning and building your website. This book explores a handful of the options available to you in terms of using off-the-shelf software and online-based turnkey solutions for creating and managing your online business venture. A turnkey solution refers to a company or service that offers you all of the tools and resources you need, often for a monthly fixed rate, to create, launch, and manage your online business. Turnkey solutions for creating an e-commerce website are offered by companies like Yahoo! and eBay. You'll learn more about these and other inexpensive turnkey solutions later in this book.

Keep in mind, the focus of this book is to help small start-up companies or small, established businesses create a presence on the Web.

You've probably heard a lot of hype about the incredible moneymaking opportunities available to anyone selling virtually anything online. If done correctly, it's true that almost anything can be sold successfully on the Web; however, it's also important to remember that many of the online business success stories we're all familiar with (Amazon.com, Yahoo!, eBay.com, and so on) . were all backed by millions of dollars in initial investment capital.

Even if you have an incredible and totally original idea for an online business venture, it's vitally important to have realistic expectations when you go online. It's extremely rare for people immediately to flock to a new online business of any type and begin placing orders, especially if the online-based business isn't a spin-off of an already successful traditional business with a strong reputation in the offline business world.

This book will help someone with an idea for creating an online business transform that idea into what will hopefully become a viable, moneymaking business venture. When you hear reports about people from all walks of life launching their own online businesses, what exactly does this mean? Can someone like you actually create and operate a successful online business?

The buying habits of consumers are changing quickly. It's no longer just highly computer literate, well-educated, high-income people who shop online. Home computers have gotten cheaper, and millions upon millions of people from all income levels are gaining access to the Web. A growing number of these

Web surfers also now have high-speed broadband or DSL Internet connections, plus they're willing to make purchases online. As a result, many individuals, just like you, have found success establishing online-based businesses catering to niche markets that larger companies aren't reaching—online *or* offline.

People interested in working on a part-time basis from home to supplement their incomes are among the fast-growing group of online entrepreneurs. Homemakers, senior citizens, people with physical disabilities, students, and those with an entrepreneurial spirit are also among the people launching new online business ventures every day. In addition, people looking for a career change and those who want to become their own bosses and set their own work schedules have found success launching online businesses. In reality, there is no stereotypical success story for online-based business operators. Even people with minimal computer skills but excellent business ideas have achieved success.

So could you be successful launching and managing an online-based business? The answer is yes, as long as you're willing to work hard and invest a significant amount of time (as well as money) into your venture, and your underlying idea for a business is sound. How well you market your online-based business will also be a major factor in whether it becomes successful. This book will help you gather the resources and knowledge you need, whether you're hoping to launch an online business on a shoestring budget or you have significant investment capital available.

Launching an online business requires an underlying understanding of how traditional businesses operate. You also need to understand basic marketing, have some basic computer skills (even though programming isn't actually required to start an online-based business), and be willing to spend a considerable amount of time doing research and managing your business once it's operational.

When it comes to obtaining the computer skills you'll need, the more you know, the better. However, you can get started with simply knowing how to use a Windows-based PC and off-the-shelf programs, like those found in Microsoft Office, plus how to surf the Internet. Being able to use a standard word processor plus send and receive e-mails are valuable skills.

In terms of equipment, at the very least, you'll need a reliable personal computer that's connected to the Internet, preferably via a high-speed connection. Ideally, you'll want a computer with a large hard drive and fast processor, plus such peripherals as a laser printer, a scanner, and a high-resolution digital camera (for taking your own product shots for your website). As for software, it will depend on the type of online business venture you're about to launch and how the website will be created.

Later, you'll read about turnkey options for designing, launching, and managing your e-commerce websites using services such as Yahoo! Store, eBay ProStores, and GoDaddy Quick Shopping Cart. These solutions make it easy for virtually anyone to launch his or her e-commerce business quickly and with no programming required.

Launching an online-based business isn't a get-rich-quick scheme, so before you get started, it's important to establish realistic expectations, which this book will help you develop. If you're hoping to discover a way to strike it rich overnight by reading this book, you're going to be disappointed because it's not going to happen! This book takes a realistic approach to learning about e-commerce and how to operate a successful online business venture.

In addition to walking you through the entire process of planning, creating, launching, marketing, and then operating your online business, this book offers a selection of interviews with experts from the e-commerce and website design fields. Chapter 16 of this book includes interviews with people who have already achieved success operating their own online-based businesses. These people offer extremely valuable advice that can help you follow in their footsteps and achieve success while avoiding the many potential pitfalls online entrepreneurs experience as they set up their business ventures.

Obviously, the opinions expressed in these interviews are based on each person's own experiences. Because there are no sure bets in this industry, you might choose to follow or totally ignore the advice these people offer, as there are many different options and opportunities available to you. If nothing else, however, these interviews will give you insight into some of the options and opportunities of which you, too, can take advantage.

Likewise, throughout this book, many different software packages, online services, and companies are listed as resources. With new products and services designed to help online business operators being released almost daily, it is literally impossible to list all the available products, software packages, and services you could use in the planning, creation, and operation of your online business venture. The goal of this book is simply to provide a general overview of what's available and to help you locate the exact tools and resources you need.

You'll find that *The Unofficial Guide to Starting a Business Online, 2nd Edition,* offers many answers and solutions in regard to e-commerce websites. The book also delves into the latest trends in online advertising, marketing, and promotions, such as search marketing, keyword-based advertising, and search-engine optimization. It also explores the online auction phenomenon created by eBay.com and Yahoo! Auctions.

The e-commerce industry is constantly evolving. There are no set rules or guaranteed methods for achieving success. As a result, use this book as a starting point, but be prepared to do your own research based on the type of business venture you hope to pursue. As you read this book, you'll be provided with hundreds of website addresses (URLs) that will lead you to valuable resources, services, and tools designed to help you plan, create, and manage your online business venture. Take full advantage of these resources and make an effort to benefit from the experiences and knowledge of others who already operate a business in cyberspace. Even if you've been successful operating a business in the offline world, you'll find that what works in cyberspace is often different.

The business idea you have is important and will have some impact on how successful your online business ultimately is; however, marketing your site and managing it properly are equally important.

For many people who proceed with caution and make educated decisions, operating an online business can be extremely rewarding, emotionally and financially. After all, very few types of businesses require a relatively low initial financial investment and allow you to be your own boss, set your own hours, and work from virtually anywhere. Ultimately, how much investment capital you use to launch your business will depend on many factors; however, it's possible to launch a start-up business for very little money, especially if you use a turnkey solution, like the ones described later in this book. Keep in mind, some of your business expenses as you launch your business will most likely be related to advertising, marketing, and promotions, plus inventory. Thus, the investment needed will vary greatly, based upon what you're selling, how you're selling it, and your overall business strategy.

Special Features

Every book in the Unofficial Guide series offers the following four special sidebars that are devised to help you get things done cheaply, efficiently, and prudently.

1. **Moneysaver:** Tips and shortcuts that will help you save money.

2. **Watch Out!:** Cautions and warnings to help you avoid common pitfalls.

3. **Bright Idea:** Smart or innovative ways to do something; in many cases, the ideas listed here will help you save time or hassle.

4. **Quote:** Anecdotes from real people who are willing to share their experiences and insights.

We also recognize your need to have quick information at your fingertips and have provided the following comprehensive sections at the back of the book:

1. **Glossary:** Definitions of complicated terminology and jargon.
2. **Resource Guide:** Lists of relevant agencies, associations, institutions, websites, and so on.
3. **You Sold It, Now Ship It:** Lists resources for shipping your products to customers.
4. **Important Documents:** "Official" copyright and trademark information.
5. **Index**

As you hop on the e-commerce bandwagon, if you'd like to share your experiences with the readers of future editions of this book, or if you have comments about this book, please e-mail me directly at jr7777@aol.com, or visit my website at www.jasonrich.com.

Welcome to the exciting and fast-paced world of e-commerce and operating a virtual business. As you turn the page, your introduction to this industry and the opportunities available to you will begin!

Jason R. Rich

Website: www.jasonrich.com
E-mail: jr7777@aol.com

In Business, Preparation
Is Everything

GET THE SCOOP ON...
Is an online-based business right for you? ▪
How to invest your time and money ▪ Do all
businesses work on the Web? ▪ Defining your
business idea and making it work for you

PART I

Making the Right Business Choices

So you've heard all the hype about the World Wide Web and the profit potential of starting a business on the Information Superhighway. You might have also heard about all of those "dot-bomb" companies that lost a fortune and folded a few years ago.

What's the real truth about the profit potential for an online business? In today's fast-paced business world, can someone still earn a profit by launching and operating an online business? As you're about to discover, the answer is most definitely yes!

Perhaps you've heard the opportunities available to small-business operators on the Internet equated to the Gold Rush, or you've seen statistics that depict online businesses as being the best moneymaking opportunities for the 21st century.

The prices of computers continue to drop rapidly, while with each new generation of microprocessor chips, their technological capabilities have improved dramatically. Thus, the equipment needed

Chapter 1

Moneysaver

If you need a home computer to establish your online business, and if you'll be using a turnkey solution for designing your website (and won't be doing a lot of programming and graphic design work), a basic, inexpensive desktop PC or laptop computer is more than adequate to get started. Companies such as Dell (www.dell.com) and Gateway (www.gateway.com) offer cheap, low-end computers. You'll definitely want to invest in a high-speed broadband or DSL Internet connection, however.

to operate an online-based business is minimal—far more affordable than ever before to get started. In fact, you can launch an online business with little more than a basic PC that's connected to the Internet, a great idea and a product or service to sell. Inexpensive PCs are available from mail-order companies, like Dell and Gateway, as well as from retail superstores, like CompUSA, Best Buy, and Circuit City.

Thanks to faster dial-up Internet connection speeds, DSL, and broadband Internet connections, surfing the Web is faster than ever. More and more people of all ages are becoming computer literate, and they're beginning to explore the Internet on their own. People from all walks of life and from almost all income levels are finding their way into cyberspace in record numbers, thanks in part to the popularity of America Online and the tremendous marketing efforts of other Internet Service Providers (ISPs), such as MSN, Earthlink, NetZero, Galaxy Internet Service, and many others.

Thousands of new people are making their way into cyberspace every week. These people, just like you, are consumers. Most have major credit cards, a checking account, and a PayPal (a secure online-based payment method) account for making online purchases using their computer.

The Internet's fast-growing popularity has made it an attractive and viable marketing tool for companies looking to reach a broad audience of computer users, plus niche markets made up of people with very specific interests, wants, and needs.

As you're about to discover, if you're planning to launch a successful online business, targeting niche markets with products that a specific group of consumers wants or needs offers a very viable business opportunity for you as the online business operator.

What's involved with starting an online business?

Just a few years ago, establishing a business online (or an "e-commerce website") was something that only large, well-funded companies were able to do; this is no longer the case. These days, virtually anyone with an idea for an online business, an inexpensive personal computer, access to the World Wide Web, and the tools for creating a website can launch their own business venture in cyberspace, with relative ease and with a potentially minimal financial investment. This book will show you how!

Every seller is welcome

The e-commerce industry is truly open to everyone; however, just because it's available doesn't guarantee that your online business venture will make you rich, no matter what the statistics show or how good your idea is. Out of the hundreds (or even thousands) of online businesses launched each month, only a handful will ever become profitable. An even smaller number will make their founders wealthy.

 Bright Idea

The amount of money you need to invest to successfully launch your online business will vary dramatically, based on a wide range of factors. You can start almost immediately using a turnkey service from Yahoo! or eBay, for example, that charges under $30 per month. It'll cost more to have a website custom designed if you have to maintain a light level of expensive inventory. Your advertising, public relations and marketing costs will also impact how much investment capital you need.

Bright Idea

Take your website seriously. The first impression you make with a customer, whether it's online, in person, over the phone, or by mail, is what makes the difference.

The good news is that starting an online business typically involves far less risk than opening a retail store or traditional mail-order business. But, launching an online business venture that has the potential for success will require a substantial investment of time and creativity on your part. It could also turn into a significant financial investment, depending on the decisions you make and the type of business you'll be launching. As you'll discover, you can start an online business, using a turnkey solution, for a very small initial investment.

Anyone who has explored cyberspace or studied the stock market has heard about all of the online businesses that have launched, gone public, and made their investors a fortune. But most online businesses don't become profitable. Those that have generated profits have done so only after being in business for several years. In many cases, sizable financial investments (in the millions of dollars) were also put into marketing, advertising, and promotion. You don't need to launch your business on a massive scale to earn profit. Millions of online businesses achieve success by starting out very small, targeting a niche market and growing over time.

Online businesses such as America Online, Yahoo!, Amazon.com, eBay.com, Priceline.com, and 1800flowers.com, for example, weren't launched as small start-up businesses. They were created by already-successful business entrepreneurs who raised millions of dollars in investment capital and invested that money in the formation and marketing of their online business ventures.

Still, don't let this discourage you. Whether you're contemplating starting your own online business as a full-time career move or as a part-time way of generating additional income, you certainly have many opportunities available to you in cyberspace for launching a business on a smaller scale that will make money. A great number of small-business operators have successfully established and profited from e-commerce websites. The majority of them have avoided competing head-on with large, mass-market–oriented companies such as Wal-Mart or Target. Instead, they've found a niche market and have sold their unique, customized, or narrowly focused products or services to a well-defined target audience.

As you'll quickly discover, there are no hard-and-fast rules about what works or why. *Any* product or service you're looking to sell on the Web can be viable if you design your website correctly, target the right audience, and do extensive marketing, advertising, and promotion.

Just having a good business idea isn't enough. Likewise, having a professional-looking website but a poor business idea isn't going to work, either. For an online business to be successful, every aspect of the business has to be well thought out and designed for a specific purpose—to reach your target audience with information, products, and services that they want and need, plus that they can't easily find elsewhere.

Every product is welcome

Since the Internet has become popular, virtually everything—yes everything—you could possibly imagine has been bought and sold over the Internet. If you surf over to eBay and browse through some of the auctions happening right now, you'll see the vast range of products for sale by companies as well as individuals.

 Bright Idea

eBay.com is the world's most popular online auction site and a major success story in the e-commerce industry. You can use eBay to test your online business idea and help determine whether there's a market for what you intend to sell.

On the Web, you'll easily find car dealerships successfully selling autos. You'll also see real estate (houses, apartments, condos, timeshares, and land) being sold, as well as yachts, jewelry, artwork, insurance, financial services, collectibles, and furniture.

Companies have also found success selling all sorts of mass-market products and services to the general Web-surfing public, such as

- Airline tickets and vacation opportunities
- Antiques
- Books
- CDs
- Clothing
- DVDs
- Electronics
- Equipment/supplies for hobbies
- Luggage
- Makeup and fragrances
- Movie/theater/concert tickets
- Pets and pet supplies
- Toys
- Videos
- Vitamins and other healthcare products

Chances are, if it can be sold via mail order, at a retail store, or at a flea market, someone has already tried selling it on the Web.

If the idea of operating your own business is appealing, you have at least some level of computer literacy (programming knowledge isn't necessarily required), and you have a good idea for an online-based business, you have most of what it takes to get started. You'll also need a computer with access to the Internet (preferably with a high-speed broadband or DSL connection), some type of website development tools, and a product or service to offer.

Bright Idea

If you're looking for truly unique, handcrafted items from around the world to sell on your website (or on eBay.com), visit the Overstock.com website and click on the WorldStock icon.

This book is designed to take you step by step through the process of launching your own online business, from the initial concept stages to the actual development of your website, its ongoing maintenance, and the promotion of the site once it goes online.

It won't be easy

No matter what you've heard about the ease of starting a business online—how quickly it can be done, how much profit you can make, how little time is required, and how it can be done for little or no money—don't believe it! Establishing a successful online business will require much of the same efforts and resources as starting a traditional business, only the risks are potentially much lower.

As you get started, you'll need to develop a well-thought-out business plan, invest a significant amount of time, make some type of financial commitment, and do an incredible amount of research about your product (or products), your target market, the viability of your overall business idea, and the Web itself.

There are a lot of mistakes you can make when trying to establish an online business and create an online presence for that business. There are also many scams out there targeting would-be entrepreneurs looking to go online in pursuit of riches.

This book will help you avoid many of these common mistakes, scams, and pitfalls. It will also point you directly to hundreds of useful resources available to online business operators.

As you read this book, try to formulate in your mind (and write down on paper) ideas about what type of online-based

Watch Out!

Beware of "get-rich-quick" schemes or Internet business opportunities that seem too good to be true. Many scam artists targeting would-be entrepreneurs focus on the glamour and ease of operating a home-based Internet business.

business you'd be interested in creating, what resources you already have at your disposal, and what useful skills and knowledge you possess. Also, consider what information, skills, knowledge, and resources (financial and otherwise) you know you're lacking.

Once you come up with what you consider to be a brilliant online-based business idea, test it, do research, become an expert regarding who your potential competition will be, and learn everything there is to know about your product or service. Most importantly, you need to understand your target audience and what needs or desires your online business will be fulfilling (or what problems your product/service will solve).

For the purposes of this book, an *online business* refers to any type of business venture being launched on the Internet. An *e-commerce site* refers to a website designed to accept orders for products or services. A *shopping-cart* application is the part of your website that contains the order form and is used to process orders along with credit-card, check, or PayPal payments. PayPal (www.PayPal.com) is a service, owned by eBay, which allows members to easily and securely send and receive money online for purchases made online. Once a PayPal account is created by a Web surfer, he or she can quickly make payments for items purchased online using funds from their checking account, credit card, debit card, or money stored in their PayPal online-based account. PayPal offers an assortment of value-added services to make online financial transactions more secure, especially if items are being bought and sold via online auctions or e-commerce websites.

E-commerce sites typically accept credit-card payments from customers and allow visitors to shop directly online without having to call a toll-free phone number, send a fax, or mail an order form to place an order. Keep in mind, however, that there are countless other terms tossed around this industry to describe online businesses or e-commerce sites, such as

- Virtual businesses
- Virtual stores
- E-stores
- Electronic malls
- E-businesses

No matter what type of online business you're hoping to launch, the level of planning, the steps you'll need to take, and the amount of effort required will basically be the same, although, as you'll learn from reading this book, there are many options available to you.

As an entrepreneur, you have taken the first step in identifying the Web as offering boundless opportunity. The next step is discovering how to focus on one aspect of the e-commerce industry in order to find a specific business opportunity that's viable—and of interest to you.

Is an online-based business right for you?

Just as there are many types of traditional businesses, there are many types of online-based businesses and e-commerce sites you can create. Actually planning and establishing an online based business requires a lot of time and effort. Once the business is operational, the time and money you must invest to keep your business running on a day-to-day basis will vary greatly, depending on the focus of your business—what you'll be selling or what services you'll be offering.

Bright Idea

As you begin developing your business plan, the time you put into research will pay for itself many times over with saved time and money later. As you get started, make sure you understand what you're selling, who you're selling it to, the best way to reach your intended audience, and how an e-commerce website can best be utilized to generate sales and profits.

As you investigate the online business opportunities available to you, you'll need to determine whether operating the type of business you have in mind fits your lifestyle. Just a few of the questions you'll need to ask yourself include the following:

- If you're already juggling a full-time job and a personal life, will you have the necessary time to dedicate to the operation of an online business?

- Are you prepared to operate your business for several months (or perhaps several years) before generating a profit?

- Do you have the computer technology necessary to access the Web and maintain your online presence?

- If you'll be operating your business from home, at least initially, do you have the available space to create a home office that will provide a conducive work environment?

- If your business will require you to maintain an inventory of products, do you have room in your home to store that inventory and enough money to maintain it?

- If you'll be selling a specific product, do you have access to adequate suppliers or manufacturers?

Launching your online business venture will take time, money, and plenty of preparation. In this business, knowledge is power. Enter into your business venture fully understanding the basics of online commerce, your target audience, and your products. It's also important to choose a business opportunity that you're excited about and truly believe in.

How best to invest your time and money

There's an age-old saying: "Keep it simple." This is especially true if you'll be launching a start-up business on the Web and have limited business or e-commerce experience. There's no need for you to invest a fortune in creating a website that is cutting-edge (from a technological standpoint) in order to test the viability of your business idea. Using an off-the-shelf Web-page-development and management software package, such as Microsoft FrontPage, or an inexpensive e-commerce turnkey solution (such as Yahoo! Stores or GoDaddy.com's Quick Shopping Cart), you can get your business online inexpensively and relatively easily. These and other options are all explored later in this book.

After you've developed an idea for an online business—but before investing time and money to get online immediately—invest time researching and creating a comprehensive business plan. Then consider how the day-to-day operations of your business will work once you launch it. Preparation is truly one of the key ingredients for success, especially in an industry that is changing so rapidly as new technological innovations become available. Thus, investing your time in advance is as important as investing your money later.

As you'll soon learn, simply having a great business idea and a professional-looking online presence isn't enough. To make your online-based business profitable, you'll need to generate traffic to your site. This can be one of the biggest challenges you'll face. Once people are at your site, they need to be motivated to

 Moneysaver

Remember that more is not necessarily better. Turnkey solutions, such as Yahoo! Stores, eBay's ProStores, and GoDaddy.com's Quick Shopping Cart are inexpensive and offer all the features most start-up e-commerce businesses need.

make a purchase, which often means helping potential customers overcome their concern for security and privacy issues related to participating in online transactions.

Absolutely nothing will replace the need for you to get to know your target audience thoroughly. You need to understand their needs, desires, buying and spending habits, demographics (age, gender, income level, education level, and so forth), the problems they face, and how your products or services address these issues. The online presence you ultimately create for your business needs to cater specifically to your target audience, look professional, and be easy to navigate, even for novice Web surfers.

By spending the necessary time doing research, you should be able to answer the following questions:

- What products and services have good market potential for sale online?

- Who is the target audience for the products and services you'll be selling?

- What type of content will your website need in order to cater to your target audience?

- How does your product or service address the needs, wants, or interests of your potential customers?

- What is the best layout/design for your website, keeping in mind its primary goal is to communicate your marketing message?

- What are the best ways to promote and advertise your website in order to reach your target audience? (At the time this book was written, search marketing and search-engine optimization were popular online promotional opportunities.)

Once you have the necessary knowledge about your product or service, determine how you plan to use the Web as a marketing and sales tool, and determine how you'd like to promote your website to your target audience. Then you'll be in a better position to decide how best to spend whatever business start-up capital you have available to launch your venture.

Educating yourself about all of the options available to you in terms of creating, managing, and promoting your online presence will ultimately save you money and can make the difference between a successful or failed venture.

Which business ideas are best suited to the Web?

Obviously, the business idea you come up with will help to determine whether your online-based business will be successful, but it's only one ingredient. As you explore the Web, you'll find many successful businesses that, judging only from the product or service they offer, might seem likely to fail. This is because in addition to the idea itself, a lot depends on how the idea is executed and marketed.

Unless you have a huge budget (say, millions of dollars) to execute your business idea, it's bad business practice to attempt to compete head-on with well-established and very large online businesses (such as Amazon.com and Travelocity.com), which have spent millions changing the buying habits of online consumers. Instead, as an entrepreneur planning to launch a small online business, you should focus on some type of niche market that isn't cost-effective for the larger, well-established companies to serve.

As you kick around ideas for your online business venture, don't rule out anything initially. From the list of ideas you generate, choose the ones you're most interested in. Then, do research

 Bright Idea

As you begin formulating plans to launch an online-based business, invest your time and energy first. Never invest your money before you've done the necessary research and have formulated a business plan you're confident will lead to success.

to determine their viability. Finally, take your top one or two ideas and develop detailed business plans around them.

Early on, even if an idea is outrageous, don't immediately dismiss it until you've closely examined its viability and have done the necessary research. Ideas that wouldn't necessarily work as traditional retail or mail-order businesses might have potential on the Web. Make sure, however, that the ideas making your final cut are manageable, based on your available resources and budget.

Forget the fads; watch the trends

At any given time, one fad or another is sweeping across America. People will spend almost anything in order to participate in the fad and get their hands on whatever items relating to the fad are for sale. Recent fads over the years have included Beanie Babies, Furbies, merchandise related to the movie *Napoleon Dynamite* and Pokémon toys, which at one time were highly popular and selling on the secondary market for 10 times (or more) their suggested retail prices.

If you're looking to capitalize on a fad by operating an online business selling products or services relating to that fad, watch out. Just as quickly as a fad starts, it can (and will) end, causing the market for those products to dry up almost instantly. Don't invest a lot of time and money creating an e-commerce site that caters to a specific fad, unless you're looking to make a quick buck and get out fast.

The fast-in, fast-out approach goes against most of the rules for establishing an online-based business. Typically, if you don't have a huge budget, you have to invest lots of time in planning, and then months of operation to build traffic to and sales from your site.

Instead of developing an entire e-commerce site or online-based business around the exploitation of a current fad (which will take time and money), consider selling these goods through one of the online auction sites, such as eBay (www.ebay.com).

Watch Out!

When evaluating your top business ideas, make sure the idea you decide to run with is manageable based on the resources and budget at your disposal. You might have a wonderful idea, but if it'll require millions of dollars in marketing alone and you are planning to launch a small business using your own financial resources, you're sunk.

Auction sites allow anyone to buy or sell items of any price and pay a small fee to the site operator. With the fast-growing popularity of these services, people have managed to supplement their incomes selling all sorts of new and used items via online auctions.

On eBay alone, there are more than 45 million active members in the U.S. and more than 15 million auctions taking place this very moment. You'll learn more about the business opportunities eBay offers in Chapters 4 and 14.

The growing competition in cyberspace

It's the American dream to become your own boss, pursue your own professional destiny, and strike it rich doing something you love to do. In an era when giant corporations and mass merchants are putting small businesses and mom-and-pop retail stores out of business in record numbers, the Internet provides small-business operators the chance to reach a global audience of Web surfers relatively inexpensively.

Upon realizing that virtually anyone can launch a successful business in cyberspace, people from all walks of life, as well as companies of all sizes, are now marking their turf on the Information Superhighway. Almost every Fortune 500 company has some type of Web presence. Likewise, large retail-store chains, such as Gap, Abercrombie & Fitch, RadioShack, The Sharper Image, Barnes & Noble, and countless others are well established online, as well as at your local mall or strip shopping center. These traditional retail-store chains have branched out into cyberspace because they see it as a fast-growing trend in how consumers shop.

There's no doubt that in the near future, for the average person in America, surfing the Internet will be as commonplace as watching television, playing a video game, or using the telephone. As a result, entrepreneurs and businesspeople alike are seeing dollar signs and coming up with ideas for generating income by marketing their products or services to Web surfers.

Thousands of new websites are popping up every day. Although not all of these sites are designed to sell products or are based on an e-commerce business model, the number of individuals, businesses, and corporations trying to exploit the Internet to generate revenue is growing extremely rapidly.

No matter what type of business you ultimately launch on the Web, there's going to be competition. Thus, you'll need to do things better, faster, cheaper, or more aggressively than the many other businesses in cyberspace, or find innovative ways to differentiate your product (or products). The problem is, if you do come up with an innovative idea that's a tremendous success, you can count on that idea being copied many times over by your competition, sometimes in a matter of days or even hours.

Despite the ever-increasing level of competition from companies and organizations of all sizes, people from all walks of life continue to launch new online business ventures. Should you be intimidated by all of the competition? No! You should, however, be aware that it exists and that the competition in cyberspace will probably become even more fierce in the future. If you plan accordingly and have the resources available to conduct your business in a way that's better (but not necessarily bigger) than the competition, your chances of long-term success increase dramatically.

Part of doing business online better than your competition is having a website that people enjoy visiting, and creating an online shopping experience that's truly intuitive. Providing top-notch customer service also is critical because repeat business and word-of-mouth are important methods for generating traffic to your website.

Defining your business idea

The early chapters of this book will deal with the concept of defining your business idea in greater detail. Unless you're equipped to launch a business venture with the capital needed to compete with the major players, it's important to develop an idea that caters to a specific niche audience. You need to truly understand what your product or service offers and why your target or niche market wants, needs, or would have an interest in it. This concept is repeated throughout this book because it's extremely important!

You must clearly define your business's goals and objectives, who its audience is, and what exactly you're offering to the public. If you can't do this in your own mind, there's no possible way your potential customers will understand what you're trying to do, and chances are they won't support your efforts.

With so much competition in cyberspace, *branding* is becoming increasingly more important. Unlike traditional business, how you brand your business, product, or service has little or no relevance to the actual size of your company. Branding refers to the overall image you create for your business and the reputation you develop among your customers. This creates a more even playing field between you (the small online business operator) and the big businesses that have established a presence on the Web. The playing field is far from being truly equal, of course, but in cyberspace, your chances of competing successfully with

 Moneysaver

Don't increase your advertising budget at the expense of offering excellent customer service. Great advertising (and even low prices) is no substitute for superior service and communication online, via telephone, by fax, by U.S. Mail, or in person. Remember: Word-of-mouth and customer referrals are free!

large companies or a handful of smaller companies is far greater than if you were operating a traditional retail, mail-order, tele-marketing, or locally focused service-type business.

As a small online business operator, it's important to define, develop, and then stick to your business idea, yet be flex-ible enough to compete in this ever-changing and evolving e-commerce industry.

Should you give up your day job?

All it really takes is a good idea, time, a bit of money, and a com-puter with Internet access to launch an online business venture. So just about anyone with basic computer and business knowl-edge and an entrepreneurial spirit can start an online business. Entrepreneurial spirit is important here because as a business operator, you'll need to dedicate a lot of time, energy, and per-haps money toward making your venture successful.

Unfortunately, although everyone who starts an online busi-ness aspires to success and wealth working part-time from home (or whatever location they choose), there is no substitute for hard work and dedication.

Businesspeople, homemakers, work-at-home mothers, stu-dents, retired people, existing traditional business operators, people with a physical disability or long-term illness, and anyone else looking to supplement their existing income are among the ever-growing group of people establishing some sort of business on the Web. Do such people achieve financial success operating their own online businesses? Some become rich, some earn a respectable second income, and, unfortunately, some people

Bright Idea

No matter how much time and effort you initially expect to invest in starting your business venture, in reality it'll take more. Unless you're prepared to make the necessary time investment, think twice about establishing your own online business. However much time you estimate you'll need, double it (at least initially).

fail. The primary reasons people fail when they launch an online business venture include the following:

- Lack of planning
- Trying to sell a product or service people have no interest in buying
- Poor (unprofessional-looking) website design
- Inferior customer service or technical support
- Ineffective advertising, marketing, or promotion
- Insufficient financial resources for the type of online business being launched
- Following a poorly thought-out business plan

One of the primary goals of this book is to offer you step-by-step directions for designing, creating, launching, and maintaining your online business, while at the same time helping you avoid common pitfalls people run into when they attempt to launch an online business.

If you have an incredible business idea, and after doing extensive research you're convinced it will be the basis for a hugely successful online business, you have several choices. You can make launching this business venture a part-time project that you work on after meeting the responsibilities of your full-time job, or you can dedicate your professional life to this business project on a full-time basis.

Choosing to leave your full-time job and pursue a somewhat risky start-up venture is a decision that will have a major impact on your life because you'll be giving up the security of a regular paycheck and perhaps a full benefits package. It could take several months before your online business makes its first sale, so you need to have the financial resources available to support yourself without receiving a steady paycheck. In addition, you'll also need money to invest in your business, to get online, to pay for inventory (if applicable), and to cover the cost of marketing, advertising, and promotion.

Watch Out!

Don't make rash decisions about quitting your job and starting an online business venture, thinking you're going to strike it rich. Test your idea first. If it seems viable, seriously consider the ramifications of quitting your job before doing so. It's important to develop realistic expectations regarding the profit potential of your business idea.

Any money you invest in your online business should be funds you can afford to lose because if your venture fails, the money you invested will most likely be lost. Before giving up your full-time job, consider launching your online business venture as a part-time project to test its viability. You might also want to solicit outside investors to ensure you'll have the financial resources available to keep your venture operational until it becomes profitable.

For homemakers, students, and retired individuals, starting an online business can be an ideal income generator because it's possible (in most cases) to work from home, set your own hours, and get started with minimal financial investment. Although computer programming skills are no longer required to establish a business presence on the Web, basic computer literacy skills and a general working knowledge of business management and marketing will certainly be useful.

How much does it cost to get started? Putting a dollar amount on what it'll take to establish your online business depends on many factors, including what type of business you'll be operating, whether you hire a professional to design your website, what hosting service or ISP you use, what company you establish your merchant account with, your inventory costs, and the cost of hiring employees.

As you create your business plan, you'll need to make a series of financial projections in order to develop your budget. Throughout this book, we explore the costs associated with various aspects of starting an online business venture and the steps required to create a business plan.

Establishing your existing business on the Web

Established businesses of all sizes and in all industries are venturing onto the Web for many reasons:

- To expand their customer base and reach a global market
- To improve the customer service they offer (and reduce related costs)
- To make it easier for customers to place orders anytime (day or night)
- To distribute information about the company (to customers, potential clients, and investors)
- To broaden brand awareness
- Simply because it's perceived as an important strategic business move for the company's future

Whether you operate a small retail store, a service-based business, or one of the few Fortune 500 companies that still hasn't created an Internet presence, there are many reasons why your business should create a website. An existing company that sells products or services should seriously consider taking advantage of e-commerce technology in order to allow customers to make purchases directly online.

If a traditional company already exists and is well established, expanding into cyberspace is in many ways much easier than launching an online-based business from scratch. Although many of the steps to get online and create a website are the same for everyone, there are slightly different considerations and possible

---

 Bright Idea

One way to expand any traditional business is to cater to a national or worldwide market by creating a presence on the Web. This will allow you to offer your (potential) customers information about your products or services, provide better customer support, and reach people you wouldn't ordinarily reach.

pitfalls to consider for existing businesses looking to expand onto the Web. For example, an existing business already has its image, brand, reputation, and product-line well-defined. It's important to ensure that all translate seamlessly into the company's new online presence to ensure continuity. These considerations are explored later in this book.

Be careful what you get involved in

In case you've spent the past few years living in a totally non-digital world and haven't yet begun exploring the power, vast penetration, and incredible growth of the Internet, the World Wide Web offers people a great opportunity to market and sell virtually anything.

This amazing resource has attracted thousands of con artists developing all sorts of scams, quasi-illegal "business opportunities," and countless other misrepresented offers. These swindlers target the would-be entrepreneur who isn't yet computer savvy and promise limitless riches for doing little or no work, simply by exploiting the power of the Internet. There are countless franchise opportunities, multilevel marketing "opportunities," pyramid schemes, and get-rich-quick scams being offered.

Because thousands of online businesses and e-commerce sites are being launched every week, many services—promoted as time- and moneysaving solutions—are offered to would-be entrepreneurs. Some of these are totally legitimate and extremely useful tools and services, whereas others are promoted by fly-by-night operations looking to capitalize on the ignorance of others.

 Bright Idea

If you come across a business opportunity that sounds too good to be true, or you want to do research about a potential supplier before doing business with that company, contact your local Better Business Bureau (www.bbb.org). The more research you do in advance, the better off you'll be later.

Watch Out!

The only people who get rich from "get-rich" schemes are the dishonest people perpetuating the scams. Of course, there are, for example, some legitimate multilevel marketing opportunities, but it's important to be extremely careful about anything you choose to become involved in.

Chapter 8, "Fine-Tuning Your Business Before Going Online," is dedicated to showing you how to avoid the many online scams and rip-offs. As a general rule, as you begin to formulate plans for your online business venture, it's critical that you take it upon yourself to do your own research. Don't rely on what others tell you. Make well-thought-out and educated decisions about which directions you choose to go. Always proceed with caution, be suspicious if something sounds too good to be true, ask lots of questions, do research, and never make rash decisions about anything relating to your business.

If you're being offered an online business opportunity that sounds sketchy, contact your local Better Business Bureau (www.bbb.org) and learn what you can before getting involved.

E-commerce in the new millennium

We're living in an exciting time. The power, capabilities, and worldwide reach of the Internet are quickly changing the way the world does business. By reading this book, you'll learn how to get into the world of e-commerce while this industry is still in its relative infancy.

For people starting new online-based business ventures or existing companies looking to expand onto the Internet, there's never been a better time to go online. The website-development tools and resources available right now have never been easier to use. They're powerful, and what's more, they're becoming extremely inexpensive and usable by people with little or no programming knowledge.

Bright Idea

Although programming knowledge is not required for launching and operating an online business, basic computer skills and a strong familiarity with how to surf the Web are required. If your computer skills aren't up to speed, consider taking classes at a local computer store, community college, or adult-education program.

What the Internet can do for you is limited only by your imagination and the amount of time and resources you put into your venture. You've taken the right first step by purchasing this book.

Just the facts

- With the decreasing prices of computers and increased technological capabilities, more and more people are becoming computer literate and exploring the Internet.

- An e-commerce site is not just an electronic brochure or interactive marketing tool; it sells products or services.

- These days, anyone with an idea for an online business, a computer, access to the World Wide Web, and the right software can launch a cyberspace business venture.

- Small-business operators are most likely to succeed when they sell their customized products or services to a well-defined niche audience.

- Before investing time and money to get online, spend time doing research, create a comprehensive business plan, and consider how the daily operations of your business will work.

- To beat the competition, you'll need to do things better, faster, cheaper, and more aggressively, or find innovative ways to differentiate your product from those of other cyberspace businesses.

GET THE SCOOP ON...
Developing your business's infrastructure ▪
Creating a setup checklist ▪ Generating a
business plan ▪ Seeking professional advice ▪
Establishing your office or workspace

Laying the Groundwork for Your Online Business

Chapter 2

At the heart of every successful online business is a solid infrastructure and well-thought-out business plan. Without these two elements, you'll find it extremely difficult to operate your business today and plan for the future. Developing a professional-looking website to sell or promote a product or service is extremely important, too. But before going online and opening for business, make sure everything else is in place in terms of planning and implementing day-to-day operating procedures.

Starting your business: some considerations

Operating your own online business is very different from working for someone else because you're responsible for everything—you're the boss. Poor planning or lack of follow-through on your part can and will lead to failure, especially if you don't have a detailed business plan in place to help you stay on track.

Advantages of self-employment

Aside from the obvious perks of being able to control your professional destiny by operating your own online business, you'll have control over your income potential. Being your own boss certainly has its advantages:

- You won't have a boss constantly looking over your shoulder.

- If you'll be operating your online business from home, there's never a commute to and from work (and no traffic jams).

- You can work at your own pace and set your own work hours.

- There's no dress code. Many people who work from home report their typical business attire (at least until mid-morning or lunchtime) is a robe or just underwear.

- It's usually easier to juggle your personal and professional life.

- There are excellent tax advantages to owning and operating your own business. You'll want to contact your accountant or financial planner for details.

Questions to ask yourself

If you've been stuck in an office job up until now, being your own boss might sound like paradise, which is why so many people are taking advantage of this type of opportunity. There are,

 Bright Idea

If you have young children and want to spend more time with them, switching from an office job to an at-home Internet business can be an attractive choice. Just be sure to think about how feasible it will be to set up a usable workspace and get work done when the kids are around.

Watch Out!

Be honest with yourself. In the evenings, at night, and on weekends, once your work day is complete and you have no pressing deadlines to meet, will you be able to focus on your personal life instead of spending extra time in your at-home office, catching up on paperwork or checking your e-mail? If not, working at home might not be for you.

however, a few things to consider before making this transition in your professional life:

Yes No

❑ ❑ Do you have personal drive and leadership qualities?

❑ ❑ Are you able to endure long hours—at least in the beginning—before your business is fully operational?

❑ ❑ Are you psychologically ready to take some risks?

❑ ❑ Are you prepared to wait several months before making a profit?

❑ ❑ Do you have specific expertise in the business you want to start?

❑ ❑ Do you know how to find your particular niche in the market and how to identify your customers?

❑ ❑ Do you know how to sell enough of what you have, at a price that will return an adequate profit for you?

❑ ❑ Can you obtain the money you will need to start and keep the business running without getting into cash-flow problems?

❑ ❑ Do you like to think ahead and plan for your future, and then work to make it happen?

❑   ❑   Are you motivated and focused enough to do all
        of your work in a timely manner when you could
        be watching television, listening to the radio,
        catching up on your housework or errands, or
        just enjoying the weather if it happens to be a
        nice day?

❑   ❑   If you'll be working from home, do you live in
        an environment that's conducive to working
        productively? Do you have a separate room in
        your home that can be transformed into an
        office? Can this area be shut off from the rest
        of the house, so that you can have your privacy
        and quiet when you're hard at work and need
        to concentrate?

❑   ❑   Are you extremely organized and detail-oriented?
        (There's nobody else to pick up the slack for you
        or cover for your mistakes.)

❑   ❑   Are you customer service–driven? Will you be
        willing to take extra steps to keep your customers
        happy and win over new customers?

❑   ❑   Do you have the support of your family in terms
        of the time commitment and potential financial
        investment that'll be required? Will your loved
        ones be able to accept the risk involved with
        starting any type of business venture?

Developing a business plan

The true backbone of America's economy is the more than 20
million small businesses, which account for the majority of new
jobs created. (A small business is defined as one with fewer than
500 employees.)

When you decide to start your own small business online,
you'll need to take the following steps:

1. Come up with an awesome business idea.

2. Develop a detailed business plan and marketing campaign.

3. Perform the necessary research.

4. Raise the required start-up capital.

5. Seek out free or low-cost guidance, especially if you lack business experience or computer literacy.

Assuming you have the intelligence, personality type, motivation, and financial backing to launch your own online business, the first step is to determine what product your online business will offer. Ideally, you want to create a business opportunity for yourself that makes full use of your background, knowledge, and talents. Next, you want to determine what opportunities are available based on the resources at your disposal.

Before investing your time and money in your idea, create a detailed *business plan* that specifically defines your business, identifies the goals of the business, and includes a balance sheet and cash-flow analysis.

Upon creating a business plan, doing extensive research, and analyzing the demand for the products your business will offer, you should be able to accurately project start-up costs, operating costs, revenues, and profits. Keep in mind that accurately predicting initial traffic to your site and customer demand for your product might be a bit challenging.

If you don't have a financial background, consider hiring an accountant, bookkeeper, or someone with the expertise to help you create a financial model for your company (in advance) and help you set up the financial aspects of your business. Right from the start, be sure to have an adequate accounting and recordkeeping system in place.

QuickBooks Pro (www.quickbooks.com), from Intuit, Inc., for example, is an excellent accounting and bookkeeping software package that's ideal for small-business operators. Whether you plan on doing the necessary recordkeeping and accounting by hand or using an off-the-shelf computer software program is up to you.

Figure 2.1. No matter what type of business you'll be operating, QuickBooks is an off-the-shelf software package designed to make managing a company's finances relatively easy, even if you're not a finance whiz.

Maintaining a current balance sheet and income statement (a profit-and-loss statement) along with accurate banking records is important for keeping your business on track financially. This represents the bare-minimum level of accounting work that'll need to be done on an ongoing basis.

Unless you're planning to tap your savings or get a home equity loan to finance your business venture, you'll either need

Bright Idea

For small businesses, QuickBooks Pro (Intuit Software, www.quickbooks.com) is one of the top-selling accounting and bookkeeping software packages on the market. This and other good programs can save you time managing your finances.

Watch Out!

Don't get caught with insufficient funds. Most experts recommend that you should have enough money up front to cover all start-up costs and operating expenses for six months to one year. If you rely on profits from your first-year sales to create cash flow, you are setting yourself up for disappointment.

to find investors or take out business loans in order to generate the start-up capital you require. No matter how you intend to raise your start-up capital, potential investors and financial institutions will look carefully at your business plan, projected financial statements, and how much of your own funds you're investing in the business.

Unfortunately, no matter how strong your business concept is, there are no guarantees that it will succeed. To greatly minimize your chances of failure, implement well-defined management practices, ensure that you have as much industry expertise as possible, and make sure you also have whatever technical support you'll need to properly manage and operate your business. Carefully planning every aspect of your business is critical.

Creating a well-thought-out business plan is an important first step for any business owner. This document will help you determine whether your idea for a business is viable, and can later be used to attract potential investors or to help you obtain loans from financial institutions. The more detail your business plan offers, the better your long-term chances for success will be.

Getting help—people and software

A CPA, financial planner, accountant, or professional bookkeeper will be able to assist you with the financial aspects of a business plan, while someone who studied business in school (at the undergraduate or graduate level) should have the basic know-how to create a coherent business plan once the necessary research has been done.

To help you format your business plan and compile the information you'll need, the Small Business Administration's website offers several free and downloadable shareware and public-domain software programs designed to help you create a business plan. For a directory of these programs, point your Web browser to www.sba.gov/shareware/starfile.html.

There are also a variety of commercially available, off-the-shelf software packages designed to assist start-up companies in the creation of business plans.

Figure 2.2. PaloAlto Software offers a comprehensive, off-the-shelf software package for creating a professional business plan.

Business Plan Pro 2005 (PaloAlto Software, Inc.; 888-PLAN-PRO; www.pasware.com) is a bestselling and easy-to-use business plan package featuring context-sensitive audio help, more than 450 sample business plans, a large database of venture capitalists, customizable business charts, and professional-looking full-color printouts. This software uses what it calls the "Easy Plan Wizard" to guide business plan writers through every step of the process. A free demo version of this $99.95 program is available for downloading from the company's website. A more elaborate edition, Business Plan Pro Premier Edition, is priced at $199.

Other developers of business plan creation software include the following:

> **BizPlanBuilder 2005 Interactive**
> JIAN Tools for Sales
> 800-346-5426
> www.jianusa.com
> PC CD-ROM, Windows XP
> Retail Price: $99

> **PlanWrite**
> Business Resource Software
> 800-423-1228, 512-251-7541
> www.brs-inc.com
> PC CD-ROM, Windows XP
> Retail Price: $119.95

Using a specialized software package to develop a business plan is an excellent idea for someone who hasn't done this type of thing before. The majority of the available software packages will guide you through the process and help you determine what information needs to be incorporated into your business plan and how best to format this information.

Basically, a business plan is a resumé for your business idea. This is a professional-looking document that combines text and graphics (charts, graphs, pictures, and so forth), as well as a spreadsheet with projected financial information.

Elements of a business plan

Depending on the type of business you're creating, a well-written business plan will probably include most, if not all, of the following sections:

The Company Name   The first line on the first page of any business plan.

Executive Summary   A text-based overview of the business that can be anywhere from a few sentences to several pages long.

Objectives   Using bulleted points or short paragraphs, this section describes the goals of the business.

Mission Statement   A one-paragraph description that explains the overall purpose of the company's existence.

Keys to Success   What will the company offer that will make it successful? What will the company do differently?

Risks   What risks, financial or otherwise, is the company facing?

Company Summary   More detail about the company, including information about its products or services, is described in this section.

Company Ownership   Who are the executives or founders involved with the company?

Start-Up Summary   What will be required to get this company launched? What costs are involved? Financial projections and a list of start-up costs and expenses should be included here.

Start-Up Assets Needed   This is a listing of the assets the company must acquire prior to its launch. Depending on the type of company, what's included in this list will vary, as will the listed costs of the assets.

Investment   Based on the total start-up costs, this section of the business plan should itemize and describe where the initial start-up capital is coming from (such as loans and private investors).

Company Locations and Facilities   This section of the business plan describes where the company will be located. From a business standpoint, what are the benefits and drawbacks of these facilities and the company's location?

Watch Out!

When you are preparing a business plan, don't sugarcoat the difficulties or exaggerate numbers in your favor. Potential financial backers will not be fooled. You're better off being completely honest and indicating how you plan to surmount the challenges.

Detailed Product/Service Descriptions   Use this section to explain, in detail, what the company will be offering.

Competitive Comparison   Describe your company's key competitors. What will your company offer that sets it apart from the competition?

Sourcing   Who will be your company's suppliers or manufacturers?

Technology   How will technology be used as a tool within your company?

Future Products/Services   What new or specific types of products or services will your company launch in the future?

Market Segmentation   How does your company fit within its industry? Will your company cater to a specific (or niche) market? If so, what is this niche, and how will the company address it?

Overall Industry Analysis   Provide a brief description of the industry in which you will do business. Describe the state of the industry, who the key players are, and whether the industry is expected to expand in the future.

Market Analysis   Describe the target customer/audience for your company's products. Break down this information geographically, by demographics, or however you can best demonstrate to the reader exactly who will be interested in your company's products. This is just one section of the business plan where charts and graphs can come in handy.

Marketing Strategy   How will your company promote its website, products, and services in order to capture the attention of its target audience? This section can be broken down into subsections that describe your company's marketing, promotions, advertising, and public-relations plans.

Sales Strategy   How will your company sell and distribute its products? How will your company make use of the Internet?

Service and Support   What type of service and support will your company offer?

Strategic Alliances   How will your company benefit from developing and implementing strategic alliances with other companies in order to achieve its goals?

Organizational Structure of the Company   Using a chart or text, describe the hierarchy of the company from the founder/president/CEO down to entry-level people. Include projected salary costs for at least the first three years of business.

Financial Plan   This section of the business plan should contain detailed financial statements and projections.

Once your business plan is complete, make sure that you have it reviewed and critiqued by your lawyer, accountant, or someone who is an expert in business before submitting it to potential investors or financial institutions (to apply for a loan).

Seeking expert business advice

Even if you've graduated with a degree in business administration, you're an expert in your particular field, and you have a great idea for a business, if you've never run a business before, the one thing you lack is experience. To help make up for your own lack of experience in the business world, you can hire someone with experience as a partner or employee. You can also take advantage of the free resources available to small-business owners from the Service Corps of Retired Executives (SCORE).

Moneysaver

Promote your business for free using the Business to Business Directory on American Express's Small Business Exchange (http://home.americanexpress.com/home/open.shtml). The site provides business planning advice as well as answers to your questions from business experts.

SCORE, a division of the Small Business Administration that was founded in 1964, is dedicated to aiding in the formation, growth, and success of small businesses nationwide. This is a nonprofit association comprised of more than 12,400 volunteer business counselors throughout the U.S. and its territories. SCORE volunteers are trained to serve as counselors, advisers, and mentors to aspiring entrepreneurs and business owners. The organization's services are offered free of charge.

To date, more than four million Americans have used SCORE's services, which include offering general business advice and helping entrepreneurs create and write detailed business plans. To reach SCORE volunteers in your area, call 800-634-0245 or take advantage of the services offered on the SCORE website, www.score.org.

American Express also offers information and services to small-business owners on the World Wide Web. Learn more about American Express's small business services at its website, http://home.americanexpress.com/home/open.shtml.

Visa offers its own website targeted to small businesses that can be accessed at www.usa.visa.com/business.

Setting up an office

If you plan to launch your online business from home, hopefully you're motivated, focused, and disciplined, and have what it takes to be your own boss. This is the personal investment you'll have to make. As you'll discover, operating from an office (located in your home, in an office building, or elsewhere) will also require an investment in supplies and equipment. Here are some of the basics you'll need to run your business from a small home office.

The computer

A core business tool needed in virtually any office is a desktop or laptop computer equipped with a dial-up or high-speed Internet connection (a DSL or broadband connection is definitely preferred). The computer will be the hub of your online business; you will use it for designing and maintaining your website(s), surfing the Internet, accessing online services, and sending and receiving e-mail, plus inventory control and perhaps bookkeeping.

The computer should also have an assortment of core applications installed, including a word processor, spreadsheet, database, contact manager, scheduler, and any specialized programs (such as accounting, inventory control, credit-card processing, and shipping software) your business needs to operate.

Software

Microsoft Office Professional Edition for Windows (www.microsoft. com) is a popular and relatively inexpensive suite of business-related applications on one CD-ROM. The software bundle includes Microsoft Word, Excel, Access, Publisher, Outlook, and PowerPoint.

One good software package for handling your bookkeeping and accounting is QuickBooks Pro (888-729-1996; www. quickbooks.com). Using the EasyStep Interview and QuickBooks Navigator, QuickBooks users can quickly set up their business on this software and create custom invoices, enter sales, perform electronic banking and bill payment, track customer contacts, track time, perform job costing, manage inventory, handle payroll, and prepare for tax time.

QuickBooks Pro offers a full range of services and features. It is a Windows-based program. The single-user version has a suggested retail price of about $299. For more information about this software, visit the company's website or any computer superstore, such as CompUSA, Staples, and OfficeMax. It can also be purchased online from Amazon.com.

Bright Idea

QuickBooks Pro is compatible with the electronic banking services offered by many banks and financial institutions. Utilizing this feature can save you time and money handling the everyday banking-related tasks you'll be responsible for. Contact your bank or financial institution to determine whether its electronic banking services support this software.

Printer, fax, and data backup device

Your office should also be equipped with a laser printer and a data backup device. Another important tool is a plain-paper fax machine. You might also need between two and four telephone lines to accommodate a personal phone number, a work/ business phone number, a fax line, and a modem line. Ideally, if you're operating an online business and spending a lot of time on the Web, a high-speed broadband or DSL Internet connection is ideal. In addition to offering much faster connection speeds, this will eliminate the need for an extra modem line.

If you don't want to invest in a traditional fax machine and a separate phone line for it, an alternative is an online-based service, called eFax (www.efax.com). This transforms your computer (that's connected to the Web) into a virtual fax machine. Upon registering for this inexpensive service, you'll be provided with a fax telephone number in your local area code. Your incoming faxes, however, will arrive as e-mail messages in whatever e-mail account you specify. You can then view and print your faxes using your computer. One advantage of this service is that you can send and receive faxes from anywhere.

You can also purchase off-the-shelf software, like WinFax Pro (Symantec Software, $99.95, www.symantec.com/product/ index_smallbiz.html) that gives your PC-based computer the ability to send and receive faxes.

While receiving faxes using eFax or WinFax Pro, for example, is easy and convenient, if you want to send a fax which is in the form of a printed sheet of paper, to send it electronically,

Moneysaver

To save money and space, consider investing in an all-in-one laser printer, which is a laser printer, copier, and scanner in one. Some units can also be used as fax machines.

you'll also need a scanner. Thus, for a small business, having a traditional fax machine may ultimately prove more beneficial.

The phone

Your telephone should be capable of handling at least two phone lines and should have a hold feature, along with an auto-dialer that can store your most frequently dialed numbers. Depending on the size of your home office, consider connecting a high-quality cordless telephone to give you added convenience and mobility.

When ordering telephone service, consider adding call waiting, three-way calling, caller ID with name, call forwarding, and call answering to your plan. All are optional services offered for an additional monthly fee from your local phone company. Call answering will replace the need for an answering machine or voice-mail system. Having the ability to retrieve messages remotely from a touch-tone phone is a must.

Many local phone companies across America now offer unlimited local and long-distance calling services for a flat monthly fee of about $50 (or less) per month. This service includes many of the added calling features such as call waiting and caller ID, which most small-business operators will appreciate.

An alternative to traditional telephone service is to use *Voice-Over-IP (VoIP)* telephone service, which uses your high-speed Internet connection to give you unlimited local and long-distance calling, plus a variety of calling features.

Voice-Over-IP phone service is priced at a flat monthly fee, which varies depending on the provider. One such provider is

Vonage (800-986-4VON; www.vonage.com), which charges individuals $24.95 per month for the unlimited calling service (plus your Internet access fees). Business plans are also available.

For people who travel a lot or spend time on the road, a cellular phone is a critical tool for staying in touch with business associates and clients. Sprint PCS/NEXTEL (800-480-4727; www.sprintpcs.com), Cingular/AT&T Wireless (800-331-0500; www.cingular.com), and T-Mobile (866-464-8662; www.tmobile.com) are among the companies that offer nationwide digital (PCS) cellular service, often at competitive rates. You can also go with one of the many pre-paid cellular services available throughout America.

Other elements

If you have the money available, a desktop copy machine is also a valuable business tool in any home office. You'll also need basic supplies, such as business letterhead, envelopes, business cards, and everything from pads of paper to paper clips. (For basic office supplies, visit your local office-supply superstore, such as OfficeMax or Staples.)

If you have the space, set up two desks for yourself to help boost productivity and organization. You will use one desk for your computer and another for your paperwork.

The desk you use for your computer should have a built-in keyboard drawer or keyboard arm. This ensures that you'll have ample desk space and helps you avoid clutter. Make sure that the desk chair you select is comfortable and provides adequate back support.

 Watch Out!

Voice-Over IP service is still relatively new. Thus, some users report problems with dropped calls and unclear connections. For a small business operator, this might not yet be the ideal solution for handling all of your incoming and outgoing call needs.

Moneysaver

Small-business operators can save money on a wide range of products and services simply by shopping around for the best prices. LowerMyBills.com (www. lowermybills.com), for example, will help you find the best rates for telephone service, cellular service, insurance, Internet access, credit cards, and a wide range of other services. Nextag.com (www.nextag.com) will help you find the lowest prices for virtually any item or product, such as home-office equipment, computers, telephones, and furniture.

Other furniture and home-office equipment you should consider purchasing includes the following:

- A desk set (desk pad, business card holder, letter tray, and so on)
- Bookshelves
- Briefcase and pad/paper folio (for when you go out on appointments)
- Calculator
- Cassette or microcassette recorder (for dictation or keeping track of ideas)
- Credit-card processing software and equipment (if your business will be accepting credit cards as payment for your products or services). Establishing a merchant account to accept credit-card payments is covered in Chapter 3. What equipment and software you'll need will depend on the merchant account provider or financial institution you use for this service.
- File cabinets
- Floor lamps and a desk lamp
- Office-supply storage cabinet
- Postage machine and postage scale
- Printer stand

- Telephone answering machine (if you don't have call answering from your telephone company)

- Wastepaper basket and paper shredder (for destroying confidential documents before discarding them)

As you set up your office, visit furniture showrooms and office-supply superstores to help you choose the right office furniture to meet your needs.

Also, request the following mail-order catalogs or visit the websites of the following companies that cater to small/home-office operators:

- **BackSaver Products Company** (800-251-2225; www.backsaver. com)   An assortment of chairs, desks, and products designed to protect your back from pain and stress in a home-office environment.

- **Day-Timer** (800-225-5005; www.daytimer.com)   Offers a catalog of time-management and organizational products useful to business professionals and home-office operators.

- **Dell Computer** (800-WWW-DELL; www.dell.com)   Offers inexpensive PCs and laptop computers via mail order.

- **FolderExpress** (800-322-1064; www.folderexpress.com) A printing company that specializes in high-quality, yet inexpensive, full-color press-kit folders and custom-printed presentation folders.

 Bright Idea

A personal digital assistant (PDA) is a hand-held computer that can store thousands of names, phone numbers, addresses, and appointments. These devices can easily transfer data to a desktop computer. The most popular PDA manufacturer is Palm, Inc. (www.Palm.com), which offers standalone PDAs and SmartPhones. PDAs are extremely valuable organizational tools used by businesspeople and entrepreneurs in all industries.

- **Gateway Computer** (888-888-2075; www.gateway.com)
  Offers inexpensive PCs and laptop computers via mail
  order.

- **Getz Color Graphics** (800-562-7052; www.getzcolor.com)
  A printing company that specializes in inexpensive, high-
  quality, full-color promotional materials, such as posters,
  fliers, bookmarks, greeting cards, business cards, catalog
  covers, and brochures.

- **FedEx/Kinko's** (www.FedEx.com; 800-Go-FedEx)
  Located throughout the country, FedEx/Kinko's locations
  can satisfy many small business printing and shipping
  needs.

- **Hello Direct** (800-435-5634; www.hellodirect.com)
  A complete catalog of telephone equipment, including
  traditional telephones, multiline phones, cordless phones,
  cellular phones, and all sorts of telephone accessories.

- **Home Office Direct** (877-709-9700; www.homeoffice
  direct.com)   An online source of office furniture (including desks, chairs, computer carts, and cabinets) designed
  for home offices.

- **Levenger** (800-667-8034; www.levenger.com)   A catalog of
  fancy pens, home-office furniture, and other home-office
  equipment.

- **Lizell** (800-718-8882; www.lizell.com)   This catalog is
  filled with home-office furniture, small-business equipment, and other products useful to people who work
  from home.

- **OfficeMax** (800-283-7674; www.officemax.com)   An
  office-supply superstore that sells office supplies, furniture,
  computers, and related equipment.

- **Palm, Inc.** (888-223-4817; www.Palm.com)   The leading
  developer and manufacturer of personal digital assistants
  (PDAs) and SmartPhones.

- **Reliable Home Office** (888-898-7008; www.reliablehome office.com/main.asp)   This catalog also is filled with home-office furniture, small-business equipment, telephone equipment, and other products.

- **Staples** (800-3-STAPLE; www.staples.com)   An office-supply superstore that sells office supplies, furniture, computers, and related equipment.

Finally, don't forget about your shipping needs. You'll need supplies for fulfilling orders and generating a wide range of business correspondence. Boxes, packing tape, packing filler (such as Styrofoam popcorn chips), and address labels are among the core shipping items you'll need right from the start. You'll also want to set up accounts with The United States Post Office (www.USPS.com), UPS (www.UPS.com), FedEx (www.FedEx. com), and perhaps DHL (www.DHL.com). Many useful services targeted to small business operators are listed in Appendix C.

Just the facts

- The advantage of operating your own online business is that you are your own boss; poor planning on your part, however, can lead to failure. Be sure to create a detailed business plan.

- Work with a financial planner or accountant to help you define your needs and take advantage of the tax benefits of being a business owner.

- There are many reasonably priced software programs on the market to help you manage your business's finances.

GET THE SCOOP ON...
Getting insurance ▪ Choosing the form of your
business ▪ Accepting credit cards ▪ Strategies for
obtaining a merchant account ▪ Financing your
business venture

Your Online Biz's Finances

D on't be fooled by all of the e-commerce hype. Chances are, you've received junk e-mails explaining how you can start an online-based business for no money down, or for a very small investment. Even the promotional materials for Yahoo! Store state that the start-up costs are a mere few hundred dollars.

Realistically, if you're planning on launching a fully functional e-commerce site, there's going to be a financial investment of at least several thousand dollars (usually more) involved. A few hundred dollars might allow you to set up a very basic website and have an online presence, but you'll still have to make an investment in technology, marketing, advertising, inventory, merchant account fees, website hosting fees, office supplies, labor, and so forth. There is an ongoing cost to doing business, which you must calculate into your ongoing operating budget. Keep in mind, these fees and expenses will exist whether or not your company is generating revenue.

Benefits plans and compensation packages

Perhaps the biggest drawback of working for yourself is that you'll be giving up all of the benefits and perks an employer would typically provide. This means that in addition to your homeowner's or renter's insurance and auto insurance—insurance everyone typically has to pay for—you'll now have to acquire and pay for your own additional insurance. This can include the following:

- Health insurance (along with dental and vision-care insurance)

- Life insurance

- Long-term disability insurance

- Umbrella insurance

- Various types of business-related insurance (including fire, workers' compensation, and business interruption policies)

- Malpractice insurance

- Liability insurance

As a self-employed person who is adequately insured against various types of disaster, you could have monthly premiums anywhere from a few hundred to several thousand dollars, depending on your level of coverage and the types of insurance you acquire for yourself, your business, and your family.

In addition to having to pay for your insurance, you also have to deal with insurance agents personally, shop around for the best available policies, and then maintain all of the paperwork associated with having each type of policy.

 Watch Out!

Because insurance agents are typically paid on commission, what they offer you might not always be the best policy to meet your personal needs. Knowing what you want and need in advance, and then shopping around by speaking with several insurance agents, is an excellent strategy.

No longer will your contribution to your insurance premiums simply be deducted automatically from your paycheck while someone in your employer's benefits office administers the various types of policies and works with the insurance agents on your behalf.

Because paying for your own benefits (insurance in particular) will be expensive, it's an excellent idea to sit down with a personal financial planner, accountant, or some other impartial person who can help you define your needs.

Try to find an insurance agent you can trust, someone you feel comfortable developing a long-term relationship with. Make sure that the agent (or agents) you choose represents only the top insurance providers, and that they're familiar with the types of insurance policies you're looking to purchase.

The best way to find a reliable insurance agent is

> **❝** The basic business insurance package consists of four fundamental coverages—Workers' compensation, general liability, auto, and property/casualty— plus an added layer of protection over those, often called an umbrella policy. In addition to these basic needs, you should also consider purchasing business interruption coverage and life and disability insurance. **❞**
>
> —Yahoo! Small Business

through a referral from someone you know, someone who already has a positive business relationship with his/her insurance agent. At the same time, you can also research what the best (or highest-rated) insurance companies are for the types of insurance you want to receive, and then call those insurance companies directly for the names of their authorized agents.

As you review all of the different types of insurance policies that are available, try to avoid too much overlap, or you could easily wind up paying multiple times for the same coverage.

Moneysaver

You can often save money on monthly premiums by choosing an insurance policy with a higher deductible. The drawback to this is obvious. With a $1,000 deductible, for example, the first $1,000 of a claim comes out of your pocket before the insurance benefits kick in.

Likewise, pay careful attention to the premiums, deductibles, and benefits each policy offers.

When it comes to life insurance, for example, the lower the benefit you desire, the lower the premiums will be. (What you'll actually pay for life insurance will also depend on several factors, including your age and current health.)

A few words about hiring employees

One of the biggest expenses associated with operating a small business involves hiring full-time or part-time employees (unless they're unpaid interns—an excellent source of inexperienced, but often talented, labor as you establish your business).

Once your business reaches a certain size, you'll need to expand, which means finding, hiring, and managing honest, hardworking, and dedicated people. Although you might be hiring additional people to help reduce your personal workload, the extra responsibilities of hiring those people could easily require an even bigger time commitment on your part.

If the business you launch grows large enough that you need to hire additional employees on a full-time (or permanent part-time) basis, you'll probably have to offer these employees benefits, plus obtain the appropriate workers' compensation insurance to protect yourself if they're working from your home (or your office).

You'll also have to begin withholding federal and state income tax payments, Social Security taxes and funds for other benefits, such as health insurance or a 401(k), from their paychecks, and establish employee policies and procedures. These should be offered in writing to the people you hire.

Your level of responsibility also increases becai
have people looking to you for ongoing guidanc
on the success of your company for their paychecks. If you do
already have excellent managerial skills, you'll need to develop
them if you plan on running a business with employees.

Hiring freelance consultants or workers such as Web programmers, graphic artists, writers, photographers, or marketing
people can become costly, even if you don't have to offer them
benefits. You should factor these costs into your operating budget and monitor them carefully.

Should you incorporate?

For tax and legal reasons, you'll need to decide what form your
business will take. Generally, all businesses fall into one of these
broad categories: sole proprietorship, partnership, corporation,
S corporation, or limited liability corporation (LLC).

Your choice of business form will affect your exposure to
personal liability, how you draw profits and pay taxes, your ability to raise capital, and how you run the business. Here are short
descriptions of the various types of business forms.

Sole Proprietorship   This is the quickest and easiest way to
start a business. Just check with a knowledgeable attorney
about any licensing or legal requirements, and you're in
business. In a sole proprietorship, profits and losses are
simply included on your individual tax returns. On the
downside, if someone sues your business, they may be
able to sue you personally, and your personal assets
are subject to those claims. Depending on the type of

Bright Idea

For more information about the different types of corporations and which is best
for your situation, visit the AllBusiness.com website (www.allbusiness.com) for
information about its *Practical Guide to Incorporation* eBook ($49) and corpo-
ration kit (sold separately).

product or service you plan on offering through your online business, this might not be the best option in terms of your own protection.

Partnership   This type of business is an association of two or more people working as co-owners of a business with the intent of making a profit. The involvement of two or more people in the business generally increases the complexity and the amount of paperwork. Also, general partners can share unlimited liability, and each is usually responsible for the acts of the other. Depending on the type of product or service you plan on offering through your online business, this might not be the best option in terms of protection for the partners.

Corporation   A corporation is a legal entity that functions somewhat like an individual, legally and for tax purposes. Liabilities are held by the corporation, minimizing the personal liability for owners. The corporation operates as a business and can be owned wholly or partially based on registered certificates, called stock. Some of the responsibilities involved with setting up a corporation include filing an application for a legal name, paying a corporate franchise fee to the state in which you file, appointing a board of directors and corporate officers, and keeping minutes of periodic meetings of the board. Some states, such as Nevada, have far fewer rules and regulations for setting up a corporation.

S Corporation   This is a unique type of corporation. It provides the advantages of a corporation; but, unlike a corporation, it is treated for income-tax purposes as a flow-through entity. Income is reported individually by the owners or stockholders on their personal income tax returns. Also, the owners can deduct the corporation's losses against other sources of income. If your new business will have fewer than 35 stockholders, you may want to talk with your accountant and attorney about this option.

Bright Idea

Consult with an attorney and an accountant before you decide what form to use for your new business. These professionals can advise you on tax advantages and which business form offers you the best protection of personal assets. The right choice will also help you avoid costly problems down the road, especially if your company fails or winds up being sued.

Limited Liability Corporation   This is another alternative in which income and income tax are distributed among partners, but generally the partners are not personally liable for debts. If you are interested in setting up such a corporation, be sure to consult a knowledgeable attorney.

To learn more about how incorporating can benefit you financially and legally, contact both an accountant and a lawyer. Although there are many "kits," books, and online services that allow you to form your own corporation in minutes for a flat fee, your best strategy (although it's a bit more expensive initially) is to seek the guidance of a lawyer to help you with this process.

Other considerations involved with launching a business

Prior to selling any product or service online, you must first establish the infrastructure for operating your business. This requires establishing an office, filing the necessary legal documents to establish yourself as a business, and determining how incoming orders will be taken and processed.

Here are just a few of the questions you'll need to answer:

- Will you need a toll-free phone number for incoming orders?
- Who will answer the phone?
- Is it necessary to hire an independent order-taking or order-fulfillment house?

- Will it be necessary to accept credit cards as payment? (If you're starting an e-commerce website, this will be important!)
- How will your orders be shipped to customers?
- How much inventory will you need to keep in stock? Where will this inventory be stored?

Once an online business is established, there are specialized software packages designed to automate such tasks as order entry and processing, inventory control, credit-card authorization, ad tracking and management, bookkeeping, customer database management, and sales-lead management. Some turnkey e-commerce solutions handle many of these functions with no additional software required.

Aside from the basic equipment and software you'll need to help your business get started, you'll also need various supplies, such as company letterhead, business cards, envelopes, press kits/ folders, invoices, packing slips, shipping labels, and packaging for your products, all of which should have your company logo imprinted on them.

One of the first things you'll need to do is develop a company logo and identity for your business. You can do this yourself using a graphics program on your computer, or you can hire a freelance graphic artist (or a graphic design firm).

As you design your letterhead, business cards, and other printed materials, keep in mind that these tools should all convey a highly professional image for your company. Also, you'll want all of your printed materials (as well as your online identity) to be consistent in terms of the look of your overall company

 Bright Idea

American Express' Small Business division (American Express Open) offers loans and credit cards to small-business operators. Point your Web browser to: http://home.americanexpress.com/home/open.shtml for details.

Watch Out!

Although you'll want to shop around for the best printing rates, don't cut corners by using cheap paper stock for your letterhead, business cards, and so forth. Remember that these items will represent your company in the eyes of your potential customers, investors, and suppliers; make sure everything looks professional.

image. Pay attention to continuity and detail. Any business print shop or graphic artist can assist you in developing your company's logo, letterhead, business cards, press kits, and other printed materials. One resource for finding a freelance graphic artist is eLance.com (www.eLamce.com). Another website, Template Monster (www.TemplateMonster.Com) has ideas if you want to design these materials yourself using pre-created templates for popular word processing and graphic development software packages.

What needs to be done before going online?

Here's a partial checklist of things you'll need to do in the planning stages of forming your online business (listed in alphabetical order, not necessarily in the order you should complete these activities).

These tasks should be completed *prior* to your business's official start date:

❑ Calculate your start-up costs.

❑ Choose a bank (after meeting several representatives and comparing services and rates).

❑ Choose a reliable lawyer and accountant. Have the accountant prepare the necessary tax forms for establishing your business.

❑ Conduct market research. Who will your customers be? How big is the market? Who are your competitors?

❑ Create a well-defined and detailed business plan.

❑ Determine how your website will be created and maintained. Will you use a turnkey service, such as Yahoo! Store; hire a programmer to create the site from scratch; or use an off-the-shelf e-commerce software (such as osCommerce)? As you'll learn shortly, osCommerce (www.oscommerce.com) is a powerful website design software ideal for creating an e-commerce site. While it requires a small amount of computer and programming knowledge, it's extremely customizable. Best of all, the software is totally free of charge and can be downloaded from the osCommerce website.

❑ Determine your business's goals, mission statement, and objective.

❑ Determine your business's legal entity (sole proprietorship, partnership, corporation, or LLC).

❑ Determine your business's location and sign a lease (if necessary).

❑ Determine your financial resources.

❑ Develop a relationship with a shipping company (such as FedEx, UPS, or the U.S. Postal Service) and determine exactly how you'll ship your products to customers.

❑ Decide what your official business mailing address will be. Do you want to list your home address on your website and on your letterhead, or would you prefer to rent office

 Bright Idea

To help keep yourself organized, Sage Software, Inc. offers an extremely powerful and robust scheduling, organizational, and contact management too, called Act!. This PC-based software is the most popular tool of its kind on the market and is ideal for entrepreneurs and start-up business operators because it allows a vast amount of information to be stored in one, customizable database and easily accessed. Data can be seamlessly synchronized with a Palm or Pocket PC PDA. ACT! retails for $199 and is available from software retailers or from www.act.com.

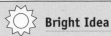

Bright Idea

Take the time to identify the risks (financial or otherwise) facing your business. Doing this might not be fun in the short run. But by thinking ahead to possible problems, you'll be equipped to deal with them efficiently if they do arise.

space or obtain a P.O. Box, for example? From shipping centers like The UPS Store, you can rent a P.O. Box that has an actual street address as opposed to a P.O. Box number, but the cost is significantly higher than renting a P.O. Box from your local United States Post Office.

❑ Develop a relationship with an Internet Service Provider or website-hosting service. Make sure your site will be able to handle secure financial transactions.

❑ Establish your company's line of credit.

❑ Identify your personal strengths and weaknesses (as they apply to operating a business), and then the strengths and weaknesses of your business idea.

❑ Join the local Chamber of Commerce and professional organizations/associations.

❑ Line up your suppliers for inventory, manufacturing, and so on. Open accounts with these vendors or suppliers and apply for credit.

❑ Obtain a merchant account so that your business can accept credit cards online. Set up a PayPal account so that you can accept PayPal payments (www.paypal.com). Accepting PayPal payments is optional as an online business operator. It does, however, make it easier for Web surfers who don't have a credit card to make purchases from your website.

❑ Obtain financing and raise start-up capital.

❑ Obtain the necessary local, state, or federal licenses or permits (most towns or cities require that you obtain some form of local business license). If you'll have employees, you'll also need an employee identification number.

❑ Plan and create your website (and hire the necessary talent in terms of programmers, graphic artists, photographers, and writers to assist you).

❑ Purchase or lease office furniture, business equipment, and related fixtures.

❑ Select an insurance agent and purchase all of the insurance you'll need (having the right insurance—and enough of it—is critical, for your own protection).

Planning your business operations

Once you have all of the pieces of your business's infrastructure in place, carefully determine how you will handle the day-to-day operations of your business. On paper (or using your computer), create detailed operating procedures for such things as order taking, order processing, website management (updating), accounting/bookkeeping, advertising and marketing implementation, credit-card authorizations, shipping, inventory management and ordering, and whatever other tasks will be key to the success of your business. How all of this is handled will vary greatly, depending on the type of online business you're running, what you're actually selling, the number of employees you have (if any) and what service you use to run your business.

Obviously, until your business is actually operating, you probably won't be able to anticipate every situation that you will need to deal with. The more prepared you are in advance, however, the lower your risk will be in terms of having to compensate for mistakes and unexpected negative situations.

Setting up a merchant account

When it comes to shopping online via a secure website, one of the fastest, safest, and easiest ways for a customer to pay for their purchases is with a major credit card.

To be competitive in cyberspace, being able to accept credit cards is an absolute necessity. Giving your customers the option to make purchases using their *PayPal* account can also be beneficial. PayPal allows people without a credit card to make purchases online, plus it offers extra security and convenience to Web surfers, even if they choose to use their major credit card or debit card. (To learn more about PayPal, point your Web browser to www.PayPal.com and click on the "Merchant Tools" icon.)

To accept credit cards (and in many cases, ATM/debit cards and electronic check payments), you must first obtain a *merchant account* through a bank, financial institution, or independent service organization. Using any Internet search engine, enter the search phrase "merchant account," and dozens of financial institutions will be listed, each offering you the ability to accept major credit cards, ATM/debit cards, and electronic check payments.

This has become a highly competitive industry, so it's important to carefully research the services being offered and shop around for the best rates. Typically, to obtain a merchant account, you'll be required to fill out an application and pay a one-time application fee (of several hundred dollars). Assuming your application is accepted, there will often be an ongoing monthly fee to maintain your merchant account, as well as transaction fees. The transaction fee on each sale might be a flat rate, or it could be a percentage of the total sale.

In addition to evaluating a financial institution's process for applying for a merchant account, you need to pay careful attention to all of the fees, how quickly the funds will be available to

 Moneysaver

Despite all of the fees associated with accepting major credit cards, assuming you obtain a competitive rate, these fees should be considered a cost of doing business. They'll pay for themselves in the long run if your business is successful.

you after the sale (if it's more than two to three days, look elsewhere), and what the steps are for processing credit-card transactions. Will you be able to perform real-time and automated credit-card processing from your website? What type of equipment will you need to lease or purchase? What special software will be required? Will you be required to use the financial institution's secure website to process credit-card transactions? Will the credit-card processing be compatible with your e-commerce software/service?

Acquiring a merchant account: strategies from Aria Financial Corporation

Aria Financial Corporation (800-731-7230; www.Arianet.com) is one of many merchant account providers that specialize in working with online business operators. It's a full-service merchant service provider that boasts an almost 99 percent approval rate for new companies getting started online.

According to the company, signing up for a merchant account can be confusing. Most companies will have websites where you can fill out a prequalification application. Once you submit your application, a sales representative will contact you.

The salesperson will determine your needs and will process your application. An application can typically be done over the phone, online, or on paper (via fax or mail). Online accounts differ from physical or retail accounts; they are considered "card not present" accounts or "Mail Order/Telephone Order (M.O.T.O)" accounts, because the credit card is not present for the transaction. This increases the risk of possible fraud. Thus, merchant account companies increase rates because of this added risk. If you're operating an online-based business with no brick and mortar (retail store) component, this is the type of merchant account you'll need.

E-commerce site operators need two tools in order to accept credit-card payments online—a merchant account and a virtual terminal/gateway.

The virtual terminal/gateway is an online credit-card interface, as well as the technology that connects the website to the merchant account so that credit-card payments can actually be processed securely and in real time.

Aria Financial Corp. has perfected the ability to set up online merchants quickly. Aria's merchant account application can be completed in minutes online or over the telephone.

The company can also assist merchants with any retail merchant solutions, including credit-card terminals with the ability to accept checks or even wireless solutions.

Ten strategies for obtaining a merchant account

To assist new online business operators in better understanding how to obtain a merchant account, Aria Financial Corp. offers the following 10 strategies:

1. **Compare prices, but beware of hidden fees.** The majority of merchant accounts will charge a percentage of the volume processed. This is called the *discount rate.* A number of merchant account companies will boast the lowest discount rates, and just make up the difference by raising other fees, such as transaction fees (a flat amount charged per transaction).

2. **Ask about rate review policies.** Once you establish a healthy relationship with a merchant bank, you may be able to request a reduction in your discount rate. Find out whether the company you're looking to work with will review your rates down the road. A small reduction in your discount rate can save a lot of money in the long run.

3. **Come up with a healthy estimate of how many transactions you will be processing monthly and at what volume; then shop accordingly.** If you plan on doing a few high-volume transactions per month, look for a company that has a lower discount rate, but possibly a higher transaction fee.

If you plan on doing many small-volume transactions with a lower monthly volume, you're better off finding a company that has a low per-transaction rate, but possibly a slightly higher discount rate.

4. **Don't sign anything until you read though the agreement (contracts) carefully.** Rushing to sign a contract because you're in a hurry to take credit-card payments can cost you a lot. Make sure you know about all the fees and the length of your contract.

5. **Make sure the solution you choose will work the way you need it to.** If you plan on setting up your merchant account to work seamlessly with a website, make sure that it will be compatible. Check with your website host or Webmaster. They can often suggest the best company to go with for ease of implementation.

6. **Do your research.** Merchant accounts can be overwhelming. Don't overpay someone because you don't understand what's out there. Most merchant accounts are very similar and so are their fees. Make an educated decision about which company you ultimately choose to go with.

7. **Consider using someone local.** If you go with a local company, you'll have easy, in-person access to your merchant account provider. Have them come to you and explain what they have to offer. You may find the best rates, however, by shopping around outside your geographic area.

8. **For traditional business operators, expand the scope of your existing merchant account.** If you already have a merchant account for an existing retail location or an established mail-order business, check with your current company about obtaining an online account.

9. **Make sure you are ready for a merchant account.** If you are just starting out online, it can take a while for business to pick up. The last thing you want to do is be responsible for paying monthly fees for a service that isn't paying for

Bright Idea

As an online business operator, being able to accept major credit cards is an absolute. According to statistics, the average American household has between 7 and 10 credit cards. The typical consumer has access to $12,190 on all of their credit cards combined. In 2004, total credit debt in the United States was $660 billion.

itself. Make sure that it is worth it to you. You may want to start off slow and pay a higher rate to a company, such as PayPal, where you won't have fees if you don't process payments. (The drawback to accepting PayPal is that the person making the purchase must also have an active PayPal account. PayPal is commonly used by frequent eBay users as a preferred method of payment.)

10. **Ask about discounts for low-risk business types.** Some merchant account providers have a sliding scale of discount rates for different types of businesses, depending on the amount of risk associated with your industry. If your company is one that is less of a risk, you may qualify for a lower discount rate. Examples of high-risk companies are escort services, credit restoration companies, and online-based gambling services.

Merchant account providers

Because your new online-based business will be operating primarily on the Internet (with no retail locations), your local banks might not offer you a merchant account. Thus, you'll need to use a financial institution or independent service organization that caters to mail-order and online-based businesses.

To find additional services and compare rates, use any Internet search engine, such as Yahoo! (www.yahoo.com) or Google (www.google.com). Enter the search phrase "Merchant Account." If you're using a turnkey solution for your e-commerce site, the service provider will often offer merchant account services (typically for an additional fee).

The following is a partial list of merchant account services you'll find on the Web:

- Aria Financial Corporation (800-731-7230; www. Arianet.com)
- Card Service International (888-869-5520; www.csicard.com)
- Credit Merchant Account Services (203-483-5751; www.merchantaccount.net)
- Electronic Clearing House, Inc. (800-233-0406; www.echo-inc.com)
- Electronic Transfer, Inc. (800-757-5453, ext. 201; www.paymentmall.com)
- Merchant Account Company (800-956-1990; www. merchantaccount.com)
- Merchant Express (888-845-9457; www. merchantexpress.com)
- Merchant Warehouse (800-574-2562; www. merchantwarehouse.com)
- Verisign (866-893-6565; www.verisign.com)

Secure Electronic Transaction Protocol (SET)

Online security is one of the top concerns of people who shop online. When people enter their credit cards into an online order form, they want assurances that their credit card numbers and personal information won't be "broadcast" throughout the Web and available to hackers. Maintaining online security on your site involves adding some form of secure transaction capabilities.

Unless your website will offer secure transactions using the *Secure Electronic Transaction Protocol (SET)*, the SSL protocol, or another form of encryption/online security, don't even consider accepting credit-card payments from your customers.

If you're using one of the popular turnkey solutions from Yahoo!, eBay or GoDaddy, for example, to operate your website, all of the necessary security is already built into the shopping cart/order form application. Likewise, most Internet Service Providers or merchant account processors offer the needed security. The Verisign (www.verisign.com) website offers extensive information on online security relating to credit-card transactions.

Beware of fraudulent credit-card transactions

One of the issues you'll need to contend with once you establish a merchant account is fraudulent transactions. According to Mindwave Research, "41 percent of merchants say the issue of online credit-card fraud is 'very serious' to their business."

Online credit-card fraud typically involves someone using a stolen credit card to make a purchase. The Merchant Account provider you choose to work with should help educate you about how to protect yourself against fraudulent transactions and avoid charge backs from customers. However, as the online business operator, you'll need to be on the lookout for unusual transactions.

Information about how to protect your business against fraud and charge backs once a merchant account is established is available from these resources:

- Merchant Seek (www.merchantseek.com/article8.htm)
- AntiFraud.com (www.antifraud.com)
- Merchant Solution (www.merchant-solution.com)
- Bank Card Law (www.bankcardlaw.com)

How much of an issue credit-card fraud will be for your company will vary, depending on what you're selling and who is your target customer.

Financing your business

Securing adequate financing is a primary concern for most new businesses. Most people don't personally possess all the resources it takes to get a business up and running, but as a business owner you'll need to invest some of your own money. Putting your funds into a business venture helps prove your commitment to potential investors or other sources of financing.

Sources of outside financing include the following:

- Banks
- Credit-card companies (like American Express Small Business)
- Loans from relatives or friends
- Private investors
- The Small Business Administration (SBA)

Be aware that many banks consider new business loans to be too risky, even when money is not tight. The SBA is usually eager to help new enterprises, but competition is keen for the SBA's limited financial resources. Before applying for financing, you need to carefully prepare a thorough loan proposal. It also helps if you, the business owner, possess a good credit history and an above-average personal credit (FICO) score.

Write up detailed figures on the capital needed, and be sure to include a salary for yourself and sufficient funds to cover start-up costs. An SBA representative or your accountant, for example, will review your business plan from a financial standpoint to be sure it's solid.

Once you obtain a loan, you'll probably have to provide updated financial statements on a regular basis. As long as your business is profitable and you're making loan payments on time, you'll probably have minimum contact with the bank or SBA. Short-term loans may require closer bank monitoring.

No matter what type of business you plan on launching, it's going to require start-up capital (probably more than you think).

 Bright Idea

You might consider seeking private investors who want to have an equity stake in your business. Relatives or friends are potential investors, too. Keep in mind, however, that these people might, understandably, expect to have a say in how the business is run. And if you tell them no, it can affect your relationship. Be sure you make the ground rules clear up front.

Starting a business has a lot of expenses associated with it. After those expenses (which vary based on the type of business) are taken into account, you still need enough operating capital at the start to keep your business going for at least one year.

Very few businesses become profitable immediately, and most of those that fail do so because there wasn't enough capital available.

Not every business has the same start-up expenses. Some of the costs you'll have to calculate into your budget and consider when creating your business plan include the following:

- Accounting and consulting
- Advertising, marketing, and public relations
- Business travel
- Communications equipment (such as telephones, telephone service, cellular service, and pagers)
- Company cars and vehicles
- Computer equipment and office technology (such as copy and fax machines)
- Custom-printed stationery, business cards, and envelopes
- Insurance
- Interest on loans
- Internet Service Provider (ISP) and website hosting fees
- Inventory
- Labor (salaries and payroll)
- Legal fees
- Manufacturing equipment or specialized equipment
- Merchant account fees
- Office furniture and fixtures
- Office supplies
- Order processing/shipping
- Printing costs for brochures, press kits, and marketing materials

- Recruiting
- Rent
- Salaries
- Taxes
- Utility bills (such as water, electricity, sewer, heat, and air-conditioning)
- Website design and maintenance

After you've figured out exactly what it'll cost you to get your business up and running and fully operational for a least one year (although you'll eventually need projections for at least three to five years), you'll need to raise the necessary capital. Once again, you have many options available to you:

- Invest your own funds (using your savings, mortgaging your home, maxing out your credit cards, or taking out a personal loan). Obviously, you want to incur the least amount of risk possible. Maxing out your credit cards, for example, offers a rather significant risk and should be used as an option only when others aren't available.
- Seek out independent partners and investors.
- Obtain small-business loans from a financial institution.
- Apply for state, federal, or private grants.
- Borrow money from close relatives or friends.
- Apply for corporate credit cards (but be prepared to pay high interest rates).
- Win the lottery (this is probably not a viable option, so don't rely on it).

Obviously, using your personal savings to launch your business provides you with the most freedom, but also exposes you to more risk if your business fails. Consult an accountant and lawyer to explore the various pros and cons of each option before deciding how you'll fund your business.

Bright Idea

Save time when researching and narrowing venture-capital options. Check out America's Business Funding Directory (www.businessfinance.com), an entrepreneurial database designed to match capital sources with people seeking funding. The service covers venture capital, equipment leasing, commercial real estate, SBA or SBIC loans, private investments, and more.

Just the facts

- For tax and legal reasons, you'll need to decide what form your business will take. Your choice of business form will affect your exposure to personal liability, how you draw profits and pay taxes, your ability to raise capital, and how you run the business.

- In order to be competitive in cyberspace, your business *must* be able to accept credit cards. To do this, you'll need to set up a merchant account.

- Consider offering PayPal (www.paypal.com) as an alternative payment method for your customers.

- Your business probably won't be profitable at first. Plan accordingly.

- Be sure you look into all the sources of financing available to you, including banks, the SBA, friends, relatives, and your own funds.

GET THE SCOOP ON...
Choosing website-creation software ▪ The basics
of online graphic design ▪ Turnkey solutions
for websites ▪ Avoiding common Web design
mistakes ▪ Using professionals

Planning Your Site

Chapter 4

The World Wide Web is packed with millions of websites. Some are interactive, highly professional, and eye-catching. Others look far less professional, take too long to load, and offer poor design and layout, a bad choice of color schemes, and ineffective or confusing text. These sites sometimes contain typos, are difficult to navigate, and have broken links or other problems that convey a poor image of the individual or company that developed the site. Even if such a site contains useful information or products, visitors probably won't stay long enough for the site to make any impact.

Making your site look professional

How do you make your site an attractive and useful one? Before you begin creating it, spend time surfing the Web looking for ideas. Knowing everything there is to know about your product is important, but understanding your customers and discovering

Bright Idea

If you're looking for website design ideas, why not start by checking out the very best and busiest sites? Visit *TrafficRanking.com*'s Top 100 websites list at www.trafficranking.com.

how to appeal to them with your website will determine how successful you ultimately become as an online business operator.

Determine what *you* think looks good and what website features you like. Next, figure out how you can incorporate those ideas into your site's content, design, and layout. At least initially, you'll most likely need and want to hire a professional website designer or graphic artist to help you achieve the website design results you're looking for.

Even if you're not a programmer; don't know HTML (HyperText Markup Language), Flash, or Java programming; and aren't a graphic artist or a talented writer, you can still create an extremely impressive site using website-creation software or services.

Many commercial Web-page-design software packages require no programming to create professional-looking Web pages. These packages (such as Microsoft FrontPage) are bundled with predefined templates created by professional graphic artists. Templates make designing your basic site much faster and easier.

Using templates as a starting point, you can simply add your own text and graphics (and audio and video clips) to customize your site and make it look professional, with content that will interest potential customers.

There are also a growing number of complete e-commerce turnkey solutions available, such as GoDaddy.com's Quick Shopping Cart (www.godaddy.com), eBay Stores for Online Auctions (http://stores.ebay.com), eBay ProStores for e-commerce (www.ProStores.com), and Yahoo! Stores (Yahoo! Small Business) (http://smallbusiness.yahoo.com/merchant).

These online-based services and design tools allow anyone to develop an online store quickly, using just a computer equipped with Internet access and Web browser software. Absolutely no programming is required. The cost of using these services is also extremely inexpensive, typically starting at well under $50 per month for the basic service.

These turnkey solutions will help get you online quickly and cheaply, but they provide only the basic functionality and design tools needed to compete successfully in the world of online e-commerce.

Whatever method you use, designing your site and creating the best content for it will take a considerable amount of time. Creativity is important if you want to make your corner of cyberspace a unique, enjoyable, and informative place to visit.

Because your website is going to be the primary way you interact with potential customers and clients, it's vital that your site convey a professional image. Your site must be all of the following:

- Easy to read and understand
- Visually appealing
- Simple to navigate through using any Web browser software
- Fast-loading
- Error-free (no broken links, misspellings, or inaccurate information)
- Loaded with the information your potential customers need and want
- Able to offer exactly the product(s) and service(s) your target customers want and need
- Able to offer fast and easy online ordering utilizing a shopping-cart application that's intuitive and encourages your customers to make online purchases

Most important, your site must build up your visitors' confidence, so that they believe they're dealing with a highly reputable company. If you'll be taking orders for your products online, you must offer easy-to-understand order forms and make it clear to customers that they'll be participating in secure financial transactions when visiting your site. This will make them more comfortable using their credit card or PayPal to place orders.

Your site should answer the most common questions your customers will have; make full use of visuals to show off your products; and display your company's logo, address, e-mail address, and telephone number (preferably a toll-free number). Visitors should be able to contact you directly with questions and comments, or to place their orders using an alternative method to online order processing.

Although you might be tempted to load up your website with lots of flashy video and audio features, they can overwhelm visitors who aren't familiar with how to navigate the Web. In addition, the browser software many Web surfers use might not be equipped with the plug-ins that allow them to hear audio or see certain types of animated graphics, such as Flash. While incorporating audio, video and flashy animations can be beneficial, it should be used to help communicate your sales message, not simply be used as eye candy.

When designing your website, choosing your color scheme and deciding on the overall look of your site, consider how the site will look on different computers that are equipped with different graphics cards, monitors, and Internet connections. Pay careful attention to compatibility issues. This is most important if you're developing your site from scratch as opposed to using a template provided by a turnkey solution provider, for example.

As you develop your site, it's important to ensure that it is compatible with the major Web browsers (Microsoft Internet

 Bright Idea

The most common resolution setting (which your website should be designed for) is 800 × 600.

Explorer, Netscape Navigator, AOL's browser, Firefox, and Opera). How your site looks when viewed with one browser may be totally different (in terms of the colors displayed and layout) from how it's displayed when viewed with another browser. The graphic resolution your visitor has set will also affect how your site is viewed. The most common setting (which your website should be designed for) is 800×600.

Some of the other common settings for graphic resolutions on a PC-based computer are 640×480, 1024×768, 1152×870, 1280×1024, and 1600×1200. (Each has 256 colors, high color [16-bit] or true color [24-bit].) True color or 24-bit color is the color of a pixel on display screens using 24-bit value. This permits 16,777,216 different colors (2 to the 24th power). Some older monitors, however, can accommodate only eight-bit color, or 256 possible colors.

People who can set their monitors to display graphics at higher resolutions have invested in high-end graphics cards and monitors.

If your online business will be targeting mass-market customers on the Web, your best bet is to design your site so that the vast majority of Web surfers can view it without having to adjust their display resolution or download additional plug-ins for their browser software. It should also load quickly, even if someone is using a dial-up Internet connection as opposed to DSL or broadband.

Plug-in applications are programs that can be installed and used as part of your Web browser. For example, Adobe's Reader lets you view documents the way they look in print. Flash is a programming language and Web browser plug-in from Macromedia (www.macromedia.com) that allows you to add fast-loading animated graphics to your website, which can be viewed by any surfer who has the appropriate Flash plug-in loaded with their browser. Other plug-ins, such as QuickTime or Windows Media Player, allow surfers to hear audio clips (music) or view streaming video.

Bright Idea

For a list of popular browser plug-ins supported by Netscape Navigator, visit http://browser.netscape.com/ns8/community/plugin.jsp. For information about the latest plug-ins supported by Microsoft Internet Explorer, visit http://windowsupdate.microsoft.com, or use the Windows Update command found under the Tools pull-down menu of Explorer 4.0 (or later). Information about the FireFox browser and compatible plug-ins can be found at www.mozilla.org/products/firefox/.

There are a handful of popular browser plug-ins, such as Flash, QuickTime, Windows Player, and Adobe Reader that most Web surfers currently have, especially if they use a high-speed broadband or DSL Internet connection. Incorporating graphic, animation, audio, or video elements into your website is okay as long as using these technologies help you communicate your sales message and help generate orders as opposed to confusing your visitors or cluttering your website (which can distract your visitors).

To accommodate all Web surfers, if you want to incorporate Flash animations into your website, for example, consider developing two versions of your site. A basic site will utilize none of the special plug-ins and best be viewed by someone with a low-end computer surfing the Web using a slow, dial-up connection.

A separate Flash-enabled site can offer fancy animations and other features for more advanced Web surfers with high-speed Internet connections. At the opening splash screen of your website, you can allow people to choose whether they want to view a basic version of your website or a Flash-enabled version. A custom programmed website can be designed to detect what browser plug-ins a visitor has and then display the appropriate version of your site automatically.

The first steps in developing your site

Before you start designing your site or putting it together, carefully evaluate and determine the exact purpose of your site. Ask yourself these questions:

- What messages or information do I want to convey?

- Will my site be an online extension of my existing business, used for customer service or technical support issues?

- Is the site being developed to enhance my existing company's image in cyberspace? Is it a marketing tool, public relations tool, sales tool, recruiting tool, or an all-purpose electronic commerce site?

- Will my site be an online catalog or interactive brochure for one or more products?

- What do I want visitors to be able to see and do when visiting my site?

- What is the overall goal of the site?

- Will I be accepting orders online?

- What features are important for my site to offer?

- How will my site be laid out and what will be contained within each of the pages? (Most sites contain a variety of individual Web pages.)

Developing your site's basic layout

One key ingredient to the success of any online business is the good design and simplicity of the site. When someone visits your site, he or she should find it intuitive to use and not at all confusing. The menus should be easy to find and understand. If someone is looking for a specific piece of information about one of your products, it should take them seconds, not minutes, to find exactly what they're looking for.

The overall production values of your site will also go a long way toward boosting customer confidence. If a visitor to your site perceives it to be amateurish, he or she will leave and won't consider buying anything. In fact, the term "Web surfers" was coined because people exploring the Web have about the same attention span as a channel surfer watching television . . . very short. If your website doesn't visually attract the attention of a visitor through high production values, the chances he or she will stay long enough to read the text or look at the pictures is slim. As a general rule, you need to capture the surfer's attention within 10 seconds.

Thus, it's important to plan your site in advance and determine what type of information will be available. You also need to think carefully about where and how that information will be conveyed.

Every website is comprised of text and images. Some images are photographs, whereas others are logos, line drawings, computer-generated graphics (bullets, arrows, and lines), or animated graphics. The use of high-quality images is an absolute must on an e-commerce website or a site designed to generate business.

As you choose which images will be incorporated into your site, keep in mind the file size of the image, as well as the color scheme. The larger the file in terms of its file size (not its displayed size on the screen), the longer it will take to load. Long load times frustrate Web surfers. For example, the background color of your product shots or the color of your logo should fit well into the overall color scheme of your site. Using colors that clash will detract from its professional appearance.

If any of your product photos, for example, look pixilated or blurry, it will cause your entire site to appear unprofessional. Ideally, you want to display small thumbnail images and allow the surfer to click on those small images to see larger, more detailed versions of the photo, image, or product shot.

 Bright Idea

When using product photos on your site, the pictures must be of professional quality and not look like they were taken with a Polaroid instant camera. Consider hiring a professional photographer to create your photos. You can also use a graphic artist to create line art of your products, which will translate into smaller graphic files. Keep the image files as small as possible (for fast loading), but don't compromise on their clarity or quality.

Choosing the perfect content

You and the people helping you design your site are the only ones who can ultimately determine what the best content is for your site because you know your company's products and services and who your target audience is. Remember, what you say, how you say it, and the graphic images you use will play a major role in the success or failure of your site.

One advantage of the Web, however, is that you can change things almost instantaneously; if something isn't working or you develop an idea that will improve something about your site, it can be fixed and uploaded quickly and easily. As you choose a company to design and host your website, make sure updates can be made quickly and inexpensively (or free).

Some of the important areas or pages of any online business (e-commerce) site include the following:

- **Home page:** When someone enters your Uniform Resource Locator (URL; such as www.yourcompany.com) into their browser, they should be taken directly to your home page. Think of it as the main lobby of your store. It should list your company's name, display your logo, and immediately inform visitors what type of content is offered on the site. You can also use the home page to offer news items, such as information about a highlighted product or an item that's on sale. As an alternative to making the home page the first place a visitor to your site sees, you could start the visitor at a "splash screen," a separate screen containing a short welcome message, animation, or your logo. A visitor must then click their mouse on the splash screen to enter the main areas of your site.

- **Company information/background:** Before people place an order with your company, they'll probably want to know something about your company—especially if they've never done business with you before. Use this page of your site to tell people about your company's background and boost their confidence in your company's products.

- **Display third-party validation logos:** To help boost your credibility among first-time visitors to your website and boost their confidence in your business, it's an excellent strategy to display the logos of third-party companies you're affiliated with. For example, displaying the Verisign or Hacker Safe logo promotes the fact that your website uses the latest security features for processing credit-card transactions. The BBBonline logo demonstrates you meet or exceed the business guidelines established by the Better Business Bureau. If you accept credit cards, displaying the Visa, Mastercard, American Express and/or PayPal logos can also help boost confidence.

- **Product description/catalog pages:** If you're developing an e-commerce site, these pages will describe each of your products in detail. In addition to offering detailed descriptions, prices, and ordering information, seriously consider offering a product photo and technical specifications, just as you would if you were creating a mail-order catalog or full-color sales brochure for the product. Using product photos in your site is an absolute must. To keep the download time of your site short, however, use thumbnail images that a surfer can click on to see a larger version of the photo. A thumbnail image is a small-size photo that downloads very quickly. There's no need for someone to wait for a large photo to load if it's not something they're interested in.

- **News, sales, specials, and promotions:** This page conveys company or industry-oriented news, late-breaking details

 Watch Out!

Using large images, especially on your site's home page, might be a huge mistake because they take longer to load. (The size of the image refers to the file size in bytes, not the physical size of the photo as it actually appears on your site.) Instead, consider a series of small images.

about new or forthcoming products, information about special sales, or other information your visitors might be interested in. One way to keep people coming back to your site is to provide an ongoing and reliable source for information about a specific topic. Yet another way to get people excited about your site is to hold contests or special promotions, allowing visitors to win prizes.

■ **Answers to common questions/technical support:** Whether customers are shopping in a retail store or online, they'll have questions about the products you're offering, no matter how detailed your descriptions are. In a traditional retail store, a customer with a question can simply ask the salesperson. In cyberspace, the customer should be able to call a toll-free phone number, send an e-mail message, or send the company a letter via fax or U.S. Mail. If you tend to get people asking the same questions over and over, you might consider creating a Frequently Asked Questions (FAQ) page for your site. This document should be written in an easy-to-understand question-and-answer format, and address the most common questions and concerns among your customers. A well-written FAQ that's available on your site should reduce the number of questions and technical support inquiries your company receives.

Some of the questions you might want to address in an FAQ document as well as in the main body of your site include the following: What forms of payment does your company accept? How will the products ordered on your site be shipped? How long before shipping? What are the shipping costs? What are the shipping options? What is your online store's sales tax policy? If a customer needs to speak with a customer service/technical support representative, how and when can someone be reached (and during what hours)? Does your site offer secure online ordering? Aside from ordering online, what other options do customers have (for example, can orders be faxed, e-mailed, or called in?)? What is your return or exchange policy? What guarantees and warranties does your company offer? Do you accept international orders? If so, what's the ordering procedure? What about additional overseas shipping charges and taxes? Will you meet or beat your competition's prices? What is your company's privacy policy in terms of sharing your customer's personal information with other companies?

- **Customer testimonials:** If you have a handful of highly satisfied customers who have written you letters or e-mails, you might want to obtain permission to reproduce these letters online as part of your site. A potential customer will find it reassuring to read testimonials from other happy customers. Of course, if you have a celebrity endorsing your product, this, too, is an extremely powerful marketing tool that goes a long way toward boosting a potential customer's confidence.

- **Online ordering/shopping cart:** One of the biggest challenges you'll face is designing an order form that's comprehensive, informative, and easy to understand. Otherwise, you risk scaring off a potential customer. Before designing your online order form (often referred to as a site's shopping cart), determine exactly what information you need to gather from the customer. This information might include the customer's name, title, company name, billing and shipping addresses (street address, city, state, ZIP code), phone number, fax number, e-mail

 Watch Out!

If you use a carrier such as FedEx or UPS that guarantees certain delivery times, part of the order-taking process should convey to the customers exactly when they can expect to receive the product they're about to order. Because Web surfers demand fast responses, it's important to be able to offer immediate shipping.

address, name of products they want to order, product numbers, quantities, sizes, and monogramming information. Your site may also need to be able to automatically calculate numbers, such as order subtotals, sales tax, and shipping charges. Finally, your order forms need to spell out exactly what forms of payment you accept, such as checks, money orders, PayPal, or credit cards. You must convince the customer that he or she is participating in a totally secure online transaction before they'll provide confidential credit-card information. A "shopping-cart" feature incorporated into your site allows visitors to easily gather items to purchase, continue shopping, and then place their order for several items in one shot. Pre-designed shopping-cart applications are readily available from many Internet Service Providers (ISPs) as well as providers of turnkey website solutions (such as the companies described later in this chapter). If you're using a turnkey solution to operate your online business, you won't need to create a shopping cart application from scratch, which makes setting up your website much easier.

■ **Order-response screens/e-mail messages:** After someone places an order, he or she should immediately see an acknowledgement screen stating that their order has been received, what the order number is, and when he or she can expect their order to be shipped and to arrive. Of course, you also want to thank the customer for their order! In addition to this order-confirmation screen, it's an excellent customer-relations strategy to send the customer an e-mail, again thanking them and confirming the details of the order.

■ **Customer newsletter or blog:** One way to keep Web surfers interested in your site is to provide them with free information that they consider valuable and extremely useful. Many website operators do this by creating an online newsletter that's updated weekly or monthly. Another method for communicating informally with potential and existing customers is to create a blog. A blog is a frequent, chronological, electronic (online) publication containing personal thoughts and Web links. It's sort of like an online, digital diary. A blog maintained by the president/founder of your company, for example, can be used to informally communicate with customers about new products, sales, special promotions, and events that relate to the company. By requiring Web surfers to subscribe or "opt-in" to receive your free newsletter or access your blog, you can obtain valuable information (market research) about your customers, plus build a valuable database of e-mail addresses, which you can use later for e-mail marketing and promotions.

E-commerce, the sale of products and services on the Web, is still a relatively new industry, compared to retail stores or mail-order catalogs. Thus, no website design is guaranteed to work, and no e-commerce model is foolproof. As you develop your site, plan to experiment and allow your site to evolve over time.

Just as with a printed document or advertisement, a Web page can be decorative, colorful, informative, nicely laid out, well organized, and visually appealing. If you're not careful, however, it can also become a confusing hodge-podge of text, pictures, and graphics.

Throughout the design process, keep in mind that in most cases, your goal isn't to wow visitors with flashy graphics, but to provide a comfortable environment in which they can shop. Likewise, just as major department stores change their displays

Bright Idea

No matter how well you think your site turns out, plan on updating and modifying it often if you want people to come back. If you can get customers in the habit of visiting your site daily or weekly by offering new content, your chances of repeat orders increase dramatically.

regularly to keep shoppers coming back, the content and even the design of your site should change periodically in order to keep people interested and keep the content fresh.

Although you'll want to update your website frequently with new information and products, for example, you don't want to drastically alter the overall design of your site too often, or it could confuse your frequent customers.

Once you've determined your target audience and the information about your company and product you want to convey, planning your website's design involves a highly creative process. Sure, basic rules of graphic design apply, but at the same time, there's plenty of room for creativity.

As a general rule, keep the site simple. Only use pictures and graphics that add meaning or value to your site; use fonts, typestyles, and color schemes that are visually appealing and will appear consistent, no matter which browser software someone is using. The fonts and typestyles you choose to convey your text-based information should be supported by the most common Web browser programs. This will ensure that your website design is displayed exactly how you want it to appear.

If you incorporate an unusual font that a program, such as Microsoft Explorer, doesn't recognize, it will automatically be converted into a more familiar font, but this conversion will change the overall look of your site.

Using color and art

Before you start creating your site, gather all of the visual assets available to you. Your assets might include your logos, artwork, images, text, photos, sound clips, video clips, animated (Flash) sequences, and any other elements that can be incorporated into your site. Once you know what assets are available, you'll be able to make intelligent and creative decisions to use these assets to get your key messages across to your site's visitors. Always be thinking about who your target customers are and how to best address them.

Regarding color, most computer monitors (and graphics cards) can display well over 256 different colors. However, Mac and Windows Web browsers have different sets of 256-color pallets that can be displayed. And if you use a color that isn't part of the palette on your visitor's browser, the browser has to "dither"—attempting to match the color as closely as possible. Unfortunately, dithering can result in a grainy appearance and detract from the design of your site. So be sure to choose your colors from among the 216 colors that are common to all Web browsers.

The Lynda.com (www.lynda.com/hex.html) website offers an article entitled "The Browser-Safe Web Palette," which helps site designers choose colors most suited for all Web browsers. Using this site, you can select colors from the 216-color Web-safe palette and see how they look.

Other useful websites that help to explain the use of the "browser-safe palette" include Web Safe Color Palette (www.visibone.com/colorlab) and The Netsider tutorial page (www.netstrider.com/tutorials/HTMLRef/color/).

Colors are like words. Just as context can alter the meaning of a word or phrase, surrounding colors can make a central color look different to the human eye. Experiment and see what effects the colors have on one another. As you do this, consider the color of your text, backgrounds, supporting graphics, and so on.

Choosing the best fonts

Fonts and typestyles play a huge role in the overall look of your site. The font you use can help set your site's attitude. Keep in mind, however, that using too many fonts on a single page can

 Bright Idea

To learn more about fonts and typestyles, visit the Adobe website at www.adobe.com. Other excellent resources are The FontSite (www.fontsite.com) and 1001Fonts.com (www.1001fonts.com).

Watch Out!

When adding standard text to your site, avoid using underlines. On the Web, underlined text usually signifies a hyperlink. If otherwise normal text is underlined, a Web surfer expects to be able to click on that text in order to find out more information about a specific topic.

make reading any type of text confusing. Likewise, you want to avoid mixing too many type sizes, and avoid using too much bold, italics, or underlining. If you incorporate unusual or non-standard fonts into your website, the only way to ensure that a viewer sees a particular font the way it's intended is to use specialized software to convert the text into a graphic image to be displayed within your site. Using Flash programming is one way to incorporate unusual fonts into your Web design and ensure they'll be viewed properly.

Times Roman, Verdana, Courier and Arial, for example, are common fonts supported by all Web browsers. If you go to a website like 1001Fonts.com and choose to use one of the more unusual fonts, it probably won't be supported by the popular browsers. Thus, unless you save and display the text as a graphic image, the font you choose will automatically be converted into a standard font that the Web surfer's computer can display. This could dramatically change the look and formatting of your site.

In terms of deciding how text should appear on the screen, it's safe to follow the same graphic-design rules you'd use for any type of traditional printed media. There are thousands of possible fonts to choose from, but for large amounts of text, it's best to stick with an easy-to-read font that looks good on the screen.

To see samples of some of the fonts available to you, visit http://store.yahoo.com/vw/fonsam.html. You can also point your Web browser to 1001Fonts.com (www.1001fonts.com), a free resource for obtaining and downloading fonts.

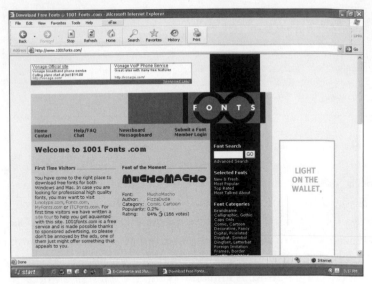

Figure 4.1. One of the best resources on the Web for downloading free TrueType (Windows-compatible) fonts is 1001fonts.com. Using eye-catching fonts within your graphics is a great way to jazz up your site's appearance.

Keep in mind that every font has a variety of different typestyles that you can use to communicate with, including normal text, **bold text,** and *italic text*. There's also ^{superscript} and $_{subscript}$. Because Web pages are displayed in full color, you can also alter the color of your text, using bright colors (such as red) to catch readers' attention or emphasize a keyword or important point.

You can also animate text on a website. You can make words flash on and off, rotate, shake, or do a wide range of other things in order to capture the reader's attention. The look of your text is as important as what the text says, if not more important. After all, if a viewer perceives your text as too wordy or confusing based on the layout, font size, or color, he or she is less likely to keep reading. It's important to balance readability with aesthetics when choosing the appropriate fonts and typestyles for your site.

Types of graphic files

As you begin creating your website and adding graphics, you'll need to start focusing on more advanced topics, like file types and file size. Many of the turnkey solutions automatically deal with many of these issues. This section is more for someone programming their website from scratch or who is using off-the-shelf website design software that doesn't automatically format graphics onto a Web page that's being created.

Graphics files—whether a company or product logo, product photos, website background graphics, small animations, navigation buttons, menu bars, or anything else that's non-text-oriented—can be created in several popular and well-supported formats for use on a Web page.

In a nutshell, GIF images are excellent for displaying small graphics files, such as logos or pieces of line art, whereas JPEG images are better suited for displaying photographs and other types of highly detailed images. TIFF files are typically large in size, but display photographs with the most detail.

TIFFs

Whatis.com offers definitions and descriptions of computer terms. The site is designed for non-technically oriented people and can be used to help you better understand technical lingo. This is a free service.

According to Whatis.com,

> A TIFF (Tag Image File Format) file can be identified as a file with a *.tiff* or *.tif* file name suffix (extension) . . . . One of the most common graphic image formats, TIFF files are commonly used in desktop publishing, faxing, 3-D applications, and medical imaging applications.

GIFs

Whatis.com reports that

> The GIF format is actually owned by CompuServe, and companies that make products that exploit the format

(but not ordinary Web users or businesses that include GIFs in their pages) need to license its use . . . . There are two versions of the format, 87a and 89a. Version 89a allows for the possibility of an animated GIF, which is a short sequence of images within a single GIF file. A GIF89a can also be specified for interlaced presentation. An interlaced GIF is a GIF image that seems to arrive on your display like an image coming through a slowly open-ing Venetian blind. A fuzzy outline of an image is gradu-ally replaced by seven successive waves of bit streams that fill in the missing lines until the image arrives at its full resolution. Among the advantages for the viewer using slower, dial-up modems are that the wait times for an image seem less and the viewer can sometimes get enough information about the image to decide to click on it or move elsewhere. GIFs are typically used for logos and rel-atively flat color pictures. GIF compression retains the entire image, as opposed to JPEG images.

Using a standalone software package, such as LViewPro (www.lview.com), you can greatly reduce the size of your site's graphic files, making them load faster. Many graphics programs, such as PhotoShop Elements, PhotoShop CS2, or Microsoft Digital Image Pro, have a built-in feature for automatically shrinking the file size of an image for use on a website.

JPEGs

According to Whatis.com,

A *JPEG* (pronounced JAY-peg) is a graphic image created by choosing from a range of compression qualities . . . . When you create a JPEG or convert an image from another format to a JPEG, you are asked to specify the quality of image you want.

To obtain the highest-quality graphic, you're going to create a file that takes up a lot of memory, which results in longer download times. It's possible to reduce the quality of the JPEG

Bright Idea

If you're looking for an extensive stock photo library, visit www.fotosearch.com. Here, you'll find thousands of photos that you can license and use on your site.

image, resulting in a smaller file size and faster download time, but you're making a trade-off. For the Web, it's usually not critical to have extremely detailed photographs. A lower-resolution photo will usually work just as well. The higher the compression you use to compress a JPEG file, the more of the image is "thrown away." The process is not reversible, so be sure to save your original file in case you need to revert back to it later.

There are many online sources of free website graphics. Some companies also specialize in creating customized graphics and offer large libraries of precreated graphics that can be incorporated into any e-commerce website.

Webpromotion, Inc. (www.webpromotion.com), is just one company that offers a full range of graphic-design and Web-page-design services. The company also offers a three–CD-ROM artwork collection for about $100, containing hundreds of animated graphic elements that can be used royalty-free. Free samples are available at webpromotion.com/propak3.html.

The Publishing Perfection Catalog (www.publishingperfection. com; 800-387-2164) is full of useful commercial software tools and CD-ROM–based graphic libraries available to website designers. One product in this catalog, WebSpice 1,000,000 (from DeMorgan), offers more than one million buttons, arrows, rules, bullets, and other images that can be used within websites.

On the Web, you'll find a vast source of exciting public-domain Web graphics you can download for free. Some of these graphics are animated (and called animated GIFs). Others are still images or graphics. Using any Internet search engine, type in the search phrase "Web graphics" or "animated GIFs," for example, to find graphics you can download for your site.

One source of free Web artwork (including animated GIFs, backgrounds, and themes) is Webpedia Animation Archive (www.webdeveloper.com/animations). Other excellent clip-art and graphic resources are Clip-Art.com (www.clip-art.com) and Free Stuff Center (www.freestuffcenter.com/sub/graphicstop.html).

The Microsoft Office website (http://office.microsoft.com/clipart/default.aspx) also offers a vast library of free clip art, photos, and animations that can be incorporated into websites. If you want to create your own graphics, there are literally dozens of graphic-creation software packages now on the market. Xara (www.xara.com), for example, offers a suite of graphic programs, such as Xara Webstyle 4, which makes creating totally customized menus, buttons, and other commonly used Web graphics easy and fast.

Although some artwork is free on the Web and can be downloaded and used in your site in a matter of seconds, keep in mind that a lot of the artwork you'll see on other sites is copyrighted. Thus, before using that artwork, you must obtain permission from the artwork's creator or the webmaster of the site where you found the artwork. Appendix D provides information about copyrights and trademarks.

How can you download a non-copyrighted piece of artwork you find on the Web? While using your Web browser software, position your mouse over the graphic you want to download. Next, click the right mouse button. Choose the "Save Picture As . . . " option, and then choose the location on your hard drive where you want to save the graphic file. Once the file is on your hard drive, you can import it into any website-creation software; adjust its size, position, and so forth; and then incorporate it into your site. Note that resizing an animated GIF image may render it motionless.

Graphics programs

To ensure that your site will look original, consider developing some of your own artwork. Computer graphics for use on a

Moneysaver

Free downloadable trial versions of the graphics programs listed below are available from each company's website.

website can be created using a number of commercially available graphics programs, such as the following:

- Adobe Illustrator CS2 (www.adobe.com/prodindex/illustrator)

- Adobe PhotoShop CS2 (www.adobe.com/prodindex/photoshop)

- Adobe PhotoShop Elements (www.adobe.com/products/photoshopelwin)

- CorelDRAW Graphics Suite 12 and Paint Shop Pro (www.corel.com)

- Macromedia Studio MX with Flash Pro (www.macromedia.com)

- Microsoft Digital Image Suite (www.microsoft.com/projects/imaging)

- Xara Webstyle 4 (www.xara.com)

Using a graphics program to create your own graphics requires knowledge of how to use the software in addition to some artistic ability.

In addition to downloading graphic files from the Web, purchasing graphic libraries on CD-ROM, or creating your own images using a graphics program, other ways you can create or obtain photos or graphic images for your site include the following:

- Using a scanner to import printed images (photos, line drawings, and other artwork). A scanner will create a digital image saved in one of the popular graphic file formats that you can then incorporate into your site.

- Using a digital camera.
- Hiring a graphic artist to create customized banners, icons, backgrounds, or other Web graphics.

Choosing website-creation software or a turnkey e-commerce solution

This section provides information you'll need if you'll be developing a start-up business online or developing a relatively small e-commerce site. To accomplish this, you can custom-program your site from scratch, using HTML, CGI, Flash, or Java programming, as well as other Web-programming languages and tools. This is one of the more complex ways of getting your business online, especially if you're not a professional programmer with a strong understanding of the latest website-development tools. This option could involve hiring a programmer, graphic designer, and writer, but will generate the most impressive results if done correctly. Many off-the-shelf website-design software packages allow you to program using HTML or Java. You'll also need to become proficient with using Flash if you want to create impressive-looking animations for your site.

Flash, Java, and CGI are examples of popular programming languages used to create websites or elements of websites. They're typically used by programmers and require significant computer and programming knowledge and training. If you'll be using one of the recommended turnkey solutions from Yahoo!, eBay, GoDaddy, or Clickincome.com for creating your online business, you *won't* need to learn any programming language in order to design a professional-looking website.

You can opt to utilize commercially available website-creation software, such as Microsoft FrontPage (www.microsoft.com/frontpage). With this program, for example, you can design a professional-looking site with little programming knowledge required. There is, however, a definite learning curve for using this software, and you must be highly computer literate and have a working knowledge of Microsoft Office and how websites work.

Another alternative is to take advantage of a full service provider that offers both website-creation and hosting services.

e-commerce software solutions for small online businesses

The following are inexpensive website-design software packages. This is only a small sampling of the many software packages available to help you create a highly professional website for e-commerce applications. These applications allow you to program a website from scratch. They require more knowledge and computer literacy than using a turnkey solution from Yahoo!, eBay, or GoDaddy, for example. These software packages can also be used to modify or edit a website created by a professional programmer.

Microsoft FrontPage

Microsoft FrontPage (www.microsoft.com/frontpage) is a popular website-creation and management program. Although FrontPage is an all-purpose website-creation tool and includes a wide range of precreated templates, if you're planning on establishing a complete e-commerce solution based around the FrontPage software, you'll need an optional add-on module, called JustAddCommerce, from Rich Media Technologies, Inc. (www.richmediatech.com/jacmain.html), which allows you to add shopping-cart functionality with ease.

FrontPage software is well supported by Microsoft and many third-party developers, so finding precreated templates is easy. You're also likely to find full compatibility with virtually all ISPs. The drawback is that the learning curve to use this software is

Bright Idea

For reviews of many software packages designed to help you set up your online store, visit the C|Net Builder.com website at www.builder.com.

steep. You'll need to familiarize yourself with HTML programming and the use of various plug-ins to really utilize this software. It's not necessarily the best bet for first-time website designers.

There are many books, videos, and other training materials available that can help you learn to use this program to develop and maintain highly professional websites. Microsoft also offers extensive online support, free website-development tools and content, and a variety of other resources to help FrontPage users.

FrontPage retails for under $200. A Macintosh version of this software is available. A free, downloadable trial version of the software is available from the Microsoft website.

Macromedia offers a complete suite of website-development tools, called Studio MX 2004 with Flash Professional (www.macromedia.com/software/studio/). This software requires some training; however, once you become familiar with this suite of applications, you'll be able to create extremely professional-looking websites. The software retails for $899; however, a free trial version is available for download. The individual programs that make up the Studio MX 2004 suite are also sold separately.

Once your website is created, if you want the ability to make small modifications to the site quickly and easily with absolutely no programming knowledge required, Macromedia offers the Contribute 3 software package for $149 (www.macromedia.com/software/contribute/). You can also use this package for creating Web pages. For additional information about Macromedia's products, call 800-457-1774 or visit the company's website.

 Watch Out!

Although using FrontPage doesn't require any programming knowledge, it does require some familiarity with using Windows XP and Microsoft Office programs, plus a basic understanding of Web-page design.

Complete turnkey solutions for website design and operation

One of the fastest, easiest, and least-expensive ways to design, create, and launch your online business, complete with shopping cart, is to utilize one of the many complete turnkey solutions available to start-up business operators. These turnkey solutions are designed for small-business operators who want to get online quickly and who have little or no programming knowledge or experience.

By using a series of predefined templates, users of these turnkey applications can design and launch a website, literally in a few hours. Depending on the decisions you make about which template, fonts, color schemes, and graphics to use, it is possible to create a basic, professional-looking site, while at the same time learning the fundamentals of website design.

These turnkey solutions by themselves are designed to offer the online business operator basic functionality and tools needed to get their business online. Ultimately, as your business begins to grow, you'll want to use more advanced website-design tools and applications, which allow you to create vastly more powerful and professional-looking sites.

Some of the most popular turnkey solutions are available from Yahoo!, GoDaddy.com, and eBay. These are the services you'll learn more about in this chapter. If you have an online business idea, a few products you'd like to start selling, and a computer that's connected to the Web, you can get started using any of these services immediately. Several of these services have a low, one time start-up fee, plus all have a monthly fee.

For an additional fee, these services can assist you with obtaining a merchant account (so that you can accept major credit cards), help you promote your business, and provide many additional services to help your online-based business become successful.

These turnkey solutions are definitely the easiest way of getting your online business up-and-running quickly and inexpensively, especially if you're not a programmer. New turnkey solutions at competitive price points are constantly being introduced. While this book was being written, eBay introduced its ProStores service to compete head-on with Yahoo! Stores. Yahoo! then transformed its offerings to what it now calls Yahoo! Small Business.

Amazon.com's Z-Shops offers a quick way to get started

For someone who wants to start selling online, but doesn't want to go through the process of creating a whole e-commerce website, Amazon.com's Z-Shops (www.zshops.com) service allows you to create an account and start selling used and collectible items in a matter of minutes, for a very low fee.

This service, along with eBay's Half.com (www.half.com), isn't the same as creating and managing your own, full-fledged online business or e-commerce website, but you can get your feet wet and experience what it's like to begin selling items online. These services are a great way to test market your online business idea before investing the time, money, and effort into developing a website.

An up-close look at Yahoo! Store

One of the best and most flexible complete turnkey solutions for e-commerce comes from Yahoo! (http://smallbusiness. yahoo.com/merchant). For an initial investment of about $40 per month (plus a one-time $50 set-up fee), you can set up and operate an online business with no programming knowledge. Available through Yahoo! Small Business, Yahoo! Store's exclusive SiteBuilder application walks you through the entire website-design process, plus allows you to customize your site with graphics, photos, fonts, and other elements.

If you want or need the help of a professional website designer to create your site, there are literally hundreds of freelancers you can hire who specialize in developing websites using this service. You can use a search engine, such as Yahoo! or Google, enter the search phrase "Yahoo Store Designer."

Using Yahoo! Store as your turnkey e-commerce solution offers many benefits. You do everything online, without special software. In addition to providing design elements to help you create your site, Yahoo! lets you register your own domain name and URL. Yahoo! Store also offers a free service that other turnkey operations charge extra for—secure order transactions using industry-standard SSL (Secure Socket Layer) encryption.

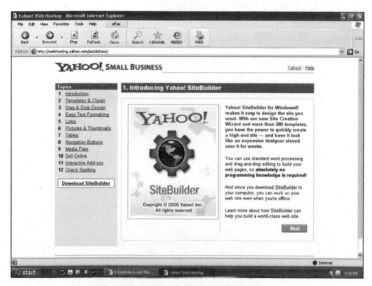

Figure 4.2. The Yahoo! SiteBuilder online-based application is the primary tool you'll use to create your website once you become a Yahoo! Store merchant.

Once your site is operational, your URL will immediately be listed with all of the major search engines if you've used Yahoo! Store. Meta tags will also be added to your site. A meta tag is a few lines of HTML programming incorporated into your site that make it easier for the various search engines to categorize your site and make it available to Web surfers. As you'll see, adding meta tags to a website is easy, and doing this will help generate traffic to your site.

If you're a start-up company with a handful of products, the price of using the Yahoo! Store "Starter" service is $39.95 per month, plus a 1.5 percent transaction fee per sale. There are no lengthy contracts to sign. For companies with more advanced needs, Yahoo! Store offers its "Standard" package for $99.95 per month (plus a 1 percent transaction fee per sale). This includes more customizability and additional tools to promote your site online. The Yahoo! Store "Professional" service, priced at $299.95 per month (with a .75 percent transaction fee per sale), offers even greater functionality and improved tools for creating a highly functional and professional-looking website. You can also maintain an online catalog of more than 50,000 items using the "Professional" service.

No matter which Yahoo! Store service you subscribe to, you can accept major credit cards using your existing merchant account, plus maintain a detailed online product catalog, handle all aspects of order processing, keep track of vital statistics pertaining to your site's traffic, utilize customized e-mail accounts, and keep your site up-to-date using a wide range of design templates. Technical support via e-mail or telephone is available 24 hours per day.

Thousands of companies use Yahoo! Store as their primary e-commerce solution. To see firsthand the capabilities of Yahoo! Store and how diverse the look of your site can be, check out some of the companies operating on the Web using this service. You can find user testimonials at http://smallbusiness.yahoo.com/merchant/testimonials.php.

You should use the same procedure for any turnkey solution you are considering: Be sure to look at how they've served other e-commerce businesses and see whether you are pleased with the results.

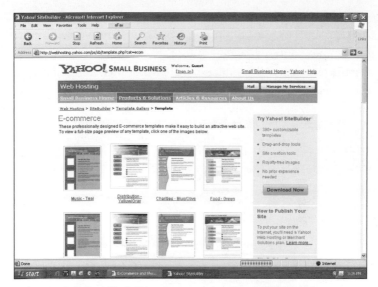

Figure 4.3. Yahoo! SiteBuilder uses a template-based website-design process. However, you can create your own templates from scratch to give your site a unique look.

Whether or not you use Yahoo! Store to design and host your online business, Yahoo! offers a free, 300+-page *Getting Started Guide,* which you can download as an eBook by pointing your Web browser to http://smallbusiness.yahoo.com/merchant/gstartdwnload.php.

For additional information about Yahoo! Store, point your Web browser to http://smallbusiness.yahoo.com or call 866-781-9246.

An up-close look at GoDaddy.com's Quick Shopping Cart

GoDaddy.com initially made a name for itself as a service that allows anyone to register domain names extremely inexpensively. The company has since expanded to offer a wide range of e-commerce and Web-hosting products and services. For the potential online business operator, GoDaddy.com offers its popular Quick Shopping Cart service.

Like the other turnkey solutions described in this chapter, GoDaddy.com's Quick Shopping Cart is an online-based website-development and management tool that allows anyone with little or no programming knowledge to create, launch, and manage an e-commerce website (complete with shopping cart).

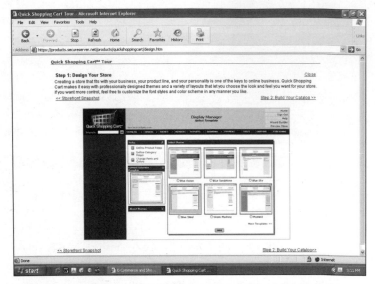

Figure 4.4. Quick Shopping Cart allows you to quickly and inexpensively launch your online business. GoDaddy.com, however, charges separate (albeit low) fees for various services, whereas with Yahoo! Store, for example, the majority of the same services are included for one flat monthly fee.

The Quick Shopping Cart Economy Edition service is priced at $9.95 per month ($7.96 per month if you pay for a year in advance) and allows you to build an online store that can display and sell up to 20 different products. This is a template-based application, which means you choose the overall design of your site from a series of predesigned templates, and then add your own text and graphics to customize the site and ultimately build your online store. The software also allows you to take products from your online store's catalog and launch eBay auctions with a few clicks of the mouse.

GoDaddy.com's Quick Shopping Cart Deluxe Edition is priced at $29.95 per month (or $20.96 per month if you pay for a year in advance). This service allows you to launch an e-commerce website with up to 100 unique products and use up to 100MB of online storage space.

For $49.95 per month ($29.97 per month if you pay for a year in advance), GoDaddy.com's Quick Shopping Cart Premium Edition allows you to build your online store and feature an unlimited number of products. Like the other turnkey services described in this chapter, this one also allows you to quickly create eBay auctions, accept major credit cards or PayPal, and automatically calculate UPS or USPS shipping charges as an order is being placed.

Other services such as inventory management, e-mail list management, and the ability to manage traffic stats for your site are all incorporated into GoDaddy.com's services. Additional services to help you market and promote your online business, establish a merchant account, and manage e-mail marketing are available for an additional fee.

Telephone and online-based technical support is available. For additional information about GoDaddy.com, point your Web browser to www.godaddy.com or call 480-505-8877. The company offers a free eBook, called *Making the Internet Work for You*, which you can download from its website. This guide offers tips for choosing and registering the perfect domain names for your business, plus strategies for launching and expanding your online presence once your site is established.

Even if you don't use GoDaddy.com to build and host your online business, it's an ideal company for easily researching, registering, and managing your domain names with the *.com, .net, .us, .biz, .info, .org, .ws, .name, .tv, .co.uk, .me.uk,* or *.org.uk* extension. Services such as domain forwarding, domain masking, domain parking, and domain locking, which other companies typically charge for, are offered free with each domain name registration. Chapter 5 offers more information about how to register your domain name(s).

An up-close look at eBay Stores

One of the fastest and easiest ways to start selling products online is to join eBay and offer your products in an online auction. For more savvy eBay users who typically have many auctions happening at once, one option is to open an eBay Store for as little as $15.95 per month.

Using a series of online-based design and development tools, anyone can create and launch an eBay Store with ease. No programming is required. Unlike more traditional online-based business and turnkey applications, an eBay Store allows you to develop a unique area, which is part of the overall eBay service, where you can host your own auctions and create a more customized shopping experience for your bidders/shoppers.

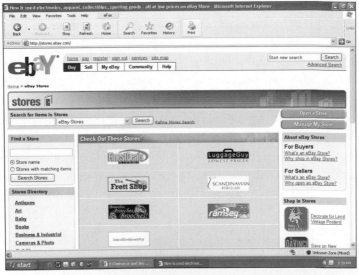

Figure 4.5. eBay Stores is the perfect solution for an online business that wants to hold multiple auctions at once using eBay. For a more traditional e-commerce solution, take a look at eBay ProStores (described in Chapter 14).

Your eBay Store will have its own, unique URL (website address), plus allow you to manage your site once it's fully designed and launched. Like Yahoo Stores, for example, eBay offers several different services for online business operators, ranging from the Basic Store ($15.95 per month) to its "Anchor Store" service ($499.95 per month).

Like the other turnkey services described in this book, eBay Stores uses template-based design tools, which allow you to totally customize your site with no programming required. You can also track sales reports, measure traffic to your site, and manage your orders using easy-to-use, online-based tools. The only equipment you'll need to get started is a computer that's connected to the Internet.

More information about how to create and launch an online business using eBay is offered in Chapter 14. You can also visit the eBay website (http://stores.ebay.com).

eBay Stores is different from the new eBay ProStores service, which offers a complete turnkey solution for creating an e-commerce-based website, as opposed to an online auction-based business.

eBay ProStores: another turnkey e-commerce solution

Not to be confused with eBay Stores, in June 2005, eBay announced the launch of eBay ProStores (www.prostores.com), a complete, online-based, turnkey solution for anyone interested in creating, managing, and launching an e-commerce website. The eBay Stores service allows people to launch an online business using an online auction business model while

 Watch Out!

Before signing up for any turnkey e-commerce solution, such as ProStores, visit a handful of the online stores currently operating using the service to ensure that you like the "finished product" in terms of the overall look and design of the online stores created using the service. You'll find vast differences in terms of the professionalism and overall design of the websites created by the different turnkey e-commerce solutions. Do your research to find the perfect solution for your online business venture.

ProStores offers more traditional e-commerce. This service is somewhat similar to Yahoo! Store and GoDaddy's Quick Shopping Cart.

Offering four levels of service at different price points, eBay ProStores offers easy-to-use, online-based tools for start-up business operators, as well as advanced tools for larger, more established online business ventures.

The tiers of ProStores service are detailed in the following sections.

ProStores Express

For those first starting out, ProStores Express will help you create an e-commerce website and begin accepting PayPal payments from customers.

eBay reports that this is a low-cost solution for individuals who want to sell a limited number of different products online. The service includes two pages, displaying up to 10 products, which can be created using the proprietary setup and design wizards built into the ProStores services, in as little as 30 minutes. The company classifies this tier of service as being an ideal first step for part-time, sideline, or hobby businesses.

Price: $6.95 per month, plus a 1.5 percent transaction fee for all successful sales.

ProStores Business

This tier of service is dubbed an "all-in-one, customizable e-commerce solution for small businesses." The service includes unlimited pages and product presentations, domain registration and hosting, 50 unique e-mail boxes, 5G storage space, data transfer, 24/7 tech support, QuickBooks integration, and the ability to easily submit products to Internet shopping engines.

Price: $29.95 per month, plus a .50 percent transaction fee for all successful sales.

Bright Idea

To see a sampling of eBay ProStores' store designs and the level of customization that's available, check out a few of the sample online stores already in existence. Point your Web browser to www.prostores.com/prostores-featured.shtml.

ProStores Advanced

A more comprehensive and powerful e-commerce solution is available through the ProStores Advanced service. According to eBay, "It's designed for small- to medium-sized retail or service businesses that want to grow their sales and streamline operations with advanced merchandising, promotion, inventory management, and payment features."

This is the perfect solution if you'll be selling services with scheduled billing or products that have multiple attributes, such as size, color, or finish.

Price: $74.95 per month, plus a .50 percent transaction fee for all successful sales.

ProStores Enterprise

According to eBay, ProStores Enterprise is ideal for medium- or enterprise-sized businesses that want to integrate online sales with existing back-end systems.

This service allows for easy drop-shipments, affiliate marketing programs, and sales team coordination. Business operators can also create customer groups and unique wholesale programs that reveal special pricing throughout your site after login.

Price: $249 per month, plus a .50 percent transaction fee for all successful sales.

eBay ProStores add-on services

For an additional fee, eBay offers a professional website-design service, allowing you to work with a team of talented programmers and graphic artists who will create a totally unique and extremely professional website for you. You'll be hiring professionals who are extremely familiar with the eBay ProStores platform, which can dramatically reduce your learning curve for creating a website, plus help you avoid common pitfalls start-up businesses encounter.

Depending on the complexity and size of your online store, complete website-design services cost anywhere from $399 to $649 (or more). Once your site is fully designed and operational, you can hire the same design team to periodically update and fine-tune your site's design for an additional fee.

For details about eBay ProStores' website-design service, call 866-908-1010, or point your Web browser to www.prostores.com/design-services.shtml.

To help you initially generate traffic to your website and successfully market your business, eBay Stores offers a team of online marketing, advertising, and promotion experts who can be hired for a predetermined fee. These professionals are extremely familiar with the eBay ProStores platform and can help you successfully launch your online business while dramatically reducing the initial learning curve involved in launching successful online marketing, advertising, and promotional programs.

For details, point your Web browser to www.prostores.com/traffic-generation.shtml or call 866-908-1010.

When your business is ready to accept credit-card payments from customers, as opposed to or in addition to PayPal payments, eBay ProStores is compatible with the services offered by a wide range of merchant account providers, including the following:

ANZ eGate	www.anz.com
Authorize.net	www.authorizenet.com
BluePay Gateway	www.onlinedatacorp.com
Concord EFSNet	www.concordefsnet.com
CyberCash	www.cybercash.com
CyberSource	www.cybersource.com

ECHO	www.eco-inc.com
Innovative Gateway	www.innovativegateway.com
iTransact	www.itransact.com
LinkPoint API	www.linkpoint.com
Payflow Pro	www.verisign.com
PayFuse	www.fnms.com
PayGateway	www.paradata.com
Paymentech Orbital Gateway	www.paymentech.net
Pay Me Now	www.paymenow.com
PSiGate	www.psigate.com
PayPal Direct Payment	www.paypal.com
QuickCommerce Pro	www.ecx.com

Whether or not you use eBay ProStores, if your company needs a merchant account in order to accept credit-card payments, you can contact any of the preceding companies, in addition to the companies listed in Chapter 3.

osCommerce: a totally free, yet powerful, website-design solution

If you have some website design know-how (or you're willing to learn), there are a wide range of extremely powerful and inexpensive website-creation software packages that offer the ultimate in customization potential.

osCommerce (www.oscommerce.com) is just one example. According to the osCommerce website, "osCommerce is an online shop e-commerce solution under ongoing development by the open-source community. Its feature-packed, out-of-the-box installation allows store owners to set up, run, and maintain their online stores with minimum effort and with absolutely no costs or license fees involved. (The software is totally free.)

"Open-source" means that the software, in this case osCommerce, has no copyrights associated with it. The programming and e-commerce community at large is allowed to take the program, customize it and use it freely, without any cost associated with its use.

While osCommerce is powerful, it is not for beginners and requires programming knowledge as well as a high level of computer literacy.

"osCommerce combines open-source solutions to provide a free and open e-commerce platform, which includes the powerful PHP Web-scripting language, the stable Apache Web server, and the fast MySQL database server.

"With no restrictions or special requirements, osCommerce is able to run on any PHP-enabled Web server, on any environment that PHP and MySQL supports, which includes Linux, Solaris, BSD, Mac OS X, and Microsoft Windows environments."

Figure 4.6. What could be better than using a powerful and extremely customizable website-design software package that's available for free to online merchants? You'll need some basic programming knowledge and a website-hosting service, but the osCommerce software is top-notch.

Because this is a free, open-source platform, many third-party companies offer add-on products, support, and training for this e-commerce solution. osCommerce was started in March 2000 and has since matured to a solution that is currently powering more than 2,000 registered shops and e-commerce websites around the world.

You can download the software and related resources, including tutorials, free of charge from the osCommerce website (www. oscommerce.com). If you'll be using this software platform, keep in mind that you'll need to find your own ISP/website-hosting service, which is as easy as opening the *Yellow Pages*. Be sure the hosting service you select supports the osCommerce software.

To see a sampling of the websites created and operated using the popular osCommerce platform (which includes a fully functional shopping-cart application), point your Web browser to www.oscommerce.com/shops/live.

There are literally hundreds of pre-created templates available for use with osCommerce that take much of the design work out of creating your website. In addition to visiting the osCommerce website, point your Web browser to Template Monster (www.templatemonster.com) for free, downloadable templates and resources.

Using "osCommerce" as a search phrase on Google or Yahoo!, you'll find listings for a wide range of resources, templates, and website-hosting services that specialize in hosting osCommerce websites.

The scoop on copyrights

As you explore and surf the Web in order to gather ideas, you may run across art, designs, photos, and texts you'd like to use for your own site. If you use these only as inspiration but create all-new material for your site, copyright issues probably won't affect you directly.

But, if you are planning on taking some elements from another website and directly incorporating them into your site, you'll need to brush up on your copyright law. See Appendix D in this book.

As a general rule of thumb, remember that when in doubt, assume the material is protected. It's always better to omit something you could have used than include it and find yourself bombarded with threatening letters from another company. Your incentive should be moral as well as legal. If you invest money in a good logo or good writing, you would think it unfair for your competitor to incorporate your work without paying for it. Apply the same standard to your own actions.

When using any type of prewritten text, artwork, music, audio, video, or photos on your website, make sure you own the copyright to that material or that you have written permission to use those assets from the copyright owner.

For additional information about how to copyright original material on your website that you've created and wish to protect, visit the U.S. Copyright Office's website at www.copyright.gov. Here, you can download forms for filing copyrights and learn the basics of copyright law.

According to the U.S. government's copyright.gov website, "Copyright is a form of protection provided by the laws of the United States (Title 17) to the authors of 'original works of authorship,' including literary, dramatic, musical, artistic, and certain other intellectual works. This protection is available to both published and unpublished works."

For information about filing a trademark for your company logo, for example, visit the United States Patent and Trademark Office's website at www.uspto.gov or call 800-786-9199.

Avoiding the most common Web design mistakes

So far, we've talked about what you *should* do. It might be helpful, however, to look at things from the opposite perspective. There are certain common mistakes Web designers make when creating a site to be used for e-commerce or to generate business.

One of the easiest ways to avoid these mistakes is to take advantage of pre-designed website templates and/or to utilize one of the turnkey solutions described earlier in this chapter. The templates available were often created by professional website designers or graphic designers and take a lot of the guesswork out of creating a professional looking website.

By familiarizing yourself with these common mistakes, you can learn *not* to repeat them when creating and managing your own website.

- **Poor spelling, grammar, or punctuation.** Proofread all of the text in your site. There should be absolutely no editing mistakes. If necessary, hire a professional writer or copy editor to proofread your online content before making it available to the public. Don't just rely on the spell-checker built into your word processor or website-creation software.

- **Excessive file size.** When choosing images for your site, make sure the file size of the electronic image isn't too large. Otherwise, it will take too long to load, and many Web surfers have no patience. They probably won't wait one, two, or three minutes for a Web page to load. As a general rule, you have about 10 seconds to capture a surfer's attention when they visit your website.

- **Poor photo quality.** If you'll be using photographs on your site, make sure they appear crystal-clear and in focus. The viewer should be able to make out visual details of the product. The quality of your photos will play a major role in building customer confidence. The overall professional image of your site is at stake. Avoid using photos that are out of focus, take too long to load, look amateurish, or add nothing to the overall content quality of your site. Also, make sure you have permission to use photos that you didn't take yourself. Be sure you don't violate any copyright laws.

 Bright Idea

To learn the basics about registering a trademark, you can download an electronic brochure called Basic Facts About Registering a Trademark for free from http://www.uspto.gov/main/definitions.htm.

- **Incompatibility.** When choosing colors of backgrounds, text, and even graphic images, maintain continuity throughout your site, paying careful attention to making your site compatible with all of the popular Web-browser programs. From a graphic-design standpoint, the overall color scheme you choose should be friendly and easy on the eyes, and shouldn't clash.

- **Frames.** Avoid using frames! They can be used so that visitors can view several windows worth of information simultaneously. But this often makes a site confusing to look at and to navigate.

- **Poor directions.** Although your goal is to get visitors to visit your main home page first and then navigate through your site from there, this doesn't always happen. Some Web search engines will send surfers directly to the page of a site that contains the keyword or search phrase they were looking for. As a result, they might find themselves visiting a sub-page of your site and not know where they are. To compensate for this, every page of your site should contain your company name and logo, a navigation bar or buttons, and an easy way for the visitor to return to your home page.

- **Hidden navigation icons.** Place your navigation icons for your site near the top of every page, so that people don't have to scroll to the bottom of a page to determine where they should go next. This is referred to as placement "above the fold," using the phrase borrowed from newspaper publishing, where lead stories are placed in the top half of the front page, above where larger newspapers are folded. In this case, "above the fold" refers to the top half of the screen, where the icons are easily visible without the surfer having to scroll down.

- **Excessive scroll.** As you plan each page on your site, don't make the visitor scroll too much. Keep the information on each page short and to-the-point, and then have him or her click on a "Next" icon to view another screen's worth

Watch Out!

Don't go overboard with Internet graphics technology. Remember that the point of your site is to convey information, inspire confidence, and convince the visitor to buy your product or service. Keep it simple and to-the-point. If you want to add animations, consider using Macromedia's Flash application.

of information, or a "Home" button to return to your site's home page. You can also offer buttons that link to other areas of your site. The visitor should not have to look for these navigational buttons or read too much text to figure out what each page of your site is all about.

- **Poor targeting.** Make sure all of the content of your site is directed to your target audience. If you don't understand who your target customers are, what their needs are, and what they're looking for, you have little hope of providing a product that addresses their needs. Even if you have the perfect product for your target customer, make sure your site conveys this information clearly.

- **Too much information.** Unlike print materials and radio or television advertising, the Web is interactive. Make sure you reshape information from your traditional advertising to take full advantage of these interactive qualities. Instead of inundating the viewer of your site with tons of information on one page, spread it out. Go from the general to the specific, allowing people to click on hyperlinks for additional information about specific topics.

- **Sensory overload.** Too many websites add tons of bells and whistles, such as flashy graphics, audio, animation, video, too many fonts and typestyles, and busy backgrounds, just to get a visitor's attention. This is overkill! Instead, focus on the facts you're trying to convey to the visitor, and use only those Web technologies and features that will help you to get your most important points across. For example, rather than several pages of text, perhaps a single color photograph will convey an important point. As the saying goes, "A picture is worth a thousand words." Also, it's easy to understand and takes less time for the viewer to comprehend and digest.

- **Shifting styles.** Once you choose a color scheme, background, and font group for your site, stick to it to maintain visual continuity. You don't want your site to appear overly busy or confusing because you used too many fonts/typestyles, or because each page has a totally different look, layout, and design. Set design standards for your site and stick to them. Using a predefined website template will help you maintain the overall look on each page of your website.

- **Poor choice of fonts.** Some fonts simply don't look good when viewed using Web browser software. Likewise, if the text is too small, it becomes very difficult to read. Stick with a basic font size of 10 to 12 points. The most common fonts to use include Helvetica, Arial, and Times New Roman. They are easy to read and visually appealing. Also, too much small type or fine print within your website will make visitors leery about placing an order.

- **Being pushy.** Never force visitors to your site to register or provide personal information about themselves until they're ready to place an order or subscribe to an online newsletter, for example. If you're going to offer a free newsletter or access to a blog, encourage people to register in order to receive that free information, but don't force them to register simply so that you can build your mailing list. If you want people to register to receive information, make sure you give them something of value in return, such as useful

---

☼ **Bright Idea**

As you're planning your site, develop storyboards or flowcharts to help you graphically plan the layout of your site and how each page will look. Remember, ease of navigation and continuity is important.

information, a discount, or some other incentive for sharing their personal contact information.

Using outside creative talent

If you're making any type of financial investment in your online business, you might consider tapping the talents of professionals to help design and launch your site. This could mean hiring a website-design service or individual programmers to create the site, graphic designers to develop the visual layout of the site, and professional writers to create the text for the site.

Some companies and consultants work on a per-project basis; others get paid by the hour. You'll find an abundance of available talent using the *Yellow Pages* or any Internet search engine (enter a search phrase such as "Website Design," "Web Graphics," or "Website Programmer"). You might also consider soliciting referrals from other people.

As you determine whom you might hire, ask to see specific examples of their work that relates to website design or specifically e-commerce websites. Also, have the agency or freelancer submit a formal written proposal and price quote based on your specific needs.

Two excellent resources for hiring professional freelance writers, artists, graphic designers, and website programmers are eLance.com (www.elance.com) and RentaCoder.com (www.rentacoder.com). These services allow you to post a message about what types of freelancers you're looking to hire as well as details about your project. The freelance professionals will then begin contacting you with bids, often within hours of you posting your message.

 Bright Idea

If you want a fully customizable, powerful, and professional-looking website, but don't want to create it yourself, Ibex Solutions (541-383-0699; www.arcticibex.com) is just one of many companies that specialize in website design and hosting, using its own, proprietary e-commerce platform. The company charges for its consulting, design, and hosting services.

If you're on a very tight budget, consider contacting a local college or university to find paid or unpaid interns to help you develop your website. A graphic-arts student or someone studying Web programming, for example, will often be willing to take on a project for little or no money, simply to gain real-world work experience and build up their portfolio. They might also earn college credit for their internship experience.

Just the facts

- Before you begin creating your own site, spend a considerable amount of time surfing the Web looking for ideas. Determine what features you like and how to incorporate them into your site.

- Avoid the temptation of overloading your website with flashy animated graphics, audio clips, and video clips. You don't want to overwhelm your visitors.

- Before you design or create your site, you must carefully evaluate and determine the exact purpose of your site and who it's targeting.

- Plan out your site. One of the first things a visitor to your site will notice is how well it's laid out and how intuitive it is to navigate through.

- You don't need to be a programmer to create an online store or website. You can use general-purpose, commercially available software or one of the turnkey website-design services described in this chapter.

- As you begin creating your site, be careful that the content you add doesn't violate any individual's or company's copyrights or trademarks.

Getting Your
Business Online

GET THE SCOOP ON...
Choosing the best domain name for your online
biz ▪ Researching and registering domain
names ▪ Costs ▪ What do to when the name you
want is taken ▪ Where to get help

PART II

Selecting and Registering Your Domain Name

Chapter 5

What's in a name? When it comes to choosing the domain name for your online business, the name you choose is everything, so keep it simple. The domain name you choose becomes your identity on the World Wide Web. Ideally, you want a name that's very easy to remember, easy to pronounce, and easy to spell—one that people will instantly associate with your company, product, or service.

Internet commerce is one of the most profitable business opportunities in the 21st century, so it's important for your online business to be readily accessible to potential consumers. Even if you manage to come up with the absolute perfect product to sell online and you also create an awesome website, if the domain name you choose isn't easy to remember and associate with your company, your online business will suffer.

Bright Idea

Don't worry that all of the good names are taken. With the *.com* extension alone, there are 31,700,000,000 (31.7 trillion) possible domain names.

With all of the hype surrounding the Internet, rumors are flying that all of the domain names are being taken, and pretty soon there won't be any left. This is a major misconception! Although it is true that many of the most desirable domain names ending with the *.com* extension have already been registered, there are still plenty of domain names available. Moreover, many other extensions, such as *.tv*, *.info*, *.biz*, *.name*, and *.us* have been created.

Understanding domain name syntax

Although a domain name helps Web surfers find a website quickly and easily, the Internet itself and the Web browser software used to surf the Internet don't pay any attention to the alphanumeric name you register for your site. When your new domain name is registered, you'll be required to provide a numeric address, called the IP (Internet Protocol). An IP is a set of four numbers separated by periods that your Internet Service Provider (ISP) or website-hosting service will assign. Each number can be between 0 and 255. For example, an IP address could be 129.52.0.203. This string of numbers is the actual address of your site. It tells computers where your site can be found on the Internet.

When someone types your website's domain name into their browser software, the Domain Name System (DNS) automatically translates the website name (such as www.your-domain-name.com) into the corresponding numeric IP address, which allows Web-browser software to locate and access the appropriate Web page.

Main URL features

A typical website's URL (uniform resource locator) looks something like this:

http://www.yourdomainname.com

or

http://www.your-domain-name.com

In reality, the domain name itself is divided into three distinct parts. The part that starts with *http://www* is common to most website addresses on the World Wide Web. This is the uniform resource locator (URL) Web browsers use to find Web pages. The second part of the domain name is the part you actually get to choose. The third part of the domain name is the extension (for example, *.com*, *.edu*, or *.org*). As you begin to think of the perfect domain names for your online business, consider the following:

- Only letters, numbers, and the hyphen (-) can be used in a domain name. Punctuation marks, such as a period, exclamation point, colon, and forward or backslash are not allowed. In addition, no spaces are allowed in the name. If necessary, use an underscore ("_") to indicate a space; however, this is not recommended for simplicity's sake.

- A domain name can be up to 26 characters long, but this includes the extension at the end of the domain name (such as *.com*, *.edu*, *.org*, or *.net*).

- The domain name you choose must be unique and can't already be registered by someone else.

Domain names are not case-sensitive, so you can't combine upper- and lowercase letters to create a unique domain name. As you promote your site, however, you can list the domain name using both upper- and lowercase because all Web-browser software (such as Microsoft Internet Explorer or Netscape Navigator) will automatically translate the address the user enters into lowercase. For example, to make your name more memorable, you can promote www.yourdomainname.com as www.YourDomain Name.com. The name www.your-domain-name.com, however, is a totally different domain name that would need to be registered separately.

Many people surf the Internet and randomly type website addresses based on the topics they're looking for, in hopes of luckily hitting a site that interests them. Thus, you want your domain name to be somewhat obvious. Network Solutions, Inc., a well-known domain name registrar, calls this type of traffic "guess traffic" because you receive visits to your site from people who don't specifically know your Web address, but who find your Internet site by guessing. For example, someone looking to order flowers online might instinctively try to visit the website www.flowers.com or www.1800flowers.com. The first is an obvious choice, and the second might be used if that person had called 1-800-FLOWERS in the past and figured the company might also have a website.

Millions of websites ending with the *.com* extension have already been registered. As a result, many of the one-word, generic domain names you might think of to describe your company, product, or service might already be taken. You'll probably have better luck registering a domain name that combines two or three words.

Common extensions

All website addresses end with some type of extension, such as *.com*, *.net*, *.org*, *.gov*, or *.edu*. There are, however, newer extensions available, such as *.tv*, *.info*, *.biz*, *.name*, and *.us*. Based on the type of website you're creating, there are guidelines for which extension you're supposed to use. Keep in mind that new extensions are always being created or adapted for more general use.

 Bright Idea

Choose a domain name that's easy to remember, intuitive, and easy to guess. The website for 1-800-Flowers (www.1800flowers.com) is a good example of a domain name that is easy to guess and remember.

Bright Idea

The *.com* extension has been around since 1985 and most Internet surfers automatically enter a *.com* extension when surfing out of habit. Thus, it's an excellent idea to have your domain name end with this extension, even though others are available. At the same time, you'll want to protect your company's online identity by also registering your domain name with several of the other more popular extensions, such as *.net*, *.biz*, and *.org*.

Choosing your domain name

There are three basic approaches you can take when deciding on a domain name for your online business. First, you can use your company name (www.yourcompany.com). When someone is looking for a specific company's website, they instinctively try a Web address that includes the company name. There are countless examples of companies whose Internet presence can be located using its company name. The following are just a few examples:

1-800-Flowers.com	www.1800flowers.com
Apple Computers	www.apple.com
AT&T	www.att.com
Brooks Brothers	www.brooksbrothers.com
Dell Computers	www.dell.com
FedEx	www.FedEx.com
Gap	www.gap.com
Honda Motors	www.honda.com
Microsoft Corporation	www.microsoft.com
MTV	www.mtv.com
National Football League (NFL)	www.nfl.com
Nike	www.nike.com
Sony Corporation	www.sony.com

The Walt Disney Company	www.disney.com
US Airways	www.usairways.com
Visa	www.visa.com

If your online business involves selling a product or service, your domain name can also be the name of that product or service.

Being creative

As you kick around domain name ideas, think about new and unique names that describe your product or service. ArtfulPups, for example, is an online business that sells designer dog collars, leads, grooming products, and accessories. The domain name for this company is www.artfulpups.com. Based on the domain name, someone not familiar with the company will have a pretty good idea of what this company offers.

You can also follow in the footsteps of several major online businesses and choose a domain name that sounds somewhat nonspecific and that can apply to anything at all. These typically are coined names that don't necessarily mean anything. Coined names are easy to trademark and protect, but as a small-business owner, they're difficult to promote, especially if your online business will be catering to a potential worldwide market.

Amazon.com, for example, started out selling books online. The company now offers books, music, videos, auctions, software, and countless other products. Based on the name, a consumer would have no clue what product(s) "Amazon.com" offers. It's only because the company has spent millions of dollars on

 Moneysaver

Unless you have a lot of extra money to invest in marketing and advertising, avoid using a nonspecific domain name for your company. It's expensive to create brand/name awareness. Your domain name should be easy to understand and remember.

Watch Out!

Make sure the domain name you choose won't accidentally be offensive to someone. Does the name mean something totally different in another language? Is there a chance the public will associate anything negative with the name you're considering? Doing your homework upfront can save you misery down the road.

marketing that Web surfers now know about Amazon.com, allowing it to become one of the most successful online businesses in the world.

Although choosing a generic-sounding domain name allows for future growth into other areas, it also requires a tremendous amount of marketing and advertising in order to inform people about what your online business offers. If your online business will be starting out small and without a multimillion-dollar advertising campaign, consider a less generic and more descriptive domain name.

Coming up with the perfect name for your business will probably take a lot of thought and creativity. As you kick around ideas in your head, seek the advice of friends, relatives, and other people you respect. Also, consider carefully what you are naming. Consider characteristics, features, advantages, and anything else that comes to mind when you think about the products or services you'll be offering. Acronyms can also be the basis for a company or domain name.

What are the goals of the company you'll be starting? Is there an image you're trying to convey? Who is your target audience? Using a pad of paper (or your computer), keep a running list of ideas and potential company/domain names. After you've compiled a list, narrow it down by selecting only those names that you really like. Next, you'll need to determine whether the domain names you like are available and whether they violate any existing trademarks or copyrights.

Watch Out!

Registering a domain name does not give you ownership of it! This process gives you the exclusive rights, however, to use the domain name as long as you pay the annual fees. The concept is very similar to getting a new telephone number from the phone company.

Getting help

If you're still having trouble coming up with potential domain names, seek the help of professionals. Consider hiring an advertising and marketing agency that specializes in helping companies create names and slogans. The NameStormers (512-267-1814; www.namestormers.com) is just one company that offers consulting services designed to help entrepreneurs and business owners create catchy company names, slogans, and domain names.

If your company name and product name differ, or you'll be selling multiple products or services through your online business, consider registering and using multiple domain names that lead to the same website. Having multiple domain names will entitle you to have multiple listings on the major Web search engines, and you can use the different names in your specialized marketing campaigns to provide target audiences with a domain name that's easy to remember based on their interests.

Thanks to "domain forwarding," having multiple domain names lead to the same website is easy. One example of this is if you're looking for paints to redecorate your home and as a Web surfer you type www.painting.com into your browser. Thanks to domain forwarding, you'll wind up at the www.shermanwilliams.com website.

Domain parking is available: plan ahead

You're not the only entrepreneur hoping to create a successful online business. In addition to the thousands of start-up electronic commerce sites created every month, huge companies and corporations are also constantly expanding and enhancing their online presence. As a result, thousands of new domain names are registered every week.

If you anticipate expanding your online business into new areas or believe that sometime in the future you might have a need for additional domain names, now is the best time to register those names—before someone else does!

When you register a domain name that you won't immediately use, it's called parking the domain name. You have the rights to it; however, the address isn't active and doesn't lead to a website. Internet Service Providers often offer complimentary "holding" or "parking" services, allowing you to reserve a domain name without having to put a website online.

Determine whether a domain name is available

Okay, you've had your brainstorming session and you've come up with several possible domain names that would be absolutely perfect for your business. Congratulations! What you need to do now is determine whether anyone has already registered your potential domain names.

First, connect to the Internet and try to access the domain name you've selected. If your Web-browser software is able to connect to that website, the name is obviously taken. Even if the domain name you like isn't currently active, that doesn't mean someone else hasn't already registered it. To determine whether a domain name is available, visit a domain name registrar, such as GoDaddy.com (www.godaddy.com) or Network Solutions (www.networksolutions.com). If you enter your ideal domain name and get a message that it's for sale, this is an independent company that's already registered the domain name, but they're willing to sell it, often at a premium price. In this situation, expect to pay several hundred dollars or more to obtain the rights to a domain name that's for sale by a broker. Keep in mind, you can negotiate!

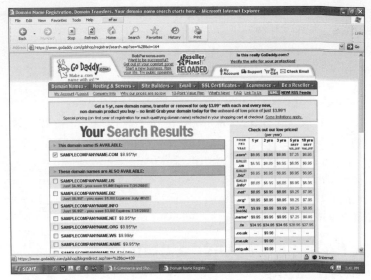

Figure 5.1. From the GoDaddy.com website, you can quickly determine whether the domain name you want is available and then register it on the spot for under $9.

From the domain registrar's website, look for the area that allows you to determine whether a specific domain name is available. In the appropriate field on the website, enter the domain name you're hoping to register, along with the appropriate extension(s).

GoDaddy.com, Register.com, Dotster.com, DomainName.com, and NetworkSolutions.com, for example, allow you to look up (for free) and ultimately register domain names (for a fee) with the following extensions:

- *.com*
- *.net*
- *.org*
- *.info*
- *.biz*
- *.tv*
- *.us*

- .cc
- .name
- .bz
- .co.uk
- .de
- .be
- .co.nz
- .at

Next, click the "Search Now" or "Search" icon (depending on which registrar's website you use), located next to the field where you entered the domain name to research. The WHOIS database, which is a centralized database of all registered domain names, will now be searched in real time. The process typically takes less than 30 seconds.

You might see the message "No match for '(your domain name).com.'" or "'(your domain name).com' is available." These messages mean that nobody has yet registered the domain name and you are free to register it immediately.

From the domain name registrar's website (such as GoDaddy.com or NetworkSolutions.com), you can then register that domain name with whatever extensions are available for an annual fee. Depending on the service you use to register your domain name, the annual fee will vary greatly. At the time this book was written, GoDaddy.com was among the least expensive domain name registrars; plus, the company offers a wide range of extra services for no additional fees.

If the domain name you entered is already registered, however, information about the registrant—including the registrant's

Bright Idea

Need help thinking of a domain name? Consider using the thesaurus! You can find one online at www.thesaurus.com.

company name, address, phone number, e-mail address, domain name, administrative contact, billing contact, and domain servers—will be listed. You now have the option to contact the domain name's owner directly. If the current owner of the domain name isn't using it, you might be able to purchase or lease it from the current registrant.

If you receive a response from the domain name registrar that the domain name you're interested in is "On Hold," this means one of the following things, according to Network Solutions:

- Payment for the domain is not current.
- The domain name is involved in a dispute with a trademark owner.
- Name server activation is pending.
- Another administrative or technical matter is pending.

If you receive an "On Hold" message relating to a domain name you're interested in, you can contact the person or company that was last in possession of that domain name or wait for a few days or weeks to see if the hold is released and the desired domain name becomes available.

Registering your domain name is easy

Once you determine that a domain name is available and you're ready to register it, all you'll need is a major credit card and a few minutes. Visit the domain name registrar of your choice, such as NetworkSolutions.com or GoDaddy.com. For a directory of domain name registrars, point your Web browser to www.internic.net/origin.html.

You'll be instructed to complete an online form, which will ask for information about you and your company (if applicable). Some of the information you'll be prompted for includes the following:

- Your full name
- Your e-mail address

- Your company name
- Your complete address (street, city, state, and ZIP)
- Your phone number
- Your fax number

You'll then be asked to provide an administrative and technical contact for this domain name registration. The person registering the domain name, the administrative contact, and the technical contact can all be the same person. You'll be asked whether the domain name will be used for personal or business purposes (or both), and whether you'll be selling products or services from the site.

For an additional fee, you can arrange to have your personal registration information kept private so that your information isn't readily available to anyone who looks up your domain name in the WHOIS database.

Upon entering the necessary information to register the domain name, you'll need to choose the term of the registration. The minimum is one year; however, the more years you pre-pay for, the cheaper the annual registration becomes. You can then pay the required fee using a major credit card, or in some instances, your PayPal account. When the term expires, you'll need to renew your domain name registration to keep it active.

Minutes after the domain name is registered, you'll need to provide the domain name registrar with details about your website-hosting service or ISP. If you haven't yet signed up with an ISP to host your website, you can park the website or forward the domain name to an existing website.

 Watch Out!

If you allow your ISP or another agency to register your domain name on your behalf, make sure that the domain name you choose is actually registered in your name and not in theirs. You don't want your company's domain name stolen or misdirected down the road because it wasn't registered in your name.

The annual fee to register a domain name is as low as $8.95 using GoDaddy.com or up to $34.99 per year using other services, such as Network Solutions. When choosing a domain name registrar, choose one that offers domain name forwarding, domain name parking, and other services.

Because the cost of registering a domain name is under $9 each (per year), it's an excellent business strategy to separately register all popular extensions of your domain name (*.org, .net*, and so on), plus any related domain names that might help Web surfers find your company online. This will help ensure that your intended customers will be able to easily find your website. Also, if your *.com* site becomes successful and you haven't registered the *.net, .org*, and other popular extensions, your competition might. This could result in you losing business.

What to do if the domain name you want is taken

Unfortunately, well over 56 million *.com, .org, .net, .biz*, and *.us* domain names are already taken. If the domain name you were hoping to obtain as the online address and identity for your business has already been registered by someone else, you have several options—including choosing another name, which is the easiest, fastest, and cheapest alternative. If the domain name you want is taken, select another one that's not and register it.

As mentioned earlier, when you do a domain name search using the WHOIS database (via your favorite domain name

 Bright Idea

If the domain name you want to register is already taken, one option is to contact the person or company that has already registered that name and ask to purchase it for a fair price (which you'll need to negotiate), assuming it's being held but not actually used. If you and the holder of the domain name can reach an agreement, transferring the domain name is a simple process that can be done through any domain name registrar, such as GoDaddy.com. There are also independent brokers that can help you negotiate the purchase of a domain name that has already been taken.

Bright Idea

As you register your domain name, consider registering all of the alternatives to that domain name as well. Examples include domain names with similar spellings, the same name but with a different extension, and your domain name with and without hyphens. This will help keep your competition from stealing some of your intended Web traffic by registering domain names that are similar to yours, hoping that surfers will accidentally enter a wrong spelling into their browser, for example. If you accidentally type "www.yahooo.com" into your browser when you meant to type "www.yahoo.com," you'll still get to the main Yahoo! website because this company registered multiple domain names with various spellings.

registrar service or directly at the WHOIS.net website), if the name you're researching is already taken, you'll be provided with that domain name's registrant information. You now have the option to contact that individual or company and offer to purchase or lease the domain name. This, however, can become a costly endeavor.

Exactly how much is a domain name worth? This is a question with no easy answer. The price range for domain names sold on the secondary market is anywhere from $100 to $150,000 or more. Some domain names have been sold for upwards of $1 million.

If an individual or company has registered a domain name that's not in use and you want to buy it, try contacting the domain name registrant directly and inquiring about the domain name's availability. You will most likely have to engage in a negotiation process if the registrant is open to giving up the domain name . . . for a price.

There are also many companies that serve as brokers for the buying and selling of domain names. You might find it easier to use a broker to obtain the domain name you're looking for if it's already been taken. The Domain Name Aftermarket (www.tdnam. com) is just one resource for buying and selling already registered domain names.

If you're not willing to pay an exorbitant price for a domain name that's already taken, you can "backorder" a domain name.

Thus, by subscribing to this type of service, if the domain name ever becomes available in the future, you'll immediately be notified and have the option to register it for yourself. (Don't put your business on hold waiting for this to happen, however.) Operated by GoDaddy.com, DomainAlertPro is just one service that allows you to backorder domain names.

Getting help registering your domain name

The best place to seek personalized help when it comes to registering a domain name is to contact your ISP directly. If you sign a long-term website-hosting agreement with an ISP, they may offer to register your domain name free of charge or for a small fee.

An alternative is to contact the technical support or customer service phone number operated by the domain name registrar of your choice. Most offer telephone and e-mail support 7 days per week, 24 hours per day. As you'll discover, however, the process for registering a domain name has become extremely fast, inexpensive, and simple.

Consider the costs

If you're using a turnkey solution to create and manage your online business, most of your expenses will be included in the flat monthly fee. In addition, here are some of the other expenses you may incur:

- Purchasing a computer with access to the Internet
- Registering your domain name

 Bright Idea

Once you register your domain with one domain name registrar, you can switch registrars at anytime. This is called a transfer. You may find that a registrar offers better rates or additional services you're interested in, such as domain name parking or forwarding.

Bright Idea

As you register your domain name, consider all of the possible domain name extensions that might be useful to you now or in the future. For a listing of the more than 100 Internet domain name extensions currently available, point your Web browser to www.domainit.com/country-domains.htm. As you'll discover, each country has its own domain name extension. For example, *.us* is for sites based in the United States. The *.uk* extension is for sites based in the United Kingdom.

- Obtaining a merchant account and paying per transaction fees
- Monthly website-hosting services (if applicable)
- Monthly Internet connection fees (for broadband or DSL) from your home or office
- Hiring a website designer, graphic designer or programmer
- Website-creation and graphic-editing software (if applicable)
- Inventory costs
- Order processing costs (including shipping products to customers)

Just the facts

- Your online business's domain name gives you an address on the Web and a unique identity. Choose your domain name (or names) wisely.
- Try to choose a domain name that's easy to remember, pronounce, and spell—one that people will instantly associate with your company or product.
- If your company name and product differ, or you'll be selling multiple products or services through your online business, consider registering and using multiple domain names that lead to the same website.

- To determine whether a domain name is available, access the WHOIS.net database of all registered domain names. You can access this database from the website of any domain name registrar, such as GoDaddy.com or Network Solutions (www.networksolutions.com).

- The cost of registering a domain name is anywhere from $3.95 to $79 (or more) per year, depending on the domain name's extension and the registrar you use.

- GoDaddy.com is one of the easiest to use and least expensive domain name registrars. This is a full-service company that includes free domain forwarding, domain parking, and other services with each registration.

- Some of the most common domain name extensions include *.com*, *.net*, *.org*, *.biz*, *.name*, *.info*, *.us*, *.tv*, and *.ws*. Several of the newer extensions include *.aero*, *.coop*, *.museum*, and *.pro*.

- More than 100 domain name extensions are available worldwide. The most common, however, is *.com*.

GET THE SCOOP ON...
What's an ISP or Web-hosting service, anyway? ▪
The cost of going online ▪ Obtaining technical
support ▪ Purchasing computer equipment

Selecting Your Host: The Ins and Outs of ISPs

As an online business operator, you'll need a
Web-hosting service to provide a server upon
which your website will exist and be made
available to Web surfers worldwide. This is your business's gateway to the Internet. All of the turnkey solutions described in Chapter 4 include website hosting
in the monthly fee. If, however, you're developing
your website from scratch or using website-design
software, you'll probably need to hire a Web-hosting
service.

You'll also need an Internet Service Provider (ISP)
to provide you with access to the Internet from your
home or office, via a dial-up, DSL, or broadband
connection, for example. Many ISPs also offer Web-
hosting services, so chances are, you'll only need to
find one company to offer you both Web hosting plus
Internet access.

Once you create your Web page, it's necessary to
hire either a Web-hosting service to get your site on

the Net. The process of uploading your website to the server and making it available to the public is called *publishing* your website. This means that the data files you create (the individual Web pages, artwork, and related files that comprise your website) will be sent to the host's server, where they will be made available to anyone surfing the Web.

It takes a lot of time and effort to create and then launch your online business. To actually get it online, however, you'll first need to register a domain name with a registrar service, such as GoDaddy.com or NetworkSolutions.com (see Chapter 5, "Selecting and Registering Your Domain Name"), and then actually create your website. You'll also have to develop a relationship with a Web-hosting service or e-commerce hosting company.

After you've read this chapter, be sure to refer to Chapter 15, "E-commerce Industry Experts Share Their Knowledge and Secrets." It includes an interview with Sandy Bendremer, the cofounder of Galaxy Internet Services. He'll offer additional advice about choosing a host that's best suited to meeting your company's needs.

The costs associated with going online

There are several different fees associated with setting up a website and getting it online. As discussed in Chapter 5, you'll need to register your domain name(s). This will cost anywhere from $3.95 (if you register many domain names) to $35 per year, per name.

Your company will also be responsible for whatever fees are involved in creating and designing your website. This could mean purchasing website-creation software. Creating your actual website might also require you to hire programmers, graphic artists, writers, photographers, and other professionals—full-time, part-time, or on a freelance basis. These costs will vary greatly.

You could create a basic website using just your own artistic ability and a website-creation program or service. The professional look of your site will probably be lacking, however. Your level of artistic ability and the time you spend creating your site will impact its overall look. Having a professional-looking website that's as nice as, if not nicer than, your competition and other e-commerce sites on the Web is critical.

Finally, to get your site online, it's necessary to sign up with an ISP (unless you have the Web-server equipment to host your own site in-house). For businesses, this typically means paying a one-time setup fee plus an ongoing monthly fee to an ISP, which also will vary greatly based on your needs and what services are offered. Some ISPs charge a flat monthly fee as low as $20 per month, but then charge you for additional services, such as technical support, maintenance, or updating.

The ISP/Web-hosting business is extremely competitive, so be sure to shop around for the best rates and the highest level of service/technical support you can find. Finding a reliable ISP is as easy as doing the following:

- Seeking out a reference from someone you know.
- Surfing the Internet, using a search engine and a search phrase such as "ISP" or "Web Hosting."
- Checking the Yellow Pages.
- Calling any of the ISP/Web-hosting services or turnkey service solutions described in this book.

Keep in mind that some ISPs and Web-hosting firms are national companies, which means they offer Web-hosting services plus dial-up, DSL, and/or broadband access from cities nationwide and cater to companies, like yours, located anywhere in the country. These nationwide providers tend to offer less-personalized service (because they're large) but highly competitive rates. If you decide to affiliate yourself with a national company, you run less of a risk that the one you choose will suddenly go out of business (due to the competitive nature of the business).

Choose an ISP/Web-hosting service that offers the services and features you need. Also, make sure you maintain an offsite backup of your website files and have 24-hour access to them. Even if the hosting service provides a backup, it's an excellent strategy to be able to restore your site at another location if this is necessary.

A local Web-hosting service/ISP is one that caters to companies in a single city or region. These services tend to be a bit more expensive; however, you'll receive much more personalized service. If you choose to work with a local Web-hosting service, make sure it has e-commerce experience and can handle your needs.

Services you need at prices you can afford

Choosing an ISP/Web-hosting service is a lot like choosing a long-distance phone company. All of the long-distance companies offer long-distance services of the same basic quality, but each has a different pricing plan, different levels of customer service, and different incentives to get you to sign up with them. Typically, you can also save money by signing up with a little-known long-distance phone service.

The same general rules that apply to choosing a long-distance company apply when choosing an ISP/Web-hosting service. Most ISPs offer the same basic services, but with subtle differences and at different price points. This is why it's important to determine exactly what you need and then shop around for the best rates and services.

Some of the things you should inquire about when investigating a possible ISP/Web-hosting service include the following:

- **Rates**   This includes setup fees, monthly rates, and extra charges.

- **Amount of storage space offered**   When you sign up with an ISP to host your website, you might be limited to a specific amount of file storage space on its server(s)—typically 20 or 30 megabytes (MB), which should be plenty of space for most sites.

Moneysaver

ISPs/Web-hosting services are cost-effective. Connecting directly to the Internet using your own server, however, can cost at least $2,000. It would also require that you establish a direct connection to the Internet (24 hours a day, 7 days a week) via a T1 phone line or ISDN phone line. This can cost hundreds or thousands of dollars every month.

- **Passwords** As the customer of the ISP, can you control/ select your own logon passwords?

- **Domain name registration services** Does the ISP offer this? If so, make sure your domain name is registered with your company name and you are listed as the owner of the domain name.

- **E-mail** Does an ISP's Web-hosting services include personalized e-mail accounts so that you can easily accept e-mail messages from customers, clients, and others? How many e-mail boxes do you receive? Is there an extra fee for e-mail boxes? Your e-mail addresses can include your domain name, such as yourname@yourdomainname.com.

- **Special software** Does the ISP offer special software for maintaining your website or monitoring traffic to your site? If so, is there an additional cost for this software? Are you able to use your own software? Are these applications online-based?

- **Compatibility** Are the website-creation software and credit-card processing services you'll be using compatible with the ISP?

- **Backup services** What type of backup services does the ISP offer? How often does the server go down? When it goes down, how long does it typically take to fix?

- **Secure services** Does the ISP offer secure services for online credit-card transactions?

Watch Out!

Some ISPs/Web-hosting firms offer free website hosting. This, however, typically means you'll be required to prominently display ads for their company or their sponsors. This can potentially look amateurish and be annoying to the visitor. Although this is okay if you're operating a personal Web page, it's not suitable for an online business/e-commerce site.

- **Bandwidth**   Does the ISP have sufficient bandwidth to accommodate the level of traffic your website will be receiving? Or will visitors to your site experience lags?

- **Terms of the contract**   What are the contract terms you'll be required to sign with the ISP? Is there a minimum length of service (three months? six? twelve? twenty-four?)? What are the penalties if you choose to end your service agreement sooner?

- **Additional services**   What additional services does the ISP offer, and at what cost?

- **Tracking**   Does the ISP offer traffic reports or other information you can use to keep track of who is visiting your site, when they're visiting, which site they linked from, which pages of your site they visited, and so forth?

- **Other website help**   Does the ISP offer website-design and creation services for an extra fee?

- **Data transfer**   How much data transfer/traffic comes with the account, and what are the charges for additional data transfer?

A typical website hosting offer

An ISP/Web-hosting service, such as Galaxy Internet Service (888-334-2529; www.gis.net) offers a variety of website hosting packages as well as Internet access.

Like so many other ISPs, with Galaxy Internet Services, for example, a "Standard Hosting" package for a website is priced at

$19.95 per month (plus a one-time $50 setup fee) and includes the following:

- 50MB of space
- 10 mailboxes
- 3 Gigabytes of transfer (This refers to the amount of data your website sends to your visitors' browser. A typical active small business will get about 300 to 500MB of transfer per month. There are 1,000MB in a gigabyte [G]. If you'll be streaming audio or video, for example, your needs will be intensified.)
- Unlimited mail mapping (customized e-mail addresses that can be forwarded to any existing e-mail account or accessed using standard e-mail software.)
- An online-based control panel to manage your website
- A real-time traffic statistic report
- Your own CGI folder
- The ability to update your site using any FTP software as well as Microsoft FrontPage.

Starting at $49.95 per month (plus a one-time setup fee of $150), Galaxy Internet Services, for example, offers e-commerce website hosting, which includes secure hosting for credit-card processing and the Miva Merchant shopping cart application. The credit-card processing application is compatible with the services of most merchant account providers.

Like so many other e-commerce hosting solutions offered by ISPs, Galaxy Internet Services offers the following:

- 200MB of space
- 20 mailboxes
- 6G of transfer
- Unlimited mail mapping
- Secure Server Enabled (SSL)
- The Miva Merchant shopping cart application

- An online-based website control panel
- Real-time traffic statistic reports
- Your own CGI folder
- The ability to update your site using any FTP or website-creation software.

All-in-one turnkey solutions

Instead of having to invest in website-creation tools (software), hire an ISP, and figure out the ins and outs of secure Internet connections to handle credit-card processing and order transactions, services such as Yahoo! Small Business (http://small business.yahoo.com/merchant/) offer a one-stop and relatively inexpensive solution.

For a monthly fee starting at about $40, Yahoo! Store will help you create an e-commerce website, host your site, and handle all secure transactions. Services like these are also easily expandable as your business grows.

Yahoo! Site (http://site.yahoo.com/site) is another website creation and hosting service. It isn't e-commerce oriented, but it can be used by businesses looking to create an online presence. The pricing for Yahoo! Site starts at a flat fee of $11.95 per month (plus a one-time setup fee of $15). This service includes the following:

- An easy-to-use site builder
- Hosting on Yahoo!'s servers
- 2G of storage
- 25 personalized e-mail addresses

 Watch Out!

As you investigate ISPs/Web-hosting services, don't be afraid to ask lots of questions. If you can't get your questions answered in a prompt and friendly manner when the ISP is first trying to get your business, just imagine what the ISP will be like once you're a customer and need technical support!

- 25G of data transfer
- Detailed traffic reports and statistics e-mailed daily
- 24-hour toll-free phone support

Getting technical support from your ISP

This book should answer many of the questions you have about launching a website. But let's face it—as you get your online business up and running, you're going to have many more questions. Being able to get your questions answered quickly, easily, and as accurately as possible will save you time and money.

How much technical support you'll need will depend on how much you already know about creating, publishing, and managing your website. At least at first, you'll want to make sure that the tech support you need (via live online chat, e-mail, or telephone) is available when you need it from your ISP and other service providers (such as your merchant account provider).

As you investigate ISPs, make sure you ask about the availability of technical support. Specifically, you should ask the following questions:

- What types of technical support are available?
- During what hours can you speak with a human? Do the tech support representatives speak English as their native language? (Many companies farm out their tech support to companies located overseas.)
- Does the ISP offer toll-free technical support, or will you rack up high long-distance phone bills each time you call and are forced to sit on hold?
- How much does telephone technical support cost?
- Is the amount of technical support you're entitled to limited?
- What other forms of technical support are available (such as online, e-mail, and fax-on-demand)?
- What is the procedure for reporting problems?

Finding an ISP/Web-hosting service

There are thousands of ISPs located around the world. Here's just a partial list of some larger Web-hosting services listed in alphabetical order:

America Online	www.aol.com
Comcast	www.comcast.net
EarthLink	www.earthlink.net
Galaxy Internet Services	www.gis.net
Juno	www.juno.com
Microsoft Network (MSN)	www.msn.com
Netscape Internet Service	www.getnetscape.com
NetZero Platinum	www.netzero.net
Verizon Online	http://dslstart.verizon.net
Yahoo!	http://site.yahoo.com

The following are free online services designed to help people find a reliable ISP to meet their needs. These services rate, review, and list hundreds of ISPs; they're sponsor-supported, however, and many of those sponsors are ISPs.

Find-A-Host.Com (http://findahost.smesource.com/hosting/)

Host Index (www.hostindex.com)

HostReview.Com (www.hostreview.com)

HostSearch.Com (www.hostsearch.com)

The List: The Definitive ISP Buyer's Guide (http://thelist.internet.com)

Once you find an ISP you might be interested in working with, refer to the questions listed earlier in this chapter to help you evaluate what's being offered.

The computer equipment you need in-house

Depending on whether you're using website-creation software or an online solution, such as Yahoo! Store, the core system requirements for creating and maintaining your website will be slightly different. If you're planning to host your own website, the equipment you'll need will be more extensive and costly.

The core system requirements needed to actually create and then manage your website will depend in part on the website-creation software and graphics-development software you'll be using. In most cases, even a low-end PC-based desktop computer, with a Pentium 4 (or equivalent) processor, a good-sized hard drive (at least 40MB), and at least 256K of RAM will be sufficient. This type of low-end PC shouldn't cost more than $500, from a company such as Dell or Gateway. At the time this book was written, Dell was offering a low-end PC package for $299.95 from its website (www.dell.com).

Visit any computer store to see the various computer models and system configurations offered. Choose a system that will be able to handle your applications, but that offers you the ability to upgrade your system as needed. Stay away from PC-based systems that offer "closed architecture." These systems are typically cheaper, but can't be upgraded, so you might wind up having to purchase new equipment sooner than you planned.

As you shop around for a computer, keep in mind that technology is changing very quickly. Within 1 year to 18 months, it might be necessary to upgrade your PC with newer and faster technology, such as a better video card, faster CD/DVD-ROM drive, more memory, or a better microprocessor. Within three years, you might need a new PC altogether to keep up with the current technology trends.

Before shopping around for a PC system, carefully define your needs. Ask yourself what the computer will be used for. You should also determine, in advance, what primary software applications you plan on running, and what types of accessories and peripherals you'll be connecting to the computer.

In addition to creating and managing your actual website, you might be using the computer to manage other aspects of your online business, such as accounting, bookkeeping, order processing, contact management, inventory control, credit-card processing, and package-shipping processing.

As you're shopping for a computer, you'll need to determine a core system configuration for your computer. To do so, look at the system requirements of the software you plan to use. For example, here are the core system requirements needed to run Photoshop CS2 (www.adobe.com/products/photoshop), a popular graphics program used by many website designers to create and edit graphics and photos:

- Intel Xeon, Xeon Dual, Intel Centrino, or Pentium III or 4 processor
- Microsoft Windows 2000 with Service Pack 4, or Windows XP with Service Pack 1 or 2
- 320MB of RAM (384MB recommended)
- 650MB of available hard-disk space
- 1,024 × 768 monitor resolution with 16-bit video card
- CD-ROM drive
- Internet or phone connection required for product activation

In addition to your computer that's equipped with a high-speed Internet connection, a high-end digital camera, scanner,

 Bright Idea

Photoshop CS2 is a high-end graphics package designed for professional website designers and photographers. A much less expensive, scaled-down version of the program, called Photoshop Elements, is also available from Adobe (www.adobe.com). This is a much better program for beginners to use in order to edit photos and graphics for use on the Web.

and laser printer are all important peripherals for an online business operator.

Your Internet connection

Because you'll definitely need access to the Internet to surf the Web, send and receive e-mail, and maintain your website, you want the fastest connection possible. Assuming it's available in your area, sign up for high-speed DSL or broadband Internet access (as opposed to a basic dial-up connection). This should cost anywhere from $29.95 to $49.95 per month. A slower dial-up connection should cost well under $20 per month. Your local phone company might offer special, money-saving bundles, which include Internet access, local phone service and long distance phone service.

It's also possible to access the Net at high speeds using a wireless connection via satellite. This service is available from DirecWay (www.direcpc.com) and is a viable option if DSL or broadband isn't yet available in your hometown or city.

Retail versus online computer vendors

Buying a computer from a retail store or computer superstore has several advantages, especially if you don't know a lot about computers. For starters, the in-store salespeople and technical staff will theoretically be able to address your needs and answer your questions on the spot.

Also, if the computer turns out to be defective, you can return or exchange it locally. The drawback to buying your computer equipment from a retail computer store is that you'll typically pay higher prices, possibly including state sales taxes. Your buying decisions will also be limited to the PC brands carried by the retail stores you visit.

The alternative is to buy your computer equipment from a reputable online merchant. Although you'll often have to pay shipping to receive your purchase, the prices are generally much lower. The trick to saving money when shopping online is to determine your exact needs and then shop around for the

Bright Idea

As you investigate ways to promote your own e-commerce site, advertising on a comparison-shopping website can generate a tremendous volume of traffic, if used correctly. In Chapter 16, Jeremy Alicandri, the founder of SimplyCheap. com, talks about how he uses comparison-shopping websites to successfully promote his online business and drive traffic to his website.

best prices. For reliable computer hardware reviews, visit the C|Net website at www.cnet.com.

A comparison-shopping website such as Nextag.com (www. nextag.com), PriceWatch.com (www.pricewatch.com), C|Net Shopper (http://shopper.cnet.com), Shopping.com (www. shopping.com), or Shopzilla (www.shopzilla.com) can help you quickly find the lowest price for a specific computer system or peripheral you're looking to purchase online. Membership warehouse clubs, like Costco or Sam's Club, also offer good deals on computers and peripherals.

Just the facts

- To actually get your site online, you'll probably have to sign up with an ISP/Web-hosting service.

- The ISP/Web-hosting business is extremely competitive, so be sure to shop around for the best rates and the highest level of service/technical support you can find.

- Before shopping around for a PC system, carefully define your needs. How much computer power will you need to run the applications you'll be using frequently?

- The alternative to buying your computer equipment from a retail computer store is to shop at an online merchant. Although you might have to pay shipping to receive your purchase, the prices are generally much lower. Use a shopping-comparison website to find the lowest prices for the equipment you need.

An Internet Presence for Existing and New Businesses

PART III

Expanding Your Existing Business into Cyberspace

Remember high school? There were the "in crowd" and the "uncool kids." If you wanted to be part of the in crowd, you had to dress how others dressed and act exactly how others did.

Chances are you graduated from high school a while ago, but some things never really change. If you're reading this chapter, perhaps you operate your own traditional business. But when it comes to succeeding in today's business world, no matter what type of business you own or operate, it's becoming vital to join the "in crowd" and follow the latest trends by establishing an Internet presence for your business. The "in crowd" in today's business world can be found on the World Wide Web.

Some established businesses identify an immediate benefit for creating an Internet presence, whether it's to sell products to a potential worldwide audience, offer potential customers information about these products, or offer improved and more

Chapter 7

Watch Out!

If you operate a medium- to large-sized traditional company, don't take a "trial-and-error" approach and attempt to design, build, and manage your website in-house. Hire professionals. They'll know how to make your site easy to use and integrate it with your company's corporate identity, brand, and reputation.

convenient customer service. Other companies are establishing themselves on the Internet now because business operators understand that having an Internet presence is critical, and they need to offer what their demanding customers expect. Established business operators also want to reserve or register the best domain names for their business before those domain names are taken by the competition.

Sure, the Internet has been around for a while now. Thus, first establishing your business online is more of a catch-up move to keep up with your competition, but it's definitely not too late to stake your business's turf on the Web.

Establishing an Internet presence doesn't necessarily mean you have to invest a fortune to create a state-of-the-art website. If you currently operate a traditional retail store, service business, consulting business, or other traditional (non-virtual) business, a website can be used for a variety of purposes. For several hundred dollars, a basic website, capable of communicating information about your company and its products/services, can be created in a matter of hours or days, depending on your knowledge level and how much planning and preparation you've already done.

As millions of people from around the world continue to gain access to the Internet and begin surfing the Web more frequently with their high-speed DSL or broadband connections, their buying habits are changing rapidly. If you're looking to buy a major appliance, for example, you no longer need to spend hours driving from one appliance dealer to the next to learn about the latest models, their features, or their cost. You can research products and comparison-shop online in far less time and without having to deal with pushy salespeople or find a parking spot at each store.

Best of all, as a consumer, you can do your shopping any time, day or night, without ever leaving your home. Using this example, if you're an appliance dealer, you could miss out on many sales if your business isn't represented on the Web and easy to find using a search engine.

Whether you operate a local retail store or a service-oriented business, the Web allows you to offer your products or services to a worldwide market via the Web, as opposed to just the people located in your business's immediate geographic area. By expanding your potential marketplace, your sales can increase and profits for your business can grow dramatically.

Many established businesses are using the Internet simply to improve their customer service and cut costs. For example, if your business receives many phone calls from potential customers requesting information (sales brochures) for your products, there is a cost associated with printing those brochures, dealing with customer phone calls, and then mailing out the requested information. Once your website is established, you can re-create those same brochures online. Then, your company can simply promote its website's URL, and potential customers can almost instantly obtain the information they want, when they want it, without having to wait.

No longer is it just a small group of high-income, computer-savvy people who shop online. More and more consumers from all walks of life are turning to the Internet to find products and

 Watch Out!

As you plan your site's content, your primary concern should be ease of use (simple navigation), fast downloading times, and content that provides exactly what the visitors to your site will be looking for. Failing to offer these things could frustrate your site's visitors and cause them to leave.

services they need or want, and this trend is growing extremely quickly.

If you are a traditional business operator, you can use an online presence to complement your existing marketing, sales, information distribution, or customer service efforts. There is no need to abandon your existing business model. Unlike starting a virtual business, adding an online component to your traditional business can be done over time, with a relatively low financial investment, and without having to reorganize your existing business.

For an existing business, here are just some of the ways an existing business can use a website effectively, starting immediately:

- To sell products/services online to a broader customer base. (You'll need to create an e-commerce site for this.)

- To enhance your existing customer service and technical support efforts (if applicable). This can be done by posting technical (how-to) articles on your website, offering a live chat with company representatives, posting an FAQ (Frequently Asked Questions) document on your website, or developing a message board or live chat area for customers to communicate with each other. You can also use your website to distribute an online-based newsletter to your customers and clients.

- To disseminate information about your company and its products/services, by offering electronic versions of your catalogs, brochures, press kits, and marketing materials on the website.

- Communicating more frequently and efficiently with your existing customers by creating an online newsletter and promoting sales and events on your website.

- To gather useful market research data from your customers (and potential customers) to help you offer better products/services.

Bright Idea

If you already operate a successful traditional business, find ways to enhance the services you offer to your customers using the Web. The ability to shop 24 hours a day, obtain technical information about a product, or get questions answered promptly are all value-added services you could offer on your website.

- To promote your latest products/services to potential new customers.

- To recruit new employees and accept electronic resumés/ applications.

- To disseminate investor and stockholder information.

- To inform customers about hours of operation for your retail store or office.

- To provide your customers with your business's mailing address (or the address of your retail store, office or showroom), phone number, and fax number.

- To distribute online coupons and special "website only" offers that customers can redeem online or at your retail store.

- To reduce costs and personnel needs.

As you'll discover simply by surfing the Web for yourself, there's a difference between e-commerce websites (designed to actually sell products or services) and corporate websites (designed to build brand awareness and simply disseminate information about the company and its products or services).

The basic steps for getting online

The basic steps for creating an Internet presence for your existing business are pretty similar to starting a virtual (online) business. The costs associated with many of these tasks are outlined in Chapter 5.

To get your existing business online, you'll need to do the following:

- Register a domain name.

- Plan your website's content.

- Actually create your website.

- Develop a relationship with a Web-hosting service.

- Manage the day-to-day operation of your site and keep it updated.

- Promote and market your website and generate traffic to it.

Other chapters of this book go into great detail about each of these steps. The purpose of this chapter is to focus on a handful of additional steps and considerations necessary for establishing an online presence for an existing company based in the "real" world.

How virtual and traditional businesses differ

A virtual business is one that was created for the sole purpose of doing business online, typically using e-commerce technologies. A virtual business will most likely be operated from a business office or home office, but its primary existence is in cyberspace.

An online-based business is very different from a retail store, a traditional mail-order business, or a service-oriented business involving in-person contact between customers and product/service providers.

In reality, an online-based business could be operated from anywhere, by someone using a laptop computer to access and

 Bright Idea

To avoid many of the common mistakes made by existing companies creating an Internet presence, subscribe to e-commerce newsletters or publications, such as Web Marketing Today (www.wilsonweb.com/wct). Instead of trying to reinvent the wheel, learn from the successes and mistakes of other companies.

maintain a site being hosted by an independent ISP/Web-hosting company. Just as there are many types of traditional businesses, there are different types of virtual businesses. With a virtual business, however, the primary communication between the business operator and potential customers is done online.

Creating an online presence for a traditional business

When someone decides to start an online-based business, it's necessary to create an entire infrastructure for that business in advance, before going online. Until all the steps are completed— from incorporating the business to creating a company logo to developing a website to establishing procedures for order fulfillment—the virtual business shouldn't go online; it shouldn't "open" to the public. Aside from registering a domain name and planning and creating a website, a virtual businessperson needs to follow many of the same steps already completed when establishing a traditional business. Thus, as a traditional business operator, you've already done much of the initial groundwork.

The biggest challenge you're going to face is seamlessly integrating your new online presence with the rest of your business, without compromising your existing business's reputation or brand. A main reason for going online is to make it easier for your customers to take advantage of the products or services you already offer and possibly increase your customer base. Thus, to keep your existing customers happy and to cater to a potential new audience, you want to take full advantage of your traditional business's reputation, corporate identity, and brand recognition—something a start-up virtual business needs to create from scratch.

For an established business looking to go online, one important consideration is the domain name you choose. The domain name should be your existing company's name, should be easy to remember (and spell), and should be intuitive. Avoid using an extremely long domain name or one that is complicated to spell.

Bright Idea

Visit any domain name registrar's website, such as Network Solutions (www.networksolutions.com) or GoDaddy.com (www.godaddy.com) to determine whether the domain names you like have already been taken. If your company's name is a registered trademark and someone else has the domain name registered, you might have legal rights to that domain name, so contact your lawyer.

If the spelling of your company name is confusing, consider registering multiple domain names for your site, and include the most common misspellings or name alternatives. The object is to make it very easy for people to find you online. For example, if you were IBM and you were planning to create a website for your company, the most obvious domain name to register would be www.ibm.com. An alternative to using your company name for your domain name is to register your product name as your domain name. Chapter 5 offers more detail about how to choose and register your domain name (or names).

People who choose to find you on the Web will discover your domain name in one of four ways:

- They'll obtain your domain name because it will be printed clearly in your company's advertisements or traditional marketing materials (brochures, catalogs, business cards, letterhead, press kits, signage, and so on).

- They'll use an Internet search engine to find your domain name, usually by typing the name of your company or the product they're looking for as the keyword or search phrase.

- They'll experiment, use common sense, and enter your company name as part of the URL when trying to find you. Back to the IBM example, if you want to find IBM's website, the most obvious URL is www.ibm.com, so that's what most people will try.

- They'll respond to online advertising and promotions you implement, such as "Search Marketing" or "Keyword

Marketing," banner ads, promotional e-mails, links from other websites, and so on.

While still in the planning stages of the online presence for your existing company, determine the following as early as possible:

- What is the purpose of the website.

- What services or features you'd like to offer visitors.

- What visual assets you already have available (company/product logos, product photos, and other artwork).

- What printed materials (such as brochures) you'd like to make available online, and in what format.

- What content needs to be created from scratch or adapted from existing materials currently not in electronic formats. This includes text, such as product descriptions, your company's press releases, or a corporate backgrounder.

Your established corporate and brand identity should remain completely consistent as you develop your Web content. This means, for example, that the color schemes you use on your Web pages should be consistent with the look of your traditional printed materials. The look of your company/product logos should remain constant, and the overall "attitude" of your site should be consistent with your corporate image.

In terms of your website's content, if you have a well-established business, avoid using too much pre-created or generic website artwork—such as animated GIFs or clip art—or preformatted website-design templates that look generic. To enhance your company's corporate identity, you're better off having original artwork and custom website design. Obtaining

Watch Out!

Not maintaining a strong continuity online will actually be detrimental to the great efforts and expense you've already incurred in developing your corporate and brand identity in the offline business world.

Bright Idea

If you have traditional negatives or a photo you want to add to your site, but don't have direct access to the necessary scanning equipment or the time to do the work yourself, many services are available to translate the negative into an electronic file.

pre-created or generic artwork or Web page templates is easy because these assets can be downloaded for free, purchased on CD-ROM, or licensed, but they won't be exclusive to your site.

Developing original artwork and a unique website design from scratch will cost a bit more, but having a unique-looking site that builds your corporate image is beneficial and will help boost customer confidence. Of course, you can take a professional-looking template and totally customize it. You'll find templates at the Template Monster (www.templatemonster.com) website.

Almost any graphic artist or professional website designer will be able to create original artwork and visual assets for your company's website that will maintain continuity with your existing business's overall image and brand.

Many ISPs/Web-hosting companies offer fast, inexpensive, and easy ways for established companies to develop and publish a website that requires a minimal time commitment and small financial investment. If you're on a tight budget, this is definitely a good starting point. You can always expand your website and add additional functionality down the road. What's important now is simply getting your business on the Web, developing a professional-looking website, and then generating traffic to that site in order to build your overall business.

Converting hard-copy assets into an electronic format

During the life of your existing business, you've probably created or acquired a variety of artistic assets such as logos, product photos, line art, and other materials that could be incorporated easily into your website to maintain continuity between your company's online and offline branding and overall image.

Instead of having to have electronic versions of your various artistic assets re-created from scratch, there are a variety of ways to create electronic versions of existing assets using a flatbed scanner, photo/negative scanner, or high-end digital camera.

If you need to scan a large number of photos or negatives in order to create electronic GIF or JPEG files for use on the Web, consider investing in a photo scanner, which commonly connects directly to a PC via a USB interface and can be used to scan 35mm film strips (positive or negatives), 35mm mounted slides and negatives, and paper-based images up to 8.5" × 17".

Once the image is in digital form, you can use a program such as Photoshop CS2 or the less expensive Photoshop Elements program (www.adobe.com/products/photoshop) or LView Pro (www.lview.com), for example, to edit, crop, or digitally enhance the photo or image. Invest the necessary time to learn how to use the graphics program you purchase so that what you create looks professional. In many cases, you can take classes, read training guides, or obtain training videos for the popular graphics programs such as Photoshop.

After these images are created, you'll still want to use file-size-reduction software (a feature built into many graphics programs) to speed up the download time for each image and to create smaller, thumbnail images. LView Pro and Photoshop will allow you to shrink the file size of graphics for use on the Web.

 Bright Idea

To make editing and cropping photos and digital images easier when you're using a program like Photoshop CS2 or Coral, for example, consider using a digital pen-enabled graphic tablet, from a company like Wacom (800-922-1490, www.i3now.com). The Intuos3, for example, allows you to more easily edit graphic files using a pen-like interface on a digital tablet that connects to a PC or Mac (as opposed to using a less precise mouse). Graphic tablets that connect to a PC via a USB cable start in price under $100 and come in a variety of sizes.

For creating product photos from scratch, you can use a traditional camera and then have the images scanned to create electronic files, or you can use a high-end digital camera. Because product photos on a website must look totally professional, it's an excellent idea to hire a professional photographer or advertising agency to have these photos created. Your product suppliers or manufacturers might already have artwork suitable for use on your website, which will save you money.

Some online business operators invest anywhere from $500 to $3,000 to build small digital photo studios in-house in order to create and edit all of their own product photos for use on their website. This gives you total control over your artistic content, plus ensures that your content will be exclusive to your website. In Chapter 16, you'll read about Christian Girts, the founder and owner of Anglersvice.com. A major part of his Web design strategy is to create all of his own product photos in-house, using a small, digital photographic studio he set up in his basement.

For website art, you'll want to create GIF or JPEG files that can easily be added to your Web pages. As always, you'll want to pay careful attention to file sizes (which impact download times—the bigger your files are, the longer it takes for your customers to view your page) as you select which artistic files you choose to add to your site during the design phase. Also, make sure all of your photos are in focus and look professional.

 Bright Idea

Do you want to learn more about electronic photography? Hewlett Packard offers a free, informative website with all sorts of information about electronic photography and creating electronic images. Point your Web browser to www.photosmart.com. Canon also offers an excellent website relating to its digital cameras (http://consumer.usa.canon.com). The PC World website (www.pcworld.com) offers a special Digital Camera Info Center. Click on the appropriate icon to read reviews of digital cameras as well as informative how-to articles.

Thanks to Adobe Acrobat software (www.adobe.com), you can easily and inexpensively take your existing printed materials, such as full-color brochures, advertisements, and annual reports, and have them transferred into the popular PDF format. This allows Web surfers visiting your site to load and read electronic files that are exact replicas of traditionally printed and typeset files. Many companies use this software to offer downloadable versions of existing product brochures and sales information via their websites. The Web surfer, however, will need the Acrobat Reader browser plug-in or stand-alone software to open a PDF file and read it. Acrobat Reader is a free program and browser plug-in that millions of computer users already have.

What features your business could offer on the Web

Depending on the type of business you operate, the services and features you can and should incorporate into your website will vary greatly. The most important thing to consider before adding any features or content elements to your site is to analyze what each addition offers to visitors. If what you're planning doesn't directly help the visitor gather the information they need or serve a definite purpose (other than provide a bit of flash or glitz to your site), skip it.

The best way to determine what your particular website should offer is to spend time surfing the Web and examining what other businesses in your field or industry have done. You can also glean some good ideas from the websites of other types of businesses. Although you don't want to steal content for your site, it's important to gather ideas and determine what works online and what doesn't. Soliciting ideas from your existing customers can also be very beneficial.

Unless you are extremely knowledgeable about website creation and programming, don't invest a fortune trying to create the ultimate state-of-the-art website yourself, no matter what type of business you're in. If you happen to create a totally original website-design idea and you invest a fortune to make the idea a reality, chances are, it will be ripped off within a matter of days (or even hours).

Although it's important that your site look original and contain original content, designing special features for your site that involve complex programming isn't usually the best approach or best use of your time and financial resources.

Spreading the word about your online presence

There are many ways to spread the word that your business now has a website. The following are a few ideas for promoting your site's URL to your existing customers once it's online:

- Add the URL (website address) to every piece of printed sales and marketing material your company uses. This includes all of your traditional advertising, such as print ads, radio and TV ads, and billboards. In a prominent space on these materials, add a phrase like "Visit us on the Web at www.(your company).com" or "For more information, check out our website at www.(your company.com)." Wherever your company's address and phone number is listed, add a line that displays your website's URL.

- Add the URL to your company's letterhead, envelopes, business cards, brochures, sales receipts/invoices, press releases, and press-kit folders. If you're a retail store, consider having the URL printed on your shopping bags and cash-register sales receipts. Large retailers, such as Gap and Barnes & Noble, display large signs in their stores encouraging people to visit their websites.

- Knowing when people are accessing your online business, particularly what pages of your website they're accessing, and what keywords or search phrases they used to find information on your site are all pieces of information that can help you better manage your online presence. Keyword marketing is an excellent and low-cost way to drive traffic to your website. Go to Yahoo! Search Marketing (http://searchmarketing.yahoo.com) or Google AdWords (http://adwords.google.com/select) for details about these advertising opportunities on the popular search engines.

- List your URL prominently in your company's catalogs or direct-mail pieces.

- If the products your company sells include packaging or manuals, add your company's URL to these materials.

- If your business has an "on hold" message when people call you, announce your website as part of this message.

- Display the company's website on your company-owned vehicles.

- Send out an e-mail to your existing customers announcing your website's launch. To get them to visit, offer a special "online only" promotion or sale.

In addition to all these methods for attracting your existing customers to your website, be sure to promote your site to new (potential) customers. Many website promotional methods are described in detail in Chapter 9, "Generating Revenues from Your Site," and Chapter 10, "Promotion Is the Key to Success." These methods include buying paid online advertising, agreeing to ad banner exchanges, creating an affiliate program, registering your site with the Internet search engines (search-engine optimization), using keyword/search marketing, initiating online-based public relations efforts, using e-mail marketing, and establishing link exchanges with other sites.

One way to help get people to visit your site, especially if yours is a well-known and established company, is to focus on your company's reputation and brand. People feel comfortable shopping online with merchants they're already familiar with

but before going online, it's vital to develop well-thought-out answers to the following questions.

To obtain honest and accurate answers to these questions, you will need to do research. This will probably mean making a time commitment. Think of the time you spend now doing research as an investment in your company's future success. The more prepared you are right from the start, the better your chances will be for success once your online-based business is actually launched and fully operational.

Some of the important questions you want to consider include the following:

- What is the market potential for your products or services?

- Who exactly are your customers? Know their demographics: age, gender, income, race, geographic area, education level, shopping preferences, occupation, and so on.

- Why do your potential customers buy what you sell?

- What do your potential customers want and need?

- In addition to the product(s) or service(s) you plan to offer online, what else can you offer to potential customers in order to boost your profits? Can you up-sell your customers with related products or services?

- Who is your competition?

- What is the current and projected size of the market and what is its growth potential?

- How will you reach your customers?

- Are your advertising, marketing, and promotional plans well thought out? Are your expectations of how well these plans will work realistic?

- What's your monthly advertising, marketing, and promotional budget?

- How will you tap the power of the Web to achieve your business objectives—to make sales and effectively target your customers?

Watch Out!

If you don't have answers to relevant questions before launching your online business, go back and do some fine-tuning in order to avoid problems down the road.

- What Web technologies are available to help you achieve your goals?

- Which ISP/Web-host provider will you use?

- Once you receive orders, how will they be processed and shipped?

- What are your options for receiving payment from customers? Which of these options will be used on your site, and how?

- How will you obtain inventory? Who will be your main suppliers?

- How much initial investment capital is needed to help make your online business successful? Remember, plan at least one year (12 months) in advance.

- How will you manage the day-to-day operations of your business? How automated will it be? What software is available to assist in your business's management?

Unfortunately, nothing can replace research as you prepare to launch any type of business. If you've already developed a business plan, hopefully you've already done much of the necessary research and answered the preceding questions. If there's no business plan in place, creating one should become one of your top priorities.

To gather accurate and timely information, do as much research as possible online, and be sure to use industry-oriented magazines and newsletters as a resource. Also, don't just rely on one source of information when doing research. Whenever possible, try to confirm whatever facts and figures you uncover using multiple reliable resources.

Bright Idea

As early as possible, discuss with your business partners or lawyers who will be responsible for designing and maintaining your website. It might be helpful to have one person be the "go-to" person, the resident authority for questions that arise.

Nobody is an expert in every aspect of business. Some people are more adept at business-related finance and bookkeeping, whereas others have a knack for marketing, product development, customer service, or management. Once you know exactly what will be required to make your business successful, carefully analyze your own talents, knowledge base, and skills. Determine what you're good at and what you know, and pinpoint the areas where you'll need to seek guidance.

For example, if you've never designed any type of website and you have no knowledge of HTML, Flash, or Java programming, chances are you should hire an expert to design and manage your online business's website until you get up to speed on how this is done. Likewise, if you're highly computer literate and have an excellent idea for an online business, but you lack the knowledge to manage a traditional business, you might want to partner with someone with business-related skills and experience.

If your online business is simply a part-time activity and you're already financially stable thanks to a full-time job, it's a bit safer to take the learn-as-you-go approach to operating your own start-up business. However, if you're making a significant financial and time investment in the launch of your business, and you're relying on this business to generate your income, there's no substitute for doing research about every aspect of your business and acquiring, in advance, as much knowledge as possible.

There are many reasons why new businesses fail, and an equal number of mistakes you could make that might lead to serious problems. Competition is fierce out there, and customers are becoming increasingly more savvy and demanding. Unless you have the infrastructure and knowledge in place to deal with every situation that might arise, think twice about actually launching your business, because you're unprepared.

If you don't already have a long list of potential problems your business could run into (and know how you'll deal with these situations), you haven't done enough research and preparation. Lack of preparation and lack of funding are some of the common reasons why start-up businesses of any kind fail.

In the business world, chances are there will always be someone you perceive to be smarter than you operating a competing business that's better funded than yours. It's your job to take full advantage of the assets, skills, and knowledge available to you and make the most of them. When it comes to traditional business, in certain situations your chances of competing successfully are slim to none—for example, if you were to open a small sporting-goods shop or pharmacy a block away from a Wal-Mart. The Internet, however, offers a much more level playing field because your presence on the Web can evolve into something just as professional-looking, functional, and engaging as your competition, no matter how big the competition.

Every well-run business on the Web has a fairly equal chance for success, provided that the people operating the business know what they're doing. Of course, if you're planning to launch an online business, like Amazon.com, to compete head-on with traditional bookstore chains, like Borders and Barnes & Noble, it will take a significant amount of investment capital. But millions of online entrepreneurs have already successfully launched

 Bright Idea

Any information or content on your site that does not directly address a concern or provide useful information to the potential customer should either be removed or reworked, in order to make your site as informative, user-friendly, and clutter-free as possible.

online businesses that are smaller in scale and that target a niche market with a specialized or customized product.

If you have a unique idea (or at least a really good idea) for an online business, you develop a professional-looking website, and you know exactly who your target audience is and how to reach them successfully, your chances for achieving success will be excellent. Starting any type of business involves taking some risks, planning carefully, conducting extensive research, and making a significant time and financial commitment.

Becoming a niche-marketing expert

Unless you have millions of dollars to invest in an online business that will cater to the masses and compete head-on with the big players, your best chance for success in launching an online business is to cater to a niche—or specialized—market. The audience for a niche-oriented product is typically a group with a very well-defined interest, need, or desire. Your job is to determine who these people are and exactly what their interest, need, or desire is. Next, you must figure out a way to convey to this audience that you have a product that caters directly to their wants.

By carefully defining your company's niche market, determining who the people are that make up the market, examining what their needs and wants are, and then pinpointing a way to cater to the market with a unique product or service, you'll soon become a niche-marketing expert. At the very least, you'll become an expert in the niche market your business is catering to.

If you don't truly understand who your target audience is and how your product meets their wants, your sales will suffer.

 Watch Out!

If you've made the decision to launch an online-based business, dedicate yourself to doing it right and putting in the necessary effort, or don't bother. Doing it halfheartedly will doom you to failure.

Likewise, if you don't truly believe that what you're offering to your target audience is a solution to a problem or answer to a need, you won't convince a potential customer that what you're offering has any value whatsoever.

Just because you have a website that's selling a product you believe is useful doesn't mean the rest of the world will share your belief. Like a sales brochure, TV commercial, or print ad, your website should be a powerful sales tool, designed to educate visitors about your product and how it offers something a potential customer wants.

As you analyze your niche market, consider carefully whether these people are typical Web surfers and whether they have the ability to order products online using a major credit card. Young adults, kids, and teens are more apt than their elders to be computer savvy and comfortable surfing the Web. They also typically have a high level of disposable income (or a lot of influence over their parents' buying habits). But as a rule, younger surfers don't have credit cards to place orders online. Older people, on the other hand, also have a lot of disposable income, but a relatively small percentage of people over the age of 55 are comfortable shopping online.

The online buying habits of people are changing rapidly as more and more people from all walks of life gain access to the Web. Without making assumptions, be sure that the niche audience you're trying to reach is, in fact, online and able and willing to make purchases on the Internet.

Identifying the needs and wants of your potential customers

Once you determine what product your online-based business will be offering and who the target market is, it's your job to get to know your potential customers. Defining your target market means determining some or all of the following information:

- Age range
- Buying and spending habits

- Club, association, or group affiliations
- Ethnicity
- Gender
- Hobbies
- Income level
- Internet surfing habits
- Level of education
- Needs and concerns
- Occupation
- Religion
- Special interests

Only by truly understanding your target audience will you be able to design a website that caters to them. Once you have developed a profile of who your potential customers are, you must determine what their actual needs, interests, and wants are as they relate to the product you plan on offering. Will your product solve a problem, meet a need, save the customers time or money, help them achieve a goal, or provide them with something they really want?

As part of your business plan and overall business practices, figure out exactly what about your product or service someone will be interested in. Next, use a combination of the resources available on the Web (such as text, graphics, photographs, audio, video, animations, and interactivity) to inform your target audience about your product in a way they'll find engaging, informative, and easy to understand.

 Bright Idea

Don't forget to think about your competition when you plan your website. Your site needs to convey not just why a potential customer should buy from you, but also why your product tops what's available from your competition.

The more defined your niche market is, the easier it will be to find ways to reach these people and promote your website and products to them.

Understanding your target market is vitally important when developing your website. It's also important when determining how and where you'll be marketing and promoting your online business. Whatever money you allocate toward marketing, advertising, and promoting your business will be spent best if those funds allow you to reach directly the group of people your business is targeting.

In advance, come up with an extensive list of all the reasons why someone in your target audience will want your product, and then develop a list of objections or reasons they might have for not buying your product. Using your list of objections, come up with solutions or a sales pitch that addresses each objection, and determine the best way to communicate this information online.

Conducting formal or informal market research, interviewing focus groups, and sending questionnaires to customers will help you better understand your target audience.

As your online business begins to take form and you sit down to plan and design your website, make sure you're tailoring every aspect of the site to your target audience.

Beware of get-rich-quick schemes

Anyone with an e-mail address, fax machine, U.S. mailbox, TV, or access to some of the less reputable business publications is constantly bombarded with offers to get rich quick while working from home or using the Internet. Con artists have devised all sorts of scams, pyramid schemes, and multilevel marketing plans. These initially appear to be extremely attractive; but in reality, they're complete rip-offs or business opportunities for which the profit potential has been greatly exaggerated.

Yes, people have been successful establishing websites to sell legitimate multilevel marketing products. But there are many Web-based get-rich-quick schemes, franchises, and business

Watch Out!

If you conduct surveys online, remember that visitors are often hesitant to provide personal information about themselves until they're ready to place an order for your product. In addition, unless you give them an incentive—such as offering a discount or free gift—they probably won't want to take the time to answer your questions.

opportunities that you should definitely avoid. As a general rule, if the offer sounds too good to be true, it is. If you receive unsolicited e-mail (spam) offering an extraordinary business opportunity, be wary.

When it comes to determining whether you're about to get caught up in a pyramid scheme and perhaps get ripped off, the Federal Trade Commission (FTC) recommends following these basic rules:

- Beware of plans asking you to spend money on costly inventory.

- Be cautious of claims that you will make money by recruiting new "members," "associates," or "affiliates" instead of on sales you make yourself.

- Beware of promises about high profits or claims about "miracle" products.

- Be cautious about seemingly unsolicited testimonials to the effectiveness of the program; they could be from people hired by the promoter.

- Don't pay money or sign contracts in a high-pressure situation.

- Check out all offers with your local Better Business Bureau (www.bbb.org) or your state's Attorney General.

Scam artists from around the world are becoming computer savvy themselves and are cashing in on the Internet's potential by selling fraudulent Internet-related business opportunities.

Many of these scams are targeted to individuals who are not technologically savvy. Many pitches are designed to take full advantage of a would-be entrepreneur's Internet innocence.

The Federal Trade Commission (FTC) urges you to investigate Internet-related business opportunities as carefully as you would check out any business opportunity. It suggests that before you invest or buy into any online-based business opportunity, you should do the following:

- Realize that seminar "trainers" or "consultants" often are there to sell you a business opportunity, not teach you Internet basics. In fact, they might be counting on your lack of experience with computers or the Internet.

- Investigate all earnings claims. Talk to others who have purchased the opportunity to see whether their experience verifies the claims. Whenever possible, visit them in person.

- Demand to see the company's claims in writing. Get all promises in writing.

- Ask for a disclosure document if you are interested in a franchise. This document is required by law. It should provide detailed information to help you compare one business to another. Be skeptical of companies that do not have disclosure documents.

If you run into trouble, you can file a complaint with the FTC by contacting the Consumer Response Center by phone at 877-FTC-HELP (382-4357); by mail at Consumer Response Center, Federal Trade Commission, CRC-24, Washington, DC 20580; or through the Internet at http://www.ftc.gov/ftc/consumer.htm.

 Watch Out!

If you get scammed, the Federal Trade Commission cannot resolve individual problems for consumers. It can, however, act against a company if it sees a pattern of possible law violations.

The FTC reports e-mail boxes are filling up with more offers for business opportunities than any other kind of unsolicited commercial e-mail. Many of these offers are scams. In response to requests from consumers, the FTC asked e-mail users to forward their unsolicited commercial notices to the agency for an inside look at the bulk e-mail business. The FTC discovered that, more often than not, bulk e-mail offers appeared to be fraudulent, and if the recipients had pursued them, they could have been ripped off to the tune of billions of dollars.

Twelve common scams

In a press release issued by the FTC, the organization identified the top 12 scams that are most likely to arrive in consumers' e-mail boxes.

Business opportunities

These business opportunities make it sound easy to start a business that will bring lots of income without much work or cash outlay. The solicitations trumpet unbelievable earnings of $100 a day and up to $1,000 a day or more, and claim that the business doesn't involve selling, meetings, or personal contact with others, or that someone else will do all the work.

Many business opportunity solicitations claim to offer a way to make money in an Internet-related business. These messages usually offer a telephone number to call for more information. In many cases, you'll be told to leave your name and telephone number so that a salesperson can call you back with the sales pitch.

Bulk e-mail

Bulk e-mail solicitations offer to sell you lists of e-mail addresses by the millions, to which you can send your own bulk solicitations. Many companies offer software that automates the sending of e-mail messages to thousands or millions of recipients. Others offer the service of sending bulk e-mail solicitations on your behalf. Some of these offers say, or imply, that you can make a lot of money using this marketing method.

Watch Out!

Several states have laws regulating the sending of unsolicited commercial e-mail, which you might unwittingly violate by sending bulk e-mail. Few legitimate businesses, if any, engage in bulk e-mail marketing for fear of offending potential customers.

Sending bulk e-mail violates the terms of service of most Internet Service Providers. If you use one of the automated e-mail programs, your ISP can shut you down. In addition, inserting a false return address into your solicitations, as some of the automated programs allow you to do, might land you in legal trouble with the owner of that domain name.

Sending bulk e-mail to recipients who have specifically requested you to send them information or put them on your mailing list is an entirely different story. Using bulk e-mail to reach this type of audience is a powerful and acceptable marketing tool.

Incidentally, by using cookies (refer to Chapter 12, "Making Your Site Look and Sound Great") and online questionnaires and order forms, you will probably be gathering information about your customers or website visitors. So it's wise to include a *Privacy Statement* somewhere on your site, indicating that any information gathered by your company will be kept confidential and that you won't be selling their information to other companies. Visit several different established online businesses to see how they word their own privacy statements.

Chain letters

With chain letters, you're asked to send a small amount of money ($5–$20) to each of four or five names on a list, replace one of the names on the list with your own, and then forward the revised message via bulk e-mail. The letter might claim that the scheme is legal or that it's been reviewed by a lawyer, or it might refer to sections of U.S. law that legitimize the scheme.

Don't believe it. Chain letters—traditional or high-tech—are almost always illegal, and nearly all of the people who participate in them lose their money. The fact that a "product" such as a report on how to make money fast, a mailing list, or a recipe might be changing hands in the transaction does not change the legality of these schemes.

Work-at-home schemes

Envelope-stuffing solicitations promise steady income for minimal labor—for example, you'll earn $2 each time you fold a brochure and seal it in an envelope. Craft assembly work schemes often require an investment of hundreds of dollars in equipment or supplies, and many hours of your time producing goods for a company that has promised to buy them. You'll pay a small fee to get started in the envelope-stuffing business. Then, you'll learn that the e-mail sender never had real employment to offer. Instead, you'll get instructions on how to send the same envelope-stuffing ad in your own bulk e-mailings. If you earn any money, it will be from others who fall for the scheme you're perpetuating. And after spending the money and putting in the time on the craft assembly work, you are likely to find promoters who refuse to pay you, claiming that your work isn't up to their "quality standards."

Health and diet scams

Pills that let you lose weight without exercising or changing your diet, herbal formulas that liquefy your fat cells so that they are absorbed by your body, and cures for impotence and hair loss are among the scams flooding e-mail boxes. These gimmicks usually don't work. The fact is that successful weight loss requires a reduction in calories and an increase in physical activity. Beware of case histories from "cured" consumers claiming amazing results; testimonials from "famous" medical experts you've never heard of; claims that the product is available from only one source or for a limited time; and ads that use phrases

Watch Out!

The trendiest get-rich-quick schemes offer unlimited profits exchanging money on world currency markets; newsletters describing a variety of easy-money opportunities; the perfect sales letter; and the secret to making $4,000 in one day.

such as "scientific breakthrough," "miraculous cure," "exclusive product," "secret formula," and "ancient ingredient."

Free goods

Some e-mail messages offer valuable goods for free—for example, computers, other electronic items, and long-distance phone cards. You're asked to pay a fee to join a club and provide a lot of personal information. Then, you're told that to earn the offered goods, you have to bring in a certain number of participants or pay additional fees. You're paying for the right to earn income by recruiting other participants, but your payoff is in goods, not money. Most of these messages are really pyramid schemes, operations that inevitably collapse. Almost all of the payoff goes to the promoters and little or none to consumers who pay to participate.

Investment opportunities

Investment schemes promise outrageously high rates of return with no risk. One version seeks investors to help form an offshore bank. Others are vague about the nature of the investment, stressing the rates of return. Many are Ponzi or pyramid schemes, in which early investors are paid off with money contributed by later investors. This makes the early investors believe that the system actually works, and encourages them to invest even more.

Promoters of fraudulent investments often operate a particular scam for a short time, quickly spend the money they take in, and then close down before they can be detected. Often, they reopen under another name, selling another investment scam. In their sales pitch, they'll say that they have high-level financial connections, they're privy to inside information, they'll guarantee the investment, or they'll buy back the investment after a certain time. To close the deal, they often serve up phony statistics, misrepresent the significance of a current event, or stress the unique quality of their offering—anything to deter you from verifying their story.

Cable descrambler kits

For a small sum of money, you can buy a kit to assemble a cable descrambler that supposedly allows you to receive cable television transmissions without paying any subscription fee. The device that you build probably won't work. Most of the cable TV systems in the U.S. use technology that these devices can't crack. What's more, even if it worked, stealing service from a cable television company is illegal.

Guaranteed loans or credit on easy terms

Some e-mail messages offer home-equity loans that don't require equity in your home, as well as solicitations for guaranteed, unsecured credit cards, regardless of your credit history. Usually, these are said to be offered by offshore banks. Sometimes they are combined with pyramid schemes, which offer you an opportunity to make money by attracting new participants to the scheme. The home-equity loans turn out to be useless lists of lenders who will turn you down if you don't meet their qualifications. The promised credit cards never come through, and the pyramid moneymaking schemes always collapse.

Credit repair

Credit-repair scams offer to erase accurate negative information from your credit file so that you can qualify for a credit card, loan, or job. The scam artists who promote these services can't deliver; only time, a deliberate effort, and a personal debt-repayment plan will improve your credit. The companies that advertise credit-repair services appeal to consumers with poor credit histories. Not only can't they provide you with a clean credit record, but they also may be encouraging you to violate federal law.

Vacation prize promotions

Electronic certificates congratulating you on "winning" a fabulous vacation for a very attractive price are among the scams arriving in your e-mail. Some say you have been "specially selected" for this opportunity. Most unsolicited commercial e-mail goes to thousands or millions of recipients at a time. The cruise ship you're booked on may look more like a tug boat. The hotel accommodations likely are shabby, and you might be required to pay more for an upgrade. Scheduling the vacation at the time you want it also may require an additional fee.

Other online scams to watch out for

Internet Fraud Watch (www.fraud.org; 800-876-7060), operated by the National Consumers League, reported that in 2004, the average loss to fraud victims totaled $895 per person, up from $527 in 2003. Also, of the frauds initiated by e-mail, the top scams include Nigerian money offers, phishing, lotteries, and fake check scams.

Out of the top 10 Internet-based scams the Internet Fraud Watch tracked in 2004, online-based auctions accounted for 51 percent of all complains made to the agency, due to items either not being delivered or being misrepresented on the auction site.

Some online auction services, such as eBay.com, are wholly legitimate and allow anyone to buy and sell virtually anything. The problem people run into using these popular auction services is not with the services themselves, but with certain sellers who use services like eBay.com to sell their products and knowingly commit fraud. Such people, who are not affiliated with the online auction site, are dishonest and sell products that aren't as described.

Always pay attention to details

If you ask small, Web-based business owners what makes their business successful, one of the top answers you'll hear repeatedly is paying careful attention to detail. When designing and maintaining your business, attention to detail means

- Correcting spelling and grammatical mistakes *before* your website goes online.

- Making sure there are no dead links on your site.

- Making sure your site is optimized to work with each of the popular Web-browser programs.

- Ensuring that you obtain the information you need on your order forms in order to process orders accurately.

- Ensuring that your site is easy to navigate, and that all of the navigational icons and toolbars are clearly visible and intuitive.

- At the bottom of each page, there's a "Back," "Home," or "Main Page" icon that allows someone to quickly and easily link back to your site's main page.

- Your company's contact information (such as e-mail address, toll-free phone number, and fax number) is clearly displayed on each page of your site.

Designing a website can get a bit confusing if your site offers too many links. NetMechanic (www.netmechanic.com), for example, offers free online utilities to check a website for broken links, spelling mistakes, Web-browser software compatibility, and average download times. These are all details that need your attention on an ongoing basis.

 Moneysaver

Make sure your site contains accurate product information and detailed photos. Otherwise, you risk losing sales—and money.

Making online ordering fast, easy, and secure

In addition to having the capability to process secure transactions, your website's online order forms need to be easy to understand and require as few keystrokes or mouse clicks as possible. Your site should automatically calculate subtotals, shipping charges, sales tax, and so forth, and display this information in a format your customers will be able to understand.

Before designing your own site, visit several e-commerce sites and see what other companies have done to make their online ordering procedures as quick and easy as possible. Using the "shopping cart" approach, your customers should be able to easily add and delete items before checking out and processing their orders.

Placing an online order is often the most intimidating aspect of shopping online for the average consumer. If your site doesn't put customers at ease, chances are they won't place their orders there. Before requiring someone to enter any personal information, it's an excellent strategy to clearly display information regarding your site's security measures and policies to help boost customer confidence. Always give someone the option to print an order form and fax it to you, or to place the order by calling a toll-free phone number.

By clearly displaying on your website your company's return policy and product guarantees/warranties, you're more apt to enhance the consumer's confidence in your company and what it's offering.

As an online business operator, make sure your website contains no dead links or programming errors. If your customer has trouble accessing your website or can't easily complete the online order form to complete their order, they'll go elsewhere, and lose confidence in your site. Also, have a backup plan if your site encounters technical difficulties, such as your server going down for an extended period.

Bright Idea

Design your website's online order forms for a computer novice who has never purchased anything online before. The interface should be intuitive.

Make building customer confidence a top priority

In addition to providing useful information about your products on your website, it's useful to provide related information your visitors will perceive to be valuable. As you attempt to convey your message, it's important to build up your visitors' confidence by positioning yourself as a reputable company that sells top-quality products at a fair price.

Some of the things you can do to enhance confidence in your company are the following:

- Display your company logo on each of the Web pages throughout your site.

- Prominently list a toll-free number people can call for more information or to place orders if they're not comfortable placing an order online.

- Offer a "Company Information" or "Company Background" page on your website.

- Make it clear your company offers totally secure online order processing.

- Offer a guarantee of satisfaction, such as a "30-day, no-questions-asked, money-back guarantee" on all orders.

- Include detailed descriptions and multiple, full-color photos of your products.

- Add a page to your website that contains customer testimonials.

- Add a page or an FAQ document to your site that answers all of the frequently asked questions people have about

Bright Idea

The Internet Alliance (www.internetalliance.org) is a trade association repre-senting companies involved in online commerce. Along with the National Consumers League, it sponsors Project Open to help consumers get the most out of going online. Visit this site for ideas on how to boost the confidence of your site's visitors. Your site will achieve far greater success if you quickly build the visitor's confidence in your company.

your company, products, ordering procedures, payment methods, online security, return policy, and so forth. This document can be written in a question-and-answer format. Be sure to provide detailed and easy-to-understand answers to questions you would have as a customer visiting your site for the first time.

Post your privacy policies

Many companies with privacy practices post this information directly on their websites. A company's privacy policy should dis-close what information is being collected on the website and how that information is being used. If you're using cookies to gather information, this should be disclosed. Likewise, if you share or sell your customer list, this too needs to be revealed.

Just the facts

- Nothing can replace solid research as you prepare to launch any type of business.

- Once you know what is required to make your business successful, analyze your own talents, knowledge base, and skills, and then pinpoint the areas where you'll need help.

- If you have a unique (or innovative) idea, develop a professional-looking website, and know how to reach your target audience, your chances for achieving success will be excellent.

- Figure out exactly what feature of your product or service would interest someone. Then use Web resources to inform your target audience about your product in an engaging way.

- Watch out for scam artists who sell fraudulent Internet-related business opportunities.

- Placing an online order can be intimidating to the average consumer. Be sure your site puts customers at ease.

GET THE SCOOP ON...
Selling ad space and banners on your site ■
Income from downloadable products ■ Charging
for site access

Generating Revenues from Your Site

Chapter 9

Whether you're developing a website to promote an existing business or you're planning to use your site for selling your product or service, there are many ways you can generate income from the site. These include the following:

- Taking orders for your product or service online using automated credit-card processing and a shopping-cart application.

- Using your site as an interactive brochure and encouraging people to visit your retail store, call your toll-free number, or send a check to make a purchase.

- Offering software or information that can be paid for online and downloaded on the spot.

- Selling online advertising space to other companies.

- Selling access (membership) to your site.

Using your site to accept purchase requests

The purpose of many online businesses (e-commerce websites) is to encourage visitors to make purchases directly from the site, typically paying by credit card or via PayPal. Depending on the product or service sold, you might then ship the product via a traditional courier, such as U.S. Mail, FedEx, or UPS.

If the customer is purchasing software or information that can be downloaded, your e-commerce site can become a fully automated business; someone can pay by credit card and then download the software or information, such as an eBook, that they purchase directly from the site.

Offering information for sale in the form of electronic books or documents is relatively easy, especially using Adobe Acrobat (www.adobe.com) software. This software allows you to create electronic documents in the Portable Document Format (PDF). PDF is the open de facto standard for electronic document distribution worldwide, which can be accessed and printed by any type of computer or Web browser when the Adobe Acrobat Reader software (available free to the document reader) is used.

Selling advertising space

Once your online-based business is established and you have a steady flow of visitors who fall into a specific niche market or demographic, you can sell banner ads or advertising sponsorships on your site to other companies interested in reaching your audience.

This, however, is becoming less popular because banner advertising tends to be less effective than other forms of online advertising, and it could detract from the brand you're trying to create by establishing the website to begin with.

Another form of online advertising is pop-up ads. These ads are typically extremely annoying to Web surfers, many of whom now have pop-up blocker software or functionality added to their browser.

A pop-up ad is a window that suddenly and automatically appears on the computer screen (without the user's permission) and often won't disappear until the user clicks on the appropriate area to close the advertising window. While pop-up ads can get a surfer's attention, they have an extremely negative reputation and, like sending spam e-mail, should be avoided. Avoid incorporating annoying pop-up ads to your website or using this type of advertising to promote your business.

Unless your site receives hundreds of thousands of hits per week, you probably won't get rich selling online ad space. You might, however, be able to defer some of the costs involved with maintaining the site itself. There are many independent services that you can use to monitor website traffic. Advertisers use these independent services to verify Web traffic and determine ad rates.

If you plan to sell advertising space on your site, you'll need to develop specifications, be able to track the number of visitors to your site, and develop fair ad rates. Many agencies specializing in online advertising can help you sell your available ad space on a commission basis.

Make sure, however, that you maintain total control over the ads on your site. You don't want to offend a potential customer by displaying a banner ad for another company that the visitor to your site could find offensive. You also don't want to distract your visitors from the main purpose they visited your website to begin with—to learn more about *your* company and its products or services, and perhaps to make a purchase. The cost of alienating a

Bright Idea

Niche marketing can generate extra income. If the visitors your site attracts fall into a well-defined niche market, you might find that some advertisers will be willing to pay a premium in order to target your audience by advertising on your site.

potential customer is a lot greater than the revenue you might receive by displaying another company's banner ad on your site.

Membership fees

Another way companies generate revenues from their website is by charging a time-based membership fee to access the specialized information or content on the site. If you're planning to make people pay to access your site, it's necessary to provide them with information or services they perceive to be valuable and not readily available elsewhere. Many sites that specialize in distributing online adult-oriented material have become extremely successful by charging an access fee.

Some more legitimate print publications, such as newspapers and magazines, often charge a subscription fee for their Web-based content. The *Wall Street Journal* is an excellent example of a well-respected publication that charges a subscription fee for its online and traditionally printed content.

Many mainstream businesses that have attempted to charge membership, subscription, or access fees for content have had a much more difficult time getting people to pay for access to Web content, however. Many Web users believe surfing the Web should be free (once they pay for Internet access through an ISP). In addition, they believe that no matter what type of "premium information" or content your site charges people to access, chances are good that similar content is available elsewhere on the Web for free.

Whether this belief is true is irrelevant; what matters is that people believe it and therefore resist paying access fees. So the success of such a site will depend on how well you're able to alter this popular perception, at least among your target audience.

Affiliate programs have become another powerful revenue-generation and traffic-building tool for online businesses. These programs are relatively simple to participate in and are described in greater detail later in this chapter.

Selling and trading online advertising space

Although search-engine optimization and keyword advertising/ search marketing are all the rage among online advertisers these days, selling advertising space in the form of banner ads or sponsorships on your site is still a way to generate revenue. Many people visiting your site, however, may be turned off by being involuntarily exposed to additional advertising over and above the marketing information they're receiving about your business's product or service.

If, however, your site offers information your visitors perceive to be valuable or unique, they'll be more willing to accept seeing the ads from which you derive income. Also, if you spread the advertising throughout your site and keep it relatively subtle, people will be much more accepting of it. For example, placing a banner ad just at the very bottom or top of a page can be effective.

If you look at Yahoo.com, for example, you'll see banner and often animated display ads interspersed throughout the site. This site receives millions of hits per week and generates its income by selling ad space and sponsorships to advertisers in order to offer, for free, a popular and powerful service that Web surfers want.

Likewise, one of the most popular news-oriented sites on the Web, The Drudge Report (www.drudgereport.com), is seen by more than 150 million people per month, but typically displays just one banner ad per page. The site is offered free to Web surfers, but generates advertising revenue by selling limited

---

 Watch Out!

The last thing you want to do is annoy or turn off a potential customer by exposing them to too much online advertising. Use advertising creatively, but avoid overkill.

Bright Idea

Create an "Advertise Here" link on your home page, allowing potential advertisers to obtain specifications about your ad rates and target audience. Be clear about the types of advertising you will accept, and make sure the advertiser supplies its own artwork (banner ads) that meets your approval.

online advertising space. Advertisers are willing to pay for some premium online advertising space because of the level of traffic sites like Yahoo.com or The Drudge Report receive.

Choosing to accept paid advertising on your site adds an assortment of management responsibilities, ranging from carefully calculating traffic to your site, preparing reports for your advertisers, selling the advertising space, and doing the financial paperwork associated with selling advertising. You'll also need to set advertising specifications for what types of advertising you'll permit on your site (such as the size of the ads, length of the animations, and the ads' content).

It's always better to have advertising that somehow relates to your online business, so that you're offering visitors additional links to information, products, or services they are likely to be interested in, without creating additional competition for yourself.

In terms of the design and management of your site, building and maintaining a high level of customer confidence in your business should be a top priority. The advertising you display will affect how the visitors to your site perceive your company, and can either help or hurt your company's image and brand. Displaying on your site banner ads from large, well-known companies with excellent reputations creates a very different impression than offering banner ads from adult-oriented sites or poorly designed ads from small online businesses that people have never heard of.

As you outline your ad specifications, some of the things you'll need to spell out for potential advertisers include the following:

- **Accepted file formats**   GIFs, JPEGs, and so on.

- **Banner dimensions**   A typical banner is 486 × 60 pixels; however, you can also offer vertical banners, advertising buttons, and smaller or larger banners. Another popular (but smaller) banner size is 150 × 350 pixels.

- **File size limit**   You'll want to spell this out so that you limit the time it takes for a visitor to download your entire page. Each graphic you add increases the overall download time. Most websites choose a maximum banner ad size of 50K (50,000 bytes), 32K (32,000 bytes), or just 15K (15,000 bytes).

- **Animation length**   This determines how long a particular animation lasts per cycle before repeating. You'll want to keep animation lengths under five seconds so that the file size isn't too large. Some animation technologies (such as Flash), as opposed to animated GIFs, allow for longer animations with smaller file sizes.

- **Tag line text**   This is one line of text, usually a maximum of five to eight words, that is displayed directly under the actual banner ad. It can be used to convey an advertising slogan, and so on. It's your decision whether to accept tag lines and, if you do, to determine their allowed length, font size, and so forth.

- **Target URLs**   Make sure you have full approval over the site your visitors will be linked to if they click on the ad. Also, remember that if a banner ad is animated, there may be a different link associated with each frame of the animation, so you'll want to review each one to see whether it is appropriate for the image you're trying to convey for your own site.

- **Signed insertion order required**   This indicates that you require a signed order, in writing, from the advertiser. It's an excellent idea to create a written contract/insertion order for your advertisers to sign.

Make it perfectly clear that all advertisements are subject to approval by your company's management, and that you maintain the right to refuse any advertiser, graphic, text description, or URL.

You'll also need to list your rates. Online advertising rates are typically based on a predetermined number of impressions or page views, and are measured in cost per thousand impressions (CPM). Your rate card should list the number of impressions you're willing to sell and the CPM. You might consider offering a discount to advertisers who purchase higher numbers of impressions. You'll also need to offer a discount to recognized advertising agencies purchasing advertising space on behalf of clients.

Your actual ad rates should be based on how specialized your audience is and how many unique impressions an advertiser can expect to obtain. For example, if an advertiser pays for 100,000 impressions, but you have only 10,000 unique users visiting your site, each visitor will see the ad 10 times. If, however, you can guarantee at least 50,000 or 75,000 unique users based on 100,000 impressions, this makes your audience more attractive to many potential advertisers because when an individual has seen an ad a number of times, new viewings of the ad are less likely to get them to click on it or buy the product or service it features.

Once you choose to accept online advertising, you'll need to provide advertisers with up-to-the-minute traffic reports on your site so that they can calculate the number of impressions in a particular time period and determine the click-through rates of

 Watch Out!

To avoid potential misunderstandings with advertisers, clearly spell out that your business has full approval over what types of advertisers and advertising content you will accept. Consider rejecting advertising for liquor, tobacco products, pornography, or products or services that compete with your own.

Watch Out!

Of course, you don't want your banner to get too few impressions—this will result in the message not being properly communicated. But avoid "banner burnout," the point at which a banner stops delivering a good return on investment because it is seen too many times by an individual and gets stale.

their ads. To enhance your credibility with advertisers, consider using an outside service to compile traffic information to your site. In fact, larger advertisers and most advertising agencies purchasing ad space on behalf of a client will insist on this.

Comprehensive online reporting lets advertisers know how their campaign is performing and what type of users are seeing and clicking on their ads. This high-level targeting and real-time reporting is one advantage Web-based companies have over other media, such as television, radio, billboards, or traditional print advertising.

Before you can begin selling online ad space to potential advertisers, it's important to learn the basics of how the advertising industry works. Numerous print and online-only publications target advertising professionals and people who buy and sell media. Some of these publications include the following:

Advertising Age*	www.adage.com
AdWeek*	www.adweek.com
Click Z	www.clickz.com
Forrester Research	www.forrester.com
Infoscavenger	www.infoscavenger.com
SRDS Online*	www.srds.com

* also offers a print edition

Another useful resource for learning about buying and selling online advertising is Buying and Selling Online Ads, a website created by a professor of marketing at James Madison University (http://cob.jmu.edu/wrightnd/buyingsellingadsmay98.htm).

If you have an established website that's already receiving a respectable level of traffic and you're looking to sell advertising space, you can hire an agency to represent your site to potential advertisers instead of having to solicit them yourself. CyberReps (www.cybereps.com) is just one example of an agency that works with website operators looking to sell advertising space.

Affiliate programs

Affiliate programs have become an extremely popular way for online businesses to generate revenue. They're also a very viable way for website operators to generate traffic to their site. You can choose to participate in another company's affiliate program, or you can establish your own. Make sure, however, that the affiliate programs you choose are of interest to the people visiting your site. Likewise, the program you launch should attract affiliates that will really be able to generate traffic to your site.

According to LinkShare Corporation (www.linkshare.com), one of the Internet's leading affiliate program facilitators, if you choose to participate in another company's affiliate program, here's how it works:

> Affiliate programs are a way for site owners like you to be compensated for driving traffic to online merchants' sites. You drive traffic by putting links on your site that, when clicked, send visitors to a merchant's site.
>
> Some merchants will pay you a percentage of all the sales they make when visitors from your site click on a link, go to the merchant's site, and buy something. Other merchants will pay you simply for sending the traffic

 Bright Idea

Make sure your expectations are realistic. The click-through rate for banner ads is low, so don't expect to get rich quick by participating in this type of advertising or marketing program. Participating in an affiliate program should be just one part of your overall marketing, advertising, and revenue-generation plan.

their way, on a per-click or per-thousand-click basis. Still others will pay for impressions. Merchants may also offer to pay you for a combination of these. It's a win-win partnership because you get increased revenue and merchants get increased traffic.

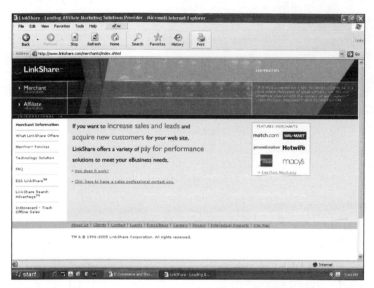

Figure 9.1. If you want to launch your own affiliate program to drive traffic to your website, or participate in another company's affiliate program to generate revenue from your site, LinkShare is one of the best services to use.

You can generate revenue from your site by becoming an affiliate with companies that offer such a program, such as 1-800-Flowers.com or Amazon.com. If you display a 1-800-Flowers.com banner on your site, for example, each time someone links from your site to 1-800-Flowers.com and places an order, you will earn a commission on the sale. Displaying advertising banners from highly respected companies, such as 1-800-Flowers.com, Amazon.com, NetFlix.com, Orbitz.com, Target, Western Union, or The Sharper Image, for example, can help boost your company's credibility among visitors to your site. When a visitor to your site sees ads from respected and nationally known companies, they will believe that these big companies have chosen to advertise on your site.

By operating your own affiliate program through a recognized service such as LinkShare, you can drive traffic to your site and hopefully generate sales without having to pay any fees in advance. You'll be obligated only to pay your affiliates a commission based on sales generated by their referrals. For companies with a limited advertising and promotions budget, establishing an affiliate program is an excellent way of boosting traffic to your site, and a marketing tool online businesses of all sizes have found useful.

LinkShare, like other reputable companies, provides clients with technology to make this type of program relatively easy. The company's software allows online merchants to alter, update, and improve their merchandising techniques.

> 66 An affiliate is a website that partners with an online merchant. The affiliate places links on its site to promote the merchant's products. In exchange, the affiliate receives a commission for all valid transactions it has referred. 99
>
> —LinkShare Corporation

If you launch your own affiliate program to promote your website, you must decide whether you'll offer your partners a pay-per-click, pay-per-lead, or pay-per-sale commission.

"Pay-per-click" means you get paid for each person that clicks on a link in order to visit a specific website. When compensated using a pay-per-lead model, you are paid a pre-set fee for each visitor you send to the merchant's site that performs a specific action. The action might include signing up for their newsletter or filling out a survey, for example. A 'pay-per-sale' compensation plan means you receive a commission from the merchant for each sale made as a result of one of your website's visitors clicking on a link or banner to another site.

Watch Out!

One potential drawback to getting involved with affiliate programs or pay-per-click programs is that you must include other banners on your website. You want to avoid cluttering your site with too many ads from organizations or companies that aren't your own, or you could take attention away from what you're trying to sell on your site.

A few words about Web rings

Another potential traffic booster is to participate in a Web ring, which is a group of sites based on a similar topic or area of interest that refer Web surfers to each other. For more information about Web rings, visit http://dir.webring.com/rw. Participating in a Web ring is free. The drawback is that you have to promote the Web ring itself and other sites affiliated with it. If you're looking to convey a highly professional image, getting involved with a Web ring might not be the ideal way to go.

Selling software or other downloadable goods

When you think of the ultimate online business model, being able to sell downloadable software or information, such as eBooks, is ideal. There are no products to ship and no inventory to maintain. After you develop a software package to sell online or create an electronic document, you can use your website to promote it. The site will accept and process real-time credit-card payments, and then allow the customer to instantly download the software or information they've purchased—directly from your site. In most cases, there will be no in-person, fax, e-mail, or telephone communication with the customer. Your business is truly virtual; and once it's set up, it will be almost entirely automated.

By operating this type of business, your primary objective once the site is operational is to promote the site's URL and drive potential customers to the site. This type of online business model works well if you have a unique software program (or utility) or information people will be willing to pay for and will want almost instantly.

Figure 9.2. The PalmOne eBook Store is the perfect example of an online-based business that sells downloadable goods (eBooks) to a very specialized market (PalmOne PDA users).

If you have a printed book, brochure, instructions, or other document you want people to be able to purchase and download, one easy way to ensure that the printed document will maintain its layout and design when transformed into an electronic file is to use Adobe Acrobat (www.adobe.com).

Using Adobe Acrobat, you can take your printed (or desktop-published) document and save it in the PDF format. A PDF file can be read by any type of computer or Web browser using a free program from Adobe (Acrobat Reader or Adobe eBook Reader) that your customers can download.

The Learn Crochet Now website (www.learn-crochet-now.com) is the perfect example of one that charges for some of its content. The site offers instructional DVDs and videos about crocheting and knitting; however, many of the videos can also be purchased, downloaded, and viewed instantly using Windows Media.

MovieLink (www.movielink.com) is the ultimate in high-tech video-rental stores. This website allows you to rent popular videos and then watch them in real-time (via streaming video) or download them to your computer for later viewing using specialized software customers download for free. The cost of renting a downloadable or streaming movie is similar to what it would cost to rent from your local video store, only you never leave your home or office, plus there are no actual DVDs or videocassettes—just a digital file you download or stream via a high-speed Internet connection.

Although eBooks have achieved only a moderate level of popularity among computer users and technology enthusiasts, some businesses have become successful selling downloadable eBooks. For the millions of PalmOS-based PDA owners, the PalmOne eBook Store (http://ebooks.palmone.com) sells more than 14,000 eBook titles specifically formatted to be downloaded and viewed on a PDA. Visitors to this site can choose what book they want to purchase, make their purchase using a major credit card, and then download and read the eBook immediately.

If you're looking to sell eBooks and other types of proprietary printed or downloadable information online, you can learn more about this business opportunity by visiting PayLoadz

 Watch Out!

There are many not-so-legitimate "get-rich-quick" schemes involving the creation and selling of eBooks online. The best way to take advantage of this business opportunity and actually generate revenue is to offer unique or proprietary information in the form of an eBook that your customers can purchase and download. Thus, you'll want to create the content yourself and ensure that what you're offering is valuable to the potential reader. You could also license the rights to other copyrighted material, but make sure what you're offering is useful and not already widely available on the Web for free.

(www.payloadz.com) or the eBook hub's website (www.ebook-hub.com).

Another useful resource for actually creating and then distributing eBooks and similar content is the Adobe eBook Mall (www.adobe.com/epaper/ebooks/ebookmall/main.html).

Charging visitors for access to your site

One of the most popular business models used by sites dealing in various types of adult-oriented material is based on membership to a website. The online business operator sells a renewable membership, issues a password to access that site, and then provides unlimited access to the site during the membership period.

Some industry-oriented publications or high-priced newsletters also use this business model to distribute information to customers, subscribers, or members who are willing to pay for it on an ongoing basis.

This type of business model works well if the information you'll be offering on your site changes regularly, and people will be returning to your site often to obtain the information.

An example of a family-oriented website that uses a paid subscription-based business model is Disney's Club Blast (http://disney.go.com/blast/specialoffers/index.html), an interactive Web-based activity center and online magazine published by the Walt Disney Company.

The Wall Street Journal Interactive Edition (www.wsj.com) is another example of a subscription-based online business model. Subscribers pay a flat annual fee for access to the electronic edition of the *Wall Street Journal*, which is constantly updated with new news stories and other features.

By visiting the online businesses described in this section, you'll discover firsthand some of the options available to you when customers, members, or subscribers pay for the privilege of accessing website content. Speak with your ISP to determine exactly what programming and technology is available to help you implement this type of pay-for-access service.

Just the facts

- To sell online advertising space on your site, you need to develop advertising specifications, track the number of visitors to your site, and develop fair advertising rates.

- Choosing to accept paid advertising on your site adds an assortment of management responsibilities, plus could detract from the main purpose or goals of your site—to promote your own business and sell your own products or services.

- Affiliate programs have become popular revenue-generation tools among online-based businesses and e-commerce sites. Launching one can be an excellent way to drive traffic to your own site with few or no upfront costs.

- By becoming an affiliate partner with one or more affiliate programs operated by other companies, you could, potentially, generate additional revenue from your website.

- Selling downloadable software or information is the ideal online business model—there are no products to ship and no inventory to maintain. For this type of business to work, you must offer information (an eBook, for example) that is valuable and unique.

PART IV

Promoting Your Site

GET THE SCOOP ON...

Paid and free promotion ▪ Banner advertising ▪
Newsgroups and mailing lists ▪ Why you
should avoid using spam ▪ Using traditional
advertising ▪ The power of public relations ▪
Blogging as a promotional tool

Promotion Is the
Key to Success

As discussed in earlier chapters, Web-page
design is a crucial part of starting your own
online business. But it's not the whole story.

If potential customers can't find your site online,
however, or don't even know of your business's existence, all your efforts will be in vain. An online business is no different from a traditional business, in
that marketing, advertising, and public relations play
major roles in the overall success of your venture.

You might not have the financial resources to
launch an advertising and marketing blitz, with network television ads, national radio spots, billboards,
print ads in national magazines, and extensive online
advertising. But you can implement an aggressive
grassroots marketing effort on almost any budget.

Next to developing an online presence for your
business that's informative, visually appealing, easy
to understand, and intuitive for user interface, it's
critical that you develop innovative ways to promote
your online business to generate traffic—and ultimately orders—for your products.

Chapter 10

215

This chapter explores some of the ways you can promote your business, with a focus on what you can do online with a relatively small budget. This includes online promotional, marketing, and public relations ideas.

No matter what size your advertising and marketing budget is, search-engine optimization, as well as search marketing or keyword marketing should definitely be a major part of the overall marketing and promotional efforts. These techniques are explored in the next chapter.

The importance of promoting your online biz

If you're making a substantial financial investment in your business and have a large advertising and marketing budget, seriously consider hiring an advertising or public relations agency to help you develop an advertising, marketing, and public relations campaign.

You're more apt to get the results you want if you hire experienced professionals to handle this aspect of your business. You can, however, do it yourself, but make sure your expectations are realistic and that you first learn the tricks of the trade for launching successful advertising, marketing, promotional, and PR campaigns.

The target audience

As you're developing your business's website, begin articulating what your marketing strategy will be, focusing specifically on determining who your target audience is and the various ways you can effectively reach this audience. Once your business goes online, you want to drive as much traffic to your site as possible. At the same time, however, you need it to be the right kind of traffic.

If you're selling designer handbags for women online, attracting to your website teenage boys who have no credit card or need for your products is utterly pointless.

Bright Idea

You want the people visiting your site to be interested in your subject matter along with your product. This means you need to choose a target audience and market directly to it.

Defining your target

A target audience can be any group of people with a specific need or desire to have your product or service. Your audience might be made up of primarily

- Males
- Females
- Adults (ages 18–49)
- Teens (ages 14–17)
- Married couples
- Singles
- Seniors
- People with a specific interest or hobby
- High-income professionals
- Homemakers
- Home-office workers (telecommuters or small-business owners)
- People with a specific career
- People with some type of physical disability
- Any other group of people you can define and reach through a targeted marketing, advertising, and PR effort

Of course, your business can have several distinct target audiences. If so, you'll probably find it easier to implement one targeted marketing effort at a time. As you define your target audience, determine early whether these people are active Internet users. If they're not, starting an online-based business could be futile.

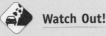 **Watch Out!**

Planning to sell a product to kids or teens online? Perhaps video games, trading cards or another hot item? Students make up a good portion of the online population, but when marketing to this younger demographic, keep in mind that they typically don't have credit cards.

Once you've determined your target audience, decide exactly what message you're hoping to get across to them. What will you be trying to accomplish with your marketing, advertising, and PR efforts? Are you simply trying to make people aware of your company or brand? Do you want them to visit your website? Is your goal for potential customers to actually order your products online?

How you convey an advertising or marketing message can mean the difference between a 1 percent and 10 percent response rate. The wording you use and the visual impact of your ad (including the colors, fonts, and ad size) will play a major role in getting potential customers to respond to your message.

If you don't have a well-defined target audience, it will be extremely difficult to reach the people on the Web who will be most interested in what your online business has to offer. Knowing your audience, however, is only the first step in developing an effective marketing, advertising, promotional, and PR campaign for your online business.

Reaching your target

After defining your target audience, the second step is to do extensive research to determine the best ways to reach them. We discussed in earlier chapters some of the concerns you'll have to keep in mind. What are their needs and wants? Are you solving a problem? Offering a benefit? Will your target audience save time or money using your product? Determine exactly what feature of your product your audience will be most interested in, and then develop a marketing message that will catch their attention.

Having defined your target audience, focus on creating the strongest possible marketing message. Then, discover the best ways to get your message across to them. Does your audience tend to visit specific websites, read certain magazines, attend specific events or functions, or have well-defined buying habits?

Effectively marketing any type of product requires such skills as the ability to communicate and a very good understanding of your audience. In addition, you need to understand at least the basics of how various media outlets work and the benefits of advertising on them, including television, radio, newspapers, magazines, direct mail, e-mail, online advertising, billboards, and PR. You also need to spend some time learning how Internet search engines and Web directories work, how to get listed on them, and how to ensure that your listing is seen by the right people. Using search engines and Web directories (such as Yahoo! and Google) as a marketing tool is critical. As you'll discover in the next chapter, there are multiple ways to best use these powerful tools to best reach your target market for the least amount of money possible.

Spend time learning who the major players in the various media are and the terminology used. Unless you hire an advertising agency to do your media placement for you, it will be your job to determine the best ways to spend your advertising, marketing, and PR dollars to generate the most impact.

Because you'll be launching a new online-based company, you'll probably want to experiment with different marketing messages and use different promotional vehicles to determine what works best. Each time you execute any form of marketing

---

 Bright Idea

Using e-mail can be a highly effective way to reach a target audience. But use a list of e-mail recipients who want information from your company. Randomly spamming strangers by the thousands, although inexpensive, is considered rude and unprofessional, and it often annoys the recipient. In some cases, it's also illegal.

Watch Out!

Make sure the advertising medium you use fits the volume of traffic your site can handle. Running a television ad can spur millions of simultaneous attempts to contact you. An ad in a monthly magazine, however, seen by the same number of people, will cause orders to trickle in over time.

campaign, it's important to track the results carefully to determine what works best and generates the most positive results.

Once your site is established, but before you begin promoting it, one of the first things you must do is to develop a strong understanding of what your site is all about. Figure out exactly how to convey this information to others. On a sheet of paper, write your site's title and URL. Next, write down a list of 25 to 50 keywords that can be used to classify or describe your site and what it offers. If someone were to begin looking for your company or your products using an Internet search engine, what keywords or search phrases would they use?

Now, write a 25-word, 50-word, and 75-word description of your site and what it offers. Choose the wording carefully so that your description catches the attention of the reader, describes what your online business is all about, and encourages the reader to visit your site. Be as specific as possible when writing your descriptions.

This information will prove crucial when registering your site with the various search engines, as well as when you send out press releases announcing your site to the media and general public. You can also use this information to attract people's interest when you begin participating in newsgroups and mailing lists.

Later, when it's time to find sites on the Web where you can advertise or exchange banner ads or links, use the same list of keywords you just compiled to find other sites of interest to a similar audience.

Promotional and advertising opportunities available online

You don't necessarily have to go any further than the Internet to reach potential customers. Of course, the best ways to reach customers for your product will vary based on the type of business you're operating. The Internet does, however, provide a variety of different promotional opportunities that you can use to target mass groups or very specific demographic audiences, depending on your needs.

If you've spent any time surfing the Web or exploring online services, such as America Online, you've seen banner advertising and display ads. Online ad banners are typically rectangular display ads (which can be animated) that viewers can click in order to visit whatever website is being promoted. You'll discover in Chapter 11 that purchasing banner-ad space is one way to generate traffic to your site; however, there are other techniques that typically generate better response rates.

Although many online business operators are now shying away from banner advertising, you can purchase or trade banner-ad space on other websites or online services that cater to the audience you're trying to reach. If you don't have a large budget to spend on online advertising, you can take advantage of services dedicated to facilitating the fair trade of banner ads among website operators.

Banner advertising can be somewhat effective if your ad message is appropriate, catchy, and placed on sites where people interested in your product or service are surfing. Trading banner ads (where you're spending no money for the advertising)

 Moneysaver

Looking for innovative ways to spend your advertising dollars? *Advertising Age,* the advertising industry's top magazine, offers an online edition featuring news and articles of interest to anyone involved with online advertising. To access the online edition, visit www.adage.com.

can be worthwhile. Many online business operators have discovered, however, that banner ads are no longer effective and typically aren't worth paying for. There are some exceptions to this, but for smaller business operators, there are definitely more effective ways of spending your advertising dollars to drive traffic to your website.

There are many other online promotional and advertising opportunities available, including the following:

- Search-engine optimization
- Search marketing/keyword advertising
- Internet newsgroups
- Internet mailing lists
- Blogging
- Electronic press-release distribution
- Sponsoring and participating in online chats, message boards, or online communities
- Publishing an online newsletter
- Sending bulk e-mails to an opt-in list (which is different from sending spam)
- Distributing online coupons
- Creating a Flash animated cartoon that conveys your marketing message. If done correctly, the cartoon will be sent from person-to-person via e-mail. This is called viral marketing and it can work extremely well. For an example of this, go to www.jibjab.com.

Internet newsgroups

Newsgroups are popular forums for computer users to communicate on the Internet. Their exact structure varies somewhat from group to group, but Microsoft's definition is still the most useful explanation. According to Microsoft,

> A newsgroup is a collection of messages posted by individuals to a news server. News servers are computers

maintained by companies, groups, and individuals, and can host thousands of newsgroups. You can find newsgroups on practically any subject. Although some newsgroups are monitored, most are not, and messages can be 'posted' and read by anyone who has access to that group. There are no newsgroup membership lists or joining fees. Your Internet Service Provider must have a link to a news server for you to set up an account with that news server . . . . After you set up an account, you can read and post messages on any of the newsgroups stored on that news server. When you find a newsgroup you like, you can 'subscribe' to it . . . . Newsgroups can contain thousands of messages, which can be time-consuming to sort through. Many newsgroup readers have a variety of features that can make it easier to find the information you want in newsgroups.

Newsgroups can provide promotional opportunities for your online business. An Internet newsgroup is very similar to a public bulletin board or discussion group that focuses on a specific topic or caters to a specific audience. Anyone can start a newsgroup or participate in the "conversation" happening there.

Some newsgroups are moderated, which means someone acts as a gatekeeper and reads and sometimes edits each text message posted to a newsgroup in order to ensure that the material is relevant. Unmoderated newsgroups often get cluttered with spam and other messages that have no relevance to the newsgroup's main topic. The difference between a newsgroup and an online chat forum is that newsgroups don't happen in real time.

The form newsgroups take has evolved. These days, online services, such as America Online, Yahoo! and Google all have their own special interest groups open to people who want to join. Becoming active in special interest groups can be a great way to reach your target audience.

Because newsgroups cater to very specific audiences and focus on particular topics, becoming an active participant in

Bright Idea

To search newsgroup content quickly, visit Google Groups (http://groups. google.com) or Supernews (www.supernews.com). Both services work like Internet search engines, but you can search newsgroup titles and message content.

newsgroups will allow you to reach potential customers with specific interests. To effectively use newsgroups, it's important to consider netiquette and avoid posting messages in the interactive discussion that are blatant ads for your product or service. Instead, by becoming active in the conversation, you can mention your online business as a resource and answer questions from others.

There are literally thousands of different newsgroups in existence, and new newsgroups are created daily. Some newsgroups have thousands of active participants who generate dozens or perhaps hundreds of messages per day, whereas others are less busy.

To obtain a complete listing of Internet newsgroups, visit www.cyberfiber.com or use the newsreader software provided by your ISP or e-mail and news reader software (such as Microsoft Outlook Express).

Internet mailing lists

Internet mailing lists are similar to newsgroups, except that messages posted to a mailing list are automatically sent to an e-mail inbox. Internet mailing lists involve groups of people discussing one of their favorite topics via e-mail. On AOL, this service is called Groups@AOL (keyword: *My Groups*).

The mailing-list format lends itself to calm, mature discussion, where relationships between the list members grow and deepen over an extended period of time. Most Internet experts feel that the mailing-list format is the most civilized type of online community. Another common type of Internet mailing list is the newsletter or announcement format, where a single writer (the list owner or moderator) broadcasts a periodical e-mail to a willing audience (and the audience doesn't participate directly).

If you're interested in establishing an Internet mailing list to communicate with clients or customers, there are several free or inexpensive services to help you do it. For example, Yahoo! Groups (http://groups.yahoo.com) hosts alumni groups, support groups, plus groups for sports fans, small-business operators, and thousands of other organizations and interests.

For a monthly fee starting at $19.95, Microsoft offers its List Builder service to small-business operators (www.microsoft. com/smallbusiness/online/email-marketing/list-builder/detail. mspx). Using this service, you can establish and manage an "opt-in" Internet mailing list. Many ISPs and website-hosting companies offer similar, but more economical, e-mail list managers to online business operators.

An opt-in e-mail list is very different from sending spam, because the people on that list have requested to be on it. Many websites allow visitors to sign up for (subscribe to) a free newsletter or to receive online promotions via e-mail. When someone provides their e-mail address in order to be included, they're opting in and requesting the information be e-mailed to them. When someone decides they no longer wish to receive your information via e-mail, they need a way to "opt-out" of the list or unsubscribe. Spam is when you send hundreds or thousands of unsolicited e-mails to people.

As an online business operator, you can communicate with your clients, customers, or anyone else using a one-way Internet-based mailing list. This allows you to broadcast newsletters, online fliers, and other information people you associate with are interested in. Creating an online mailing list and communicating with customers (or potential customers) via e-mail can be an extremely powerful way of generating business, provided that the people you're distributing your information to requested that information, and that you're offering these people something of value or information they're interested in.

There are several ways online businesses can distribute information to a large group of people online. These uses include the following:

- E-mailing a company newsletter to your customer base.

- Sending new product announcements or online coupons to existing customers.

- Distributing press releases to important media contacts.

- Building a mailing list of visitors to your site and e-mailing them special offers.

- Providing additional product information to your customers via e-mail. You can also offer special deals or promotions.

When using e-mail as a marketing tool, the people you send your promotional e-mails to should have already requested to receive information from your company, by subscribing or opting into your e-mail list when they visited your website, for example.

Sending unsolicited e-mail is considered spam, which most recipients find extremely annoying. Sending out spam e-mail messages to hundreds, thousands, or even millions of unsuspecting recipients is an extremely bad business practice and won't generate positive results for your company. After all, you don't want to be associated in the minds of your potential customers with those e-mail offers for Viagra without a prescription, penis-enlargement techniques, fraudulent wire-transfer scams, or offers for replica designer watches, for example. These are the annoying spam e-mail offers that clutter almost everyone's e-mail inbox.

Why you should avoid using spam

Let's face it, the concept of instantly sending thousands or millions of promotional e-mail messages to people on the Internet

Watch Out!

Spamming won't just annoy the people who receive it. It will also cause them to associate your company with cybersex, pyramid schemes, multilevel marketing schemes, or scams. This will hurt your brand and, ultimately, your sales.

is very appealing because the cost associated with doing this type of mailing is extremely low. The problem is, when you send someone an unsolicited e-mail message that's trying to sell them something they didn't inquire about or express an interest in, it's called *spam*.

Most Internet users absolutely hate receiving spam because it clutters their e-mail inboxes. If your online business is legitimate and offers a valuable or useful product or service, do you really want to alienate potential customers by sending them spam? Probably not!

The term *spam* refers to e-mail that is sent unsolicited to the recipient. Using e-mail as a marketing tool can, however, be a very powerful way of communicating with customers (or potential customers) who specifically request e-mail from your company. If your company sponsors an electronic mailing list through which you distribute a weekly or monthly newsletter for free, and you have people "subscribe" to this electronic publication, this is one highly effective way of using e-mail. You can also use e-mail to confirm orders, handle customer service inquiries, or answer technical support-related questions; and then in those e-mail messages, you can also convey your marketing message.

As an online business operator, you will most likely see ads for online companies that specialize in sending spam very inexpensively to many people quickly. There are also several different software packages that enable the user to gather e-mail addresses and then send junk e-mail quickly. Again, if you're attempting to create a reputable business, this is not the marketing approach you should take.

Some companies, such as PostMaster Direct (www.postmaster direct.com), develop lists of e-mail users who specifically request information on specific topics of interest to them. You can purchase or rent these targeted e-mail lists and send these people e-mail for much less money than it would cost to send a mass mailing via the U.S. Postal Service.

If you choose to use some form of e-mail to communicate with your customers or potential customers, be professional. In the subject line of your message, clearly state what the content of your message is so that the recipient can choose to read the message or delete it without having to spend time opening the message. Some companies choose to use misleading message subjects in order to get people to read their messages. Although this might get someone to open the message, it creates a sense of resentment because the recipient was tricked. Keep in mind that some people receive dozens or even hundreds of e-mail messages per day, and they don't have time to read messages that aren't of direct interest to them.

An opt-in e-mail list is one that the recipients have requested to receive in order to get information about a specific topic. One benefit of using such a list is that the audience is preselected and already somewhat interested in what you have to say. As a result, if you use an opt-in e-mail list in conjunction with a well-written e-mail message, your response rate will probably be considerably higher than the 1 or 2 percent response rate you can typically expect from sending a direct-mail piece via the U.S. mail.

When using e-mail as a promotional tool, be professional, be conscientious, and don't abuse the power of e-mail to harass the recipient.

 Bright Idea

When sending e-mails to your clients and customers, make sure your company name is in the e-mail address and in the message subject. This will help to ensure it's read by the recipient and not just deleted as spam. You want the recipient to recognize who the e-mail came from.

Paid online advertising versus free promotion

You'll discover from this chapter and the next that there are many different ways to advertise and promote your online business. Some promotional opportunities involve a financial investment on your part, to pay for things such as online advertising, a graphics artist to design your ads, or an ad agency. Other opportunities are free, and simply require a time commitment on your part.

To establish your online business and generate an ongoing flow of traffic to your site (comprised of new potential customers as well as existing customers returning to your site), you'll need to invest time and money into advertising, marketing, PR, and promotion. Simply running a few banner ads or sending out a press release concerning your website isn't enough to keep your business thriving. As we've noted before, successfully marketing and promoting your business will take creativity, time, financial resources, and the willingness to experiment in order to determine what works best for your particular type of business.

Whether you have an advertising budget of several thousand or several hundred thousand dollars (or more), don't neglect the free promotional opportunities available on the Net, such as the use of banner exchanges, participation in newsgroups, blogging, and opt-in mailing lists (the legitimate use of e-mail).

The ins and outs of banner advertising

Banner ads are display ads, often animated, that are placed on other Web pages and act as links to your site. Banner advertising can be used to enhance name, product, or brand recognition, or to lure potential customers to your site.

Online advertising is different from any other form of advertising, such as billboards and ads on TV, in print, and on the radio. One major advantage to online ads is that the people seeing the ads can respond instantly and get more information

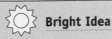

Bright Idea

Another form of online display advertising is through button ads, which are similar to banner ads. They're graphic-based, appear online, and can be animated, yet they are smaller than banner ads (typically more than 70 percent smaller). You can use button ads as a subtle way to attract people to your site, without distracting them too much.

about what's being advertised simply by clicking their mouse to link to a website created by the advertiser.

Another distinct advantage to online advertising is that it works 24 hours a day, every day, and ad campaigns can be launched, modified, or stopped almost instantly. This gives you, the advertiser, total control over when and where the public sees your ad, plus allows you to carefully target who will see your ad.

The first step to using banner advertising is to develop your advertising message and determine the specific audience you're trying to target. Next, develop the actual banner-ad artwork to be placed online. It might be helpful to hire an advertising agency that specializes in Web advertising to assist you in the creation and placement of your banner ads; however, this is something you can do yourself with relatively little artistic or programming ability.

For a banner ad to help you generate business, it has to be catchy. Its job, just like a traditional print ad, is to capture the attention of the readers and, in this case, encourage them to click on the ad in order to visit your site.

Chapter 11 describes in more detail the most common banner-ad sizes and shapes, as well as how to create them. As you create the artwork for your banner ad, keep size specifications in mind and tap your creativity to determine the best way to take full advantage of this advertising space using features such as color, fonts, artwork, text, and animation. Keep in mind that although from a creative standpoint it's easy to develop a flashy, in-your-face banner ad, research has shown that the simplest banner-ad messages often have the greatest impact on viewers.

As you develop your banner ad, remember that only a small portion of people who actually see the ad are going to use it as a link to access your site. Research shows that on average, only about 2.5 to 3.5 percent of the people who see a banner ad will respond by clicking their mouse on the banner. This statistic varies, depending on what you are advertising, but the response rate tends to be very low with banner advertising, which is why many online business operators are spending their advertising budget on other advertising and marketing techniques or use banner advertising as just a small piece of their overall advertising campaign and marketing plan.

Out of everyone who sees your banner ad, only a small percentage of people will actually click on the ad. This is called a "click-through." Your goal is to establish the highest possible click-through rate. This means developing an ad that's visually attractive, eye-catching, and informative, one that creates a sense of urgency, need, or excitement. What you say in your banner ad, how you say it, how the ad looks, and where the ad is placed will have a major impact on your click-through rate and, ultimately, the success of your business.

Ad placement is another key issue. Through research, you must determine who your customer base is and the best places on the Web to advertise in order to reach this base. Of course, you'll have to work within your advertising budget. Once you pinpoint where the best places for your banner ad are, it's important to determine the best position on a site for your ads to appear. The position on the page and the size of the ad definitely have an impact on response rates.

 Moneysaver

Click-through rate (CTR) is the response rate of an online advertisement. It is usually given as a percentage. For example, if an ad is seen 10,000 times and generates 50 responses, it would have a CTR of 0.5. When paying for advertising, you want to obtain the highest click-through rate possible in order to get the most out of your advertising efforts.

When using banner ads, you can track the results instantly. As soon as your ad goes online, you can begin measuring how many exposures your ad receives and how many people visit your site as a result of seeing your banner ad (the click-through rate). Based on this information, you can fine-tune your ad message or alter the placement of your banner ads to reach a more targeted audience. This strategy also holds true for search-marketing techniques (described in the next chapter).

The cost of banner advertising varies from a few cents per day to thousands of dollars per day, depending on the popularity of the sites where you're advertising. Rates are usually based on the number of impressions your banner ad receives (you pay for 10,000, 50,000, or 100,000 or more impressions) or the length of time your ad is displayed on a website. If your advertising space purchase is based on time, it's important to request specific information about how many hits the website in question receives; also be sure to analyze how the site is promoted, to ensure that it will continue receiving that level of hits while your ad is running.

When deciding where to buy online advertising space, do plenty of research. Part of your research should include surfing the Web looking for sites that would be appropriate for your ad and that cater to the needs of your potential customers. As you pinpoint individual sites, contact the webmaster and request advertising information and rates. Often, at the bottom of a commercial website, you will see a link that says something like "Advertise Here" or "Advertising Information." By clicking these links, you can learn more about the advertising opportunities on the site.

Finding an advertising agency you can hire to assist with the creation and implementation of your online or traditional advertising campaign is as easy as opening the Yellow Pages, using a search engine, or visiting the website sponsored by the American Association of Advertising Agencies (www.aaaa.org).

Banner ad trades: the ad barter system

If your business is considered a start-up, you're probably trying to keep your overall costs down while attempting to generate as much exposure as you can for your online-based business. One way to take advantage of banner advertising without having to pay for it is to trade banner-ad space with other commercial or noncommercial websites. This means that you offer another company website banner-ad space on your site in exchange for ad space on their site. No money changes hands, yet both sites receive the benefits of cross-promotional advertising.

Obviously, your site's traffic might be lower than an established site's, so you might have to negotiate with other website operators to determine a fair exchange of banner-ad space. For example, you might offer four weeks of banner-ad space on your site in exchange for one week's worth of ad space on another site. If you can track exposures, you might agree to keep each other's banner ads on your respective sites until they receive a predetermined number of exposures (such as 10,000, 50,000, or 100,000).

There are many banner-exchange services available on the Web to help you facilitate fair banner-ad trades with other websites. Some of these services include the following:

Banner 123	www.123banners.com
CheapClick	www.cheapclick.org
Click4Click	www.click4click.com
Datexchanges	www.datexchanges.net
Exchange-It	www.exchange-it.com
Linkshare	www.linkshare.com

 Watch Out!

Before signing up to participate in any banner-exchange programs, make sure that you have control over the types of banners that will be displayed on your site. For example, make sure no sites promoting or advertising cybersex or pornography will be displayed on your site.

Press-release distribution

A press release is a document (usually between 500 and 1,000 words) about your company that's designed to make a newsworthy announcement to the media.

A press release is a key tool for public relations professionals. This type of document has a highly defined style and format, and answers the basic questions on the minds of reporters who might be interested in reporting on the topic of your press release—who, what, when, where, why, and how. For tips on how to write a press release, visit Gebbie Press' website (www.gebbieinc.com/howto.htm).

You can also hire a traditional PR firm, an online-based press release distribution service (such as Press Flash; www.pressflash.com), or a public relations consultant to write and distribute your press releases to the media for a fee. To find a PR consultant, visit the eLance (www.elance.com) website. Many professional writers and journalists, including the author of this book (www.JasonRich.com), also do freelance PR consulting to companies. (Please pardon the blatant self-promotion.)

You can distribute press releases to the media (such as newspapers, magazines, radio news outlets, television news outlets, other webmasters, and online publications) via U.S. mail, fax, or e-mail. Once you have a press release announcing your business (or some other newsworthy event relating to your business), your goal is to get it into the hands of the editors, reporters, and journalists responsible for covering your industry or type of business. You can do this by manually gathering your own media contact list by reading bylines in newspapers and magazines, or by purchasing a media directory.

 Bright Idea

Whenever you distribute a press release, also post the release somewhere on your website, under the heading "Corporate Information," "Company Background," or "Press Releases."

To help you compile your own customized media list, consider visiting the websites sponsored by *Editor & Publisher* (www. editorandpublisher.com) or the National Press Club (http:// npc.press.org).

Broadcast Interview Source (www.expertclick.com) publishes a variety of media directories that list the contact names, phone numbers, addresses, fax numbers, and e-mail addresses of writers, reporters, producers, editors, and radio/television hosts.

The Gebbie Press's *All-In-One Directory* (www.gebbieinc.com) lists contact information for more than 25,000 media people from TV and radio stations, newspapers, magazines, African American and Hispanic media, news syndicates, networks, and AP bureaus.

Other media directories are published by the following:

Bacon's Media Directories   www.bacons.com

Burrelle's Media Directories   www.burrellesluce.com

PR Place's Free Media Guide   www.prplace.com/
                                                            mds_guide/index.html

If you choose to save money and handle your own public relations efforts, consider using the press-release-distribution services of PR Newswire (www.prnewswire.com) or MarketWire (www.marketwire.com). You supply the press release and pay the company's fee, and your release gets distributed to media representatives that you designate based on area of interest, industry, or a specific topic.

As you compile the list of media outlets to send your press releases to, don't forget to include the following:

- Television shows (especially those that cover your industry)
- Talk radio and news stations
- Newspapers
- Magazines
- Trade journals
- Newsletters

- Online publications (including popular blogs)
- The webmasters at sites that cater to your target market's area of interest
- Special-interest groups or clubs

Using traditional PR efforts to reach both online and other media outlets in order to obtain free editorial coverage is a powerful way to reach potential customers. To generate the best possible publicity for your business, make sure your press releases contain only newsworthy information the media would be interested in covering.

Another approach to take with reporters is to pitch a feature story idea or segment idea for them that someone relates to your product or service and can feature you as their expert. This takes a bit of extra creativity, but it's what professional public relations firms are often hired to do.

If you're promoting a product, your press release should discuss what the product is, why there's a need for it, and why, for example, a magazine, newspaper, or radio or TV station's audience would be interested in it. The press release should position the executives within the company as experts in their field, who are available to be interviewed. The media loves interviewing "experts" on topics they're doing stories on.

If you're not familiar with how PR works, consider hiring a PR firm or consultant to assist you in generating media coverage for your online business. You can also read how-to books on the topic. Additional information about how to launch a PR effort for your business can be found online at PR Place (www.prplace.com).

 Bright Idea

Make sure you list the URL for your online business prominently in your press release. This will help ensure that it gets listed in any article your press release helps generate.

Tips for writing an effective press release

Before sending out any press release, make sure you do the following:

1. Know who to send it to, not just where. Find out who the editor or reporter is for the section you want your release to appear in.

2. Send the release to only one person per news outlet. Any problems that develop from duplicate coverage and effort will be blamed on you.

3. Don't just send press releases—call the editor or writer directly. If you want your release covered, call the person before sending the release, and call a couple of days later to make sure they received it. Just don't become a pest.

4. Know your deadlines. Magazines, even weekly ones, are often planned months in advance. Seasonal events, such as Christmas and Easter, are great examples of this. For calendar items, know the news outlet's deadline for the section.

5. Keep it short and informative. Reporters and editors are notoriously busy. Most press releases should be kept to one page. Two is acceptable. If a reporter wants more information, they'll ask.

6. Write it in a news style. That means putting the prime information (who, what, when, where, why, and how) into the lead (first paragraph). It also means keeping the sales pitch subtle. No exclamation points!!! Many papers will directly reprint a press release, as long as it is written in a professional news style. Use short words and sentences. Make sure what you're saying is very clear.

7. Use one or two quotes from your company's executives that have meaning. Position them as industry or product "experts." Journalists will often reprint these quotes verbatim in their articles.

8. Always include, at the top corner of every page, a two- or three-word description of the story, the name and phone number of key contact people (no more than two), the page number (if there is more than one page), and the release date (usually "For Immediate Release"; otherwise "Please hold until xx/xx/xx").

9. End a press release with ### typed across the center of the margin a couple lines below the end of your text. If a release is continued on another page, type "-more-" at the bottom of the page in the center.

10. Use standard 8½" × 11" paper typed on one side only. Never break a paragraph across two pages. Leave plenty of margins for editors to write notes—an inch and a half all around should be fine.

11. Make sure the press release clearly states how the reporter can contact you via telephone *and* e-mail. It should also clearly list your company's website address.

12. Consider sending your release to the online editors at websites associated with newspapers, magazines, radio stations, and TV stations or news programs. Sometimes the online edition of a news outlet offers different coverage than its traditional media counterpart.

Online chats and communities

Hosting an online chat either through your own website or through a major online service is one way to communicate in real time to an audience. Although it's inexpensive to host an online chat, if you want potential customers to attend the chat, it's important that you offer them information of value and not simply use this as a vehicle to convey your marketing or advertising message. For example, for a special guest, you might consider having an expert, celebrity, or author who will answer questions from chat participants.

Many companies are now hosting one-on-one online chats to facilitate technical-support-related communications with customers or clients.

Creating an online community with a chat room also allows your customers to talk among themselves and discuss how they use your products, and so on. This is a great way to encourage your customers to exchange ideas and testimonials in an informal manner. Some of the turnkey solutions allow you to quickly add chat capabilities as part of your website. If you're designing your site from scratch, you can find the programming scripts for chat functionality at websites like www.hotscripts.com.

Taking advantage of traditional advertising

For some online businesses, focusing exclusively on online advertising, marketing, and PR will be extremely effective. It's important to understand, however, that the really successful online businesses also use traditional advertising media to promote their websites and generate traffic to their sites.

Traditional advertising vehicles include newspapers, magazines, radio, network television, cable television, syndicated television, billboards, in-theater advertising, direct mail, trade shows, and so on. Whether you choose to take advantage of any of these powerful media vehicles will depend on the audience you're trying to reach and your budget. One inexpensive way to tap the power of traditional print advertising is to run an ad in a special-interest magazine or newsletter that caters specifically to the target audience you're trying to reach. You can also use classified advertising as a way to get short, text-based messages across to broader groups of newspaper or magazine readers.

Millions of everyday people are Web surfers. So it makes perfect sense in some cases to promote your website using traditional newspaper, TV, radio, and magazine advertising. If your company already does traditional advertising, be sure to include your site's URL in the copy once your site goes online. The more prominently the URL is displayed in your print ads, the more traffic you'll ultimately generate for your site.

In Chapter 16, you'll read an interview with Scott Meyer (www.onlyonecreations.com), an artist and online business operator who created his e-commerce business to sell the fine writing instruments he creates from scratch. Each of his pens is a unique work of art. Meyer has determined that one of the niche markets he needs to reach through advertising is fountain-pen collectors. To reach this market, he runs print ads in a special-interest magazine called *Pen World*.

Likewise, Christian Girts, the founder of Angler's Vice (www.anglersvice.com), has discovered that advertising in special-interest fly-fishing magazines is one ideal way to reach his target audience, which is comprised of fly-fishermen.

Blogging as a promotional tool

One of the newer trends for communicating online is through the use of blogs. A blog is simply an online-based digital diary or forum where anyone can write anything and make it available for the Web-surfing public in minutes. As of mid-2005, there were more than nine million blogs currently online, with new ones being launched daily.

Although blogging has become extremely popular among computer enthusiasts as a way to keep in touch with friends and family, plus meet new people online in an informal way, online business owners have also discovered that blogging can be a powerful marketing and promotions tool. It's a great way to communicate directly (yet informally) with customers and potential customers online.

By creating a blog, written by the president or owner of your online business, for example, you can create an ongoing digital diary (that gets updated daily, weekly, or monthly) to keep potential and existing customers up-to-date on everything that's happening with your company. Furthermore, people reading your

Bright Idea

If you're planning to use a blog as a business tool, consider researching how other businesses use this technology as a marketing tool. For information about "Business Blogging," visit the Cerado website at www.cerado.com/solutions05. asp. This company specializes in helping companies use blogging to communicate with their customers.

blog can then post their own comments, ideas, and suggestions for others to read.

A blog offers an informal way to communicate with people using primarily text, graphics, and photos. You can create a blog as part of your company's website (or as a separate website) in less than a few hours initially (plus whatever time you invest on an ongoing basis to post new entries to your blog). You can easily use a blog as a communication tool, offering an alternative to a traditional (or electronic) newsletter.

Best of all, most of the popular blog hosting/publishing services are free to use and require absolutely no programming. These days, celebrities, politicians, business operators, hobbyists, families, and writers use blogs to reach out to the general public (or a specific audience) and share thoughts and ideas.

Google operates one of the most popular blogging services, called Blogger.com. There is no charge to use this service. To see a sample blog (created by the author of this book), point your Web browser to http://jasonrich.blogspot.com. Another way to add a blog to your existing website is to use the blogging tools offered by www.wordpress.org or www.moveabletype.org.

If you're using website-creation software or a turnkey solution for developing your website, chances are, blogging capabilities are already available to you. You could also link your website to your blog hosted by Blogger.com or another blog-hosting service, such as Square Space (www.squarespace.com), Type Pad (www.typepad.com), Blogomonster (www.blogomonster.com), or NeBo Group (http://nebogroup.com).

Bright Idea

Once you drive traffic to your website, one way to keep people coming back is to offer news or ever-changing information they're interested in. This could include "how-to" articles for using your product, industry news, or other information that's relevant. You can either create this content yourself or license it. The strategy is to offer ever-changing and timely information that will keep people coming back to your website. One company that syndicates content to webmasters is OSKAR (www.electroniccontent.com/conFinder.cfm).

To read an article that appeared in the May 2, 2005, issue of *BusinessWeek* about the popularity of blogging, point your Web browser to www.businessweek.com/magazine/content/05_18/b3931001_mz001.htm.

Once you've created a blog as a way to help promote your online business venture, you can use to it communicate the following:

- Information about the day-to-day operation of your company
- Details about your product/services, including previews of new products
- Announcements about sales and special promotions
- Practical tips and strategies for using your products or service
- Answers to questions from (potential) customers
- Testimonials from your customers
- Useful information relating to your industry that your (potential) customers will find informative and valuable

If you want to create a blog that (potential) customers will read and return to often, use your creativity to provide interesting, fun, and relevant content that will nicely supplement what's already available on your website. Keep the tone of your blog casual.

Podcasting as a marketing tool

Podcasting has become almost as popular as blogging when it comes to "broadcasting" information. Podcasting involves recording an audio program, like a full-length radio show, for example, and making it available for download in a special file format that can easily be transferred to an Apple iPod MP3 player (or compatible MP3 player). *Book Marketing Update* recently referred to Podcasting as "the latest Internet marketing craze."

According to Wikipedia, "Podcasting is a term that was devised as a crisp way to describe the technology used to push audio content from websites down to consumers, who typically listen to it on the iPod or other audio player . . . . Podcasting allows individuals and small businesses to publish (Podcast) radio shows that interested listeners can subscribe to."

To learn more about Podcasting as a marketing tool and listen to thousands of different sample Podcasts, point your Web browser to any of these sites:

- www.podcast.net
- www.podcastalley.com
- www.ipodder.org
- www.odeo.com
- www.podshow.com

To discover how to actually create a Podcast, the following websites will be helpful: www.gopodder.com, www.castblaster.com, www.easypodcast.com, and Liberated Syndication (www.libsyn.com). A basic Podcast can be created on your computer by hooking up a microphone and utilizing specialized software.

The Apple website (www.apple.com/podcasting/) offers information about the various iPod MP3 players and related technology, plus information about Podcasting, including a useful tutorial.

As an online business operator, you can use a Podcast to tell people about your products, how to best use them, and to offer audio tutorials, testimonials, and other information. Take some

time to listen to a bunch of Podcasts produced by other companies and determine how they're creating original audio content
to promote their company and products. Then, consider pro-
ducing your own Podcast that's targeted specifically to your customers and those interested in your products.

Online newsletters are excellent promotional tools

Another way to communicate your marketing message to potential and existing customers it to create a simple electronic
newsletter, which can be accessed, free of charge, from your
website and/or e-mailed to people on your opt-in e-mail list.

Your newsletter can be published weekly, biweekly, or
monthly and include information about your company, along
with its products and services. If you want potential customers to
read your newsletter on an ongoing basis, however, make sure it
also offers information they perceive to be useful and valuable.

The newsletter's content should not simply be advertising
for what you're selling. Consider offering how-to articles, advice,
industry-related news, interviews with experts, and other articles
that your target audience will be interested in. A newsletter is a
great way to inform potential customers about new products.

Publishing an online newsletter is extremely inexpensive
and easy to distribute online. To ensure you convey a sense of
professionalism with your online publication, consider hiring
one or more freelance writers to help you create your content.

Remember, the newsletter you create can be a promotional
tool for your company, but it should also offer useful (and relevant) information for the reader. The newsletter should also be
offered free of charge.

If you decide to offer a free newsletter, create an icon or
menu option on your website that prominently promotes the
publication and encourages visitors to subscribe to it or access it
directly from the site.

Just the facts

- Promotion and advertising are the keys to success for any online business.

- Aside from purchasing banner advertising space, you can also trade banner-ad space with other sites.

- Your mission is to drive people interested in your product to your site. This means choosing a target audience and marketing to that audience.

- Advertising and marketing opportunities include trading links with other sites, taking advantage of newsgroups and mailing lists, using e-mail, hosting online chats, blogging, and distributing press releases.

- If you can afford it, also take advantage of traditional media outlets to advertise and promote your business.

- First and foremost, your online business's advertising and marketing efforts should include search-engine optimization and search-marketing techniques (described in Chapter 11).

- Blogging can be a useful, grassroots promotional and marketing tool. It costs very little to implement and allows you to communicate informally with your (potential) customers. When creating a blog, be creative and have fun!

Search-Engine Optimization and Search Marketing Made Easy

Chapter 11

There are literally millions of websites in existence with more going online each day. So, how are typical Web surfers supposed to find your site, and why should they even care to look for it?

For Web surfers of any skill level, the fastest and easiest way to locate information on the Web is by using a search engine, Web directory, or information portal, such as the following:

- **Yahoo!** (www.yahoo.com)
- **Google** (www.google.com)
- **HotBot** (www.hotbot.com)
- **AltaVista** (www.altavista.com)
- **About** (www.about.com)
- **AOL Search** (www.aol.com)

- **Ask Jeeves** (www.ask.com)
- **Lycos** (www.lycos.com)
- **MSN Search** (www.msn.com)

Knowing that a search engine, Web directory, or information portal is the first place Web surfers go to find what they're looking for, your first step as an online business owner should be to ensure that your site is prominently listed with all of these popular services.

As you'll quickly discover, simply being listed with a search engine, for example, isn't enough. When someone sees a list of possible links as a result of their search query, your website needs to be one of the very first on that list to help ensure that the Web surfer will actually visit your site.

With so many websites available and so much intense competition, obtaining a top listing isn't always an easy task, yet it's something you need to strive for.

The process of obtaining a prominent listing placement on a search engine, Web directory, or information portal is called *search-engine optimization*. Understanding how these services work and how to obtain a great placement is a skill unto itself, plus it requires a significant and ongoing time commitment.

Thus, there are many third-party services you can hire to assist you in listing your website with the search engines and help you achieve prominent placement. You'll pay a fee to use a search-engine listing and optimization service, but you'll save a lot of time. Keep in mind, once you register your website with a search engine, unless it's a paid placement, it could take several weeks for your basic (free) listing to appear.

No matter what type of online business you operate, focusing on website optimization and achieving good placement on services such as Yahoo! or Google will, without a doubt, drive traffic to your website on an ongoing basis, especially if your search-engine optimization is done correctly.

In addition to simply getting your website listed with these services, you can better utilize the power of search engines, Web directories, and information portals by taking advantage of the paid advertising and paid placement opportunities available from many of the popular search engines and related services. Using these advertising opportunities will ensure that when someone uses a search engine and enters a search phrase or keyword that's relevant to your website, a link to your website appears. This process is called *search marketing* or *keyword marketing/advertising*.

As you'll discover from this chapter, signing up for Google AdWords and Yahoo! Search Marketing's services will require a financial investment on your part (starting as low as $30 per month), but will most likely prove extremely beneficial. The more you spend, however, the better your results will be.

Internet search engines and portals

Initially, a search engine was nothing more than a database of websites that could be searched based on a keyword or search phrase. This has changed. These days, services such as Yahoo!, Excite, AltaVista, Lycos, and many others have become information portals. Although they still work as basic search engines and Web directories, these services also offer a variety of other free services to surfers, ranging from personalized news, sports, and weather reports to private e-mail accounts, online shopping, and online chatting.

On the World Wide Web, search engines were among the first viable online businesses. Millions of Web surfers visit these sites daily to find information. In fact, most people assign a search engine to be their Web browser's home page.

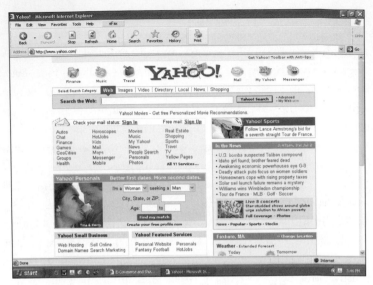

Figure 11.1. Yahoo! (www.yahoo.com) is perhaps the world's most popular search engine, Web directory, and Internet portal, all wrapped up into one.

Because Internet search engines are free to use, companies such as Yahoo! sell online advertising and sponsorships to generate revenue. Advertising on a popular search engine, Web directory, or information portal is an ideal way to reach large numbers of Internet users and even target the specific audience you're trying to reach.

In addition to helping people find specific information, search engines, Web directories, and information portals are often used as a launch pad for people exploring cyberspace. Virtually all search engines and Web directories are searchable by keyword or phrase; but like the Yellow Pages, they're also divided into categories, allowing people to pinpoint links that lead to topics of interest.

So, even if someone might not know that your online business exists, if the Web surfer happens to seek out a list of sites about a topic related to your business or finds you based on a keyword under which your business is listed, you have a good chance of catching their attention and having them visit your site.

By visiting the powerful search engines yourself, you'll quickly discover that each is slightly different in terms of its layout and design. As an online business owner, ultimately you'll want to spend time pinpointing exactly how and where you want to be listed on each of the popular Web directories.

Just like a telephone book, having your website (online business) listed with a search engine is totally free for a basic listing. In many cases, all you need to do is complete an online form when visiting each search engine. (This process is described later in this chapter.) In some situations, using what's called a *spider*, the search engine will automatically find your website based on keywords and meta tags you create as part of your website's design and HTML programming. How to do this is also described later in this chapter.

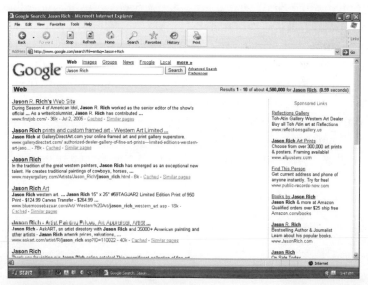

Figure 11.2. Google is an extremely popular search engine. On the right side of the screen, check out the "Sponsored Links." To place your ad here, visit the Google AdWords website (www.adwords.com).

Understanding search-engine lingo

In everyday conversation, the terms *search engine, Web directory,* and *information portal* all refer to services such as Yahoo!, Google, AltaVista, AOL Search, HotBot, and Ask Jeeves. But, strictly speaking, there is a difference between these types of services.

The key difference between a search engine and a Web directory is that search engines use "spiders" to crawl across the Web looking for new websites to add to their massive databases. Directories are hand-assembled listings of websites, put together by humans. At Yahoo!, for example, humans determine what gets listed in its Web directories, not automated spiders. AltaVista, HotBot, Go.com, Lycos, Google, and WebCrawler, however, are examples of search engines that use spiders to automatically compile their databases.

All of the search engines and Web directories offer the same basic Internet-searching features, but how these features are implemented and what additional services are offered allow companies such as Yahoo! and Google, for example, to broaden their appeal by offering value-added services. (All of these additional services, such as news, sports, weather, and entertainment headlines; free e-mail accounts; and online shopping are free to the user, thanks to paid advertising support from e-commerce companies like yours.)

When you visit Yahoo!'s main page (www.yahoo.com), one of the first things you'll see at the top of the screen is an input prompt that enables you to enter a keyword or search phrase. Based on what you enter, Yahoo! will pinpoint and list websites that might be of interest to you.

 Bright Idea

Although descriptions of search engines are good starting points, there's no substitute for visiting the sites yourself. Try several different sites to get a feel for how they work, how one differs from another, and how you might be able to tailor your own business needs to the special features of each one.

A search engine is able to match up your keywords with the content of all websites in the service's massive database. This is done using specialized software called "robots," "spiders," or "crawlers," which scan websites to create a detailed index of keywords found on sites that are registered with the search engine. The search engine's index is compared to the keyword or search phrase the surfer enters and a listing of related websites is displayed, all in a matter of seconds.

The Web-directory aspect of certain search engines

If you scroll down the Yahoo! main page, you'll discover the Yahoo! Web Directory, which begins by listing main headings. These include Arts, Business, Computers, Culture, Education, Entertainment, Health, News, Recreation, Reference, Regional, and Science. Each of these headings leads to subheadings, which are links that lead to still further subheadings. These categories enable a Web surfer to find the information they're looking for based on general topics, and then narrow down their search, ultimately finding specific websites.

Online services are also sometimes referred to as Internet (or information) portals because they provide a starting point for people to begin surfing the Web and taking advantage of a wide range of features and functions from a single website. Portals typically offer customized news, chat rooms, group forums, and other features, allowing people to customize their online experience and also to search for information.

Make sure your site contains meta tags

A *meta tag* is a search-engine indexing device that's a programming tool for helping a website get indexed correctly by a search engine's spider. Meta tags are a list of keywords (relating to the website and its content) created by the webmaster and incorporated into the HTML programming code of a website.

Bright Idea

"Robot" or "crawler" software used by search engines will scan your site for the keywords you designate for your site. Make it easy for the search engines to determine what information, products, or services your online business offers. Incorporate well-defined meta tags into the HTML programming of your site.

There are two types of tags. The first is a short, text-based website *description* (usually one or two sentences) created by the webmaster for a site. The second is a detailed list of *keywords* and search phrases (one or two words) that the webmaster believes relate directly to that site.

If a website lacks meta tags, search engines will usually take the first few words it finds on a site and make that the description. The keywords in the meta tag tell the search engine exactly which keywords you want your site to be searchable under. Without meta tags, a search engine will automatically attempt to choose keywords for your site. The results might not be beneficial to you and could prevent people from finding your site.

You should understand that meta tags are not a surefire solution for getting your site to the top of search-engine lists. They will help to get your site indexed correctly, but they do not guarantee top placement.

What a meta tag looks like

Incorporating meta tags into your site is optional, but it's extremely easy to do and something that every Web page of every website should contain. In terms of generating traffic to your site from the various search engines, the few minutes it takes to add meta tags to the HTML programming of your site will be extremely beneficial, especially because there is absolutely no cost involved.

The following is a sample of what meta tag HTML programming looks like. It was created using SiteOwner.com's MetaTag Builder (www.siteowner.com/system/meta.cfm) for a fictional website that could be used to promote this book. The first step

Watch Out!

A search engine matches only the text portion of various websites to the keywords or search phrase you enter. Any text that's incorporated into a graphic file or Flash animation within a website, such as a company logo, won't be recognized by a search engine's spider.

is to enter the relevant information about your website into the online based meta tag creation tool. You'll be asked for the website name, website description, and keywords (in this case, you can enter up to 10 keywords).

Based on the information provided, the following lines of HTML code were generated and could be placed within the site's existing source code, inserted into the head section (the codes between <head> and </head>). You can do this using any ordinary text editor or website-creation software, such as Microsoft FrontPage.

Many website-creation tools and software packages have a meta-tag-creation utility built in. As you create the page, meta tags are created and placed in the HTML code. You should definitely use this feature for each page of your website.

Web Site Name: The Unofficial Guide to Starting a Business Online, 2nd Edition

Web Site Description: A website all about the best-selling book, The Unofficial Guide to Starting a Business Online, 2nd Edition, written by bestselling author Jason R. Rich and published by Wiley. This book is a detailed, step-by-step guide for anyone interested in launching their own online-based business.

Keywords: E-Commerce, website design, online business, e-store, virtual store, Internet marketing, Wiley, Jason Rich, search-engine optimization, online marketing, website programming

Title Tag

<title>The Unofficial Guide to Starting a Business Online</title>

Description Meta Tag

<meta name="description" content="A website all about the bestselling book, The Unofficial Guide to Starting a Business Online, 2nd Edition, written by bestselling author Jason R. Rich and published by Wiley. This book is a detailed, step-by-step guide for anyone interested in launching their own online-based business.">

Keyword Meta Tag

<meta name="keywords" content="E-Commerce, website design, online business, e-store, virtual store, Internet marketing, Wiley, Jason Rich, search-engine optimization, online marketing, website programming">

Search engines: the next millennium's Yellow Pages

Information is power, and the computer users with the most information available to them are those who can quickly navigate their way around the various Internet search engines to find the information they need or want.

Although Yahoo! was the first search engine on the Web (it was created by two Ph.D. candidates at Stanford University in 1994), over the past decade, literally hundreds have gone online, each offering slightly different tools for navigating in cyberspace.

The most important search engines

Using any search engine, if you use the keyword or search phrase "search engine," you'll see listings for hundreds of other Web directories. However, more than 90 percent of the Web-surfing public uses only the top 10 search engines, which include Google, Yahoo!, AltaVista, AOL Search, HotBot, and WebCrawler. This means it's vital that you spend extra time registering your site with these popular search engines and making sure that your listing remains prominent and current.

If your online business is reachable via multiple URLs, list all of your URLs separately with each search engine to increase the probability that Web surfers will find you with ease. To register a site with Google.com, the most popular search engine, go to this URL: www.google.com/intl/en/about.html and click on link "Submitting your Site."

Registering your site with the search engines

In order for search engines to list your website, you must first register your site with each individually. When visiting any search engine, look for a link that says "Suggest a URL," "Add a URL," or "How to Suggest a Site." You'll then be provided with details on how to proceed with listing your website for free. Each search engine follows a slightly different process for site submissions.

Getting help with registration

Registering your site on each of the various search engines and keeping the listing current can be a time-consuming process. Although you'll want to take the time to personally ensure that your site gets listed with at least the top 10 search engines, for a relatively small flat fee, you can hire a company that will register your URL with hundreds of search engines and Web directories.

The cost of hiring a company can be anywhere from a flat, one-time fee of under $50 to several hundred dollars per month. The least-expensive service offers *search-engine submission* only, whereas the more expensive service, *search-engine optimization*,

actually takes steps to ensure that your site will receive prominent placement with each popular search engine.

Search-engine submission and optimization services

The following is a sampling of search-engine submission and
optimization services you can sign up for online. It will take anywhere from several days to several weeks for you to start seeing
your listings appear on the various search engines, so be patient.
Paid ads and sponsored links on the search engines, however,
appear almost instantly.

- **1-Hit** (www.1-hit.com)
- **Build Traffic** (www.buildtraffic.com)
- **Engine Seeker** (www.engineseeker.com)
- **eSiteBlast** (www.esiteblast.com)
- **Monster Web Promotion** (www.monsterwebpromotion.com)
- **Submission Pro** (www.submission-pro.com)
- **Submit Express** (www.submitexpress.com)
- **Traffic Blazer from GoDaddy.com** (www.godaddy.com)
- **WPromote** (www.wpromote.com)
- **Yahoo! Search Marketing** (http://searchmarketing.
  yahoo.com)

If you're using a turnkey solution to create and host your
e-commerce website, such as Yahoo! Store or Clickincome.com,
search-engine submission and optimization services are typically
included with your monthly fee.

 Bright Idea

By registering your domain with the top directories, you'll reach the most
surfers. Many Web directories share the same search-engine database. Thus,
for example, you might see a little icon reading "Powered by Yahoo!" on a service other than Yahoo!. If your site is listed with Yahoo!, it will automatically
be listed with Yahoo!'s various affiliates.

Generate traffic with Google AdWords

You already know the importance of having a prominent listing on the popular search engines in order to make it easy for potential customers to find you. One way to make it even easier is to use AdWords marketing from Google, or a similar service that's offered by Yahoo! Search Marketing.

In addition to the list of relevant websites that appears based on a Web surfer's keyword search when they use a search engine such as Google, AdWords displays "Sponsored Links," which are short, text-based ads that appear from advertisers like you who are offering products, services, or a website that's relevant to the Web surfer's search criteria (based on the keywords they entered).

According to Google, "Google AdWords ads connect you with new customers at the precise moment when they're looking for your products or services. The Google Network reaches more than 80 percent of Internet users . . . . Google AdWords is our global advertising program. Advertisers use our automated tools, often with little or no assistance from us, to create ads, place bids to serve their ads, select the types of sites where they'd like their ads to appear, and set daily spending budgets. AdWords features an automated, low-cost online signup process that enables advertisers to implement campaigns that can go live in 15 minutes or less.

Figure 11.3. Google AdWords, like Yahoo! Search Marketing, is an extremely cost-effective and easy way to drive traffic to your website by advertising on the popular search engines and on other participating websites. This is considered keyword-based advertising or search marketing.

Bright Idea

Because of the high number of visitors to the major search engines, placing an ad with one can be comparable to (if not superior to) placing an ad in more traditional venues. Yahoo! does not exaggerate when it claims that "being on the front page of Yahoo! is like having the largest billboard in Times Square."

"AdWords ranks ads for display in one of two ways: either by CPM (cost-per-thousand) or by a combination of the maximum cost-per-click (CPC), which is set by the advertiser, together with click-through rates and other factors used to determine the relevance of the ads. This process favors the ads that are most relevant to users, improving the experience for both the person looking for information and the advertiser looking for interested customers.

"Advertisers can deliver targeted ads based on specific search terms (keywords) entered by users or found in the content on a Web page. We also offer tools to help advertisers consider synonyms and useful phrases to use as keywords or ad text. By choosing relevant keywords advertisers can improve ad click-through rates and the likelihood that a user will become a customer."

AdWords, and services like it from companies such as Yahoo!, offers an inexpensive way to generate additional traffic from search engines. This advertising vehicle can be used by companies of any size, because your ad budget is totally controllable by you, starting as low as $1 per day. The start-up cost is as low as $5.

In addition to AdWords ads being displayed on Google, the company has a long list of affiliate websites where AdWords ads also appear, such as on AOL, Netscape Netcenter, EarthLink, Ask Jeeves, CompuServe, Shopping.com, About.com, Lycos, iVillage, and the *New York Times* on the Web. As an AdWords advertiser, you control your cost-per-impression, cost-per-click, and your overall budget. Using online-based tools, choosing the most appropriate keywords for your site becomes an easy task.

Once you begin using an advertising vehicle such as Goggle AdWords, you'll want to monitor the campaign carefully and fine-tune it as necessary based on the real-time statistics you receive from the service as well as from your ISP.

The process for launching a Google AdWords advertising campaign includes the following:

1. Setting up your Google AdWords account using a major credit card.

2. Targeting your customers (by geographic region, for example).

3. Creating your AdWords ad. Space within these ads is very limited. The wording you use is critical and must grab the reader's attention instantly using only a few well-selected words or phrases.

4. Selecting your keywords.

5. Setting your maximum cost-per-click (CPC).

6. Selecting your daily budget.

A Google AdWords ad is comprised of a bold-typeface headline, plus two lines of regular text (up to 35 characters per line) and your website's display URL (which has a 35-character limit). The actual destination URL (not displayed to Web surfers) can be up to 1,024 characters long.

An AdWords campaign can consist of just one ad that is displayed based on a wide range of keywords, or many different ads with a very narrow and defined list of keywords associated with each of them. This will determine exactly who sees your ad and how much of a targeted audience you reach with your ad(s).

 Bright Idea

To learn more about Google AdWords and how to best utilize this service, visit the *Inside AdWords* blog at http://adwords.blogspot.com.

To help you create and fine-tune your list of keywords, Google AdWords offers online tutorials and utilities. Wordtracker Keywords (www.wordtracker.com), however, is an online service that allows you to compare the most popular search terms used by Web surfers with the list of keywords you're associating with your ads. This can help you create a more defined list of keywords that you know Web surfers are actually using when they visit the search engines.

Using banner ads to boost traffic

Banner ads are perhaps the most well-known form of online advertising. They're like print ads in a magazine, except they can be animated and they're interactive. When someone sees a banner ad, they can immediately click on that ad and be redirected to the advertiser's website. From an advertiser's standpoint, you can track the success of a banner ad in real-time, so you know almost instantly which banner ad messages work and which don't, plus you have the ability to modify your advertising message (your banner ad and artwork) very quickly.

As you surf the Web, you'll see banner ads everywhere. Some are flashy and very "in your face," while others are more subtle, yet still display advertising messages that encourage Web surfers to "click here."

Banner ads continue to be a popular form of online advertising, although many online business owners agree that paying for banner advertising in many cases no longer generates the positive results that they once did. When this book was being written, many online business operators were scaling down their paid banner advertising campaigns in favor of expanding their search marketing advertising using the search engines.

As an online business operator, you can pay for online banner ad space on other websites (just as you'd buy advertising space in a newspaper or magazine), or you can participate in one of the many banner exchange programs. A banner exchange program allows you to display your banner ad(s) on other websites for free, as long as you agree to display other advertisers' ads on your site. No money changes hands in this situation, which makes it an attractive advertising vehicle for start-ups and small online businesses.

Another way to get your banner ads displayed on other sites without having to pay upfront is to develop an affiliate program. By becoming a member of a well-established affiliate program, you wind up paying your affiliates (the websites that display your ads) based on a cost-per-click, cost-per-lead, or cost-per-sale business model. For more information about creating an affiliate program, point your Web browser to www.LinkShare.com, which is one of the largest services used by online business operators to establish and implement an affiliate program.

Many well-known and well-established companies use affiliate programs to enhance their online advertising and marketing efforts. Delta Airlines, FTD.com, Cingular Wireless, 1800flowers.com, Zirh skincare products for men, American Express, JCrew, Macy's, NetFlix, Orbitz, PetCo, Target, Hallmark, and Tupperware are just a few of the companies that utilize affiliate programs to get their banner ads prominently displayed on other websites.

While placement of your banner ads is critical for their success (after all, you want people to see them), what's equally important is their appearance and the wording you use. Your marketing massage in a banner ad needs to be very concise and powerful. You'll have a few seconds to capture a Web surfer's attention and get them to click on your banner ad.

Tips for banner ad creation

Although keyword advertising (search marketing) has proven to be extremely cost-effective for most online business operators, banner advertising still has a place in the online advertising arena.

Every search engine and website you can advertise on has strict guidelines for banner ads. Typical guidelines are the following:

- 468×60 pixels for a full-size banner or 234×60 pixels for a half-size banner. Other popular sizes are 100×100 and 120×120. A popular vertical banner size is 120×240 pixels, whereas a button-size banner is typically 120×90 or 120×60 pixels.

- Typically, only *.GIF* images are accepted. Banners can, however, be created using Flash if you want to incorporate animation.

- The size of the graphic file containing your banner ad usually needs to be smaller than 15K, but the smaller the file size, the better. A 12K file for a banner graphic will load faster.

- Consider the use of a tagline directly below your banner. Taglines are offered at the discretion of the online service and are usually limited to 12 words or less.

- If you're designing an animated banner, pay careful attention to file size and the length of the animation, which can typically be no longer than four to seven seconds.

- All banner ads are subject to approval by the search engine or the site where you'll be advertising.

As you're developing the content for your banner ad(s) and choosing the wording and appearance, a few general rules apply:

- Keep the message simple and uncluttered.

- Target your audience carefully.

- Consider offering something of value for free as a way to capture someone's attention. Just make sure you follow through when someone clicks on your banner to visit your site.

- If you're not offering something free, use some other enticement that will encourage people to respond immediately.

When it comes to online banner ads, you can use animation to get the viewers' attention. Use simple animations that aren't distracting but help get your message across.

Use banner ads as a way to grab an audience's attention so that they want to visit your site for additional information. For example, you can pose a question as part of your banner ad, and require the viewer to click on the ad and visit your site for the answer.

Make sure you state the obvious. If you want someone to click on the banner and visit your site, include the message "Click Here," or use some form of graphic to make it perfectly clear what the viewer should do.

Develop several messages and approaches for your banner ads and test them to see which ones generate the best response or the most traffic. One of the great things about online advertising is that it's easy to instantaneously measure the impact the banner ad has. It might be necessary to test several messages or approaches and fine-tune your advertising until you develop an approach that works the best.

The majority of search engines offer what is called "beyond the banner" advertising opportunities, allowing advertisers to utilize new ways to build relationships with customers, build brands, and distribute content. This includes sponsorship of particular online events, specific content, or areas of a service.

Utilizing price-comparison websites

If you're selling a product that will appeal to savvy online Web surfers shopping for the lowest prices possible, you should look to the price-comparison websites that these price-conscious shoppers often use.

Services such as Nextag.com (www.nextag.com), BizRate (www.bizrate.com), PriceScan (www.pricescan.com), Price Grabber (www.pricegrabber.com), and LowerMyBills.com (www.lowermybills.com), MySimon (www.mysimon.com), and Shopzilla (www.shopzilla.com) are just a few of the popular price-comparison websites used by savvy online shoppers.

You'll also find specific price-comparison sites that specialize in specific types of products or services, such as consumer electronics, finding the best credit-card offers, automobile sales, mortgages, or insurance, for example.

A price-comparison website enables the user to enter a specific product or service they're interested in purchasing. The site then provides a detailed list of merchants selling that exact product and the discounted price each merchant is offering it for. The merchants are also rated based on customer satisfaction.

When Web surfers see the list of potential merchants, they can click on any of them to actually link to the appropriate website and place their order, typically going with the merchant with the best reputation and the lowest price.

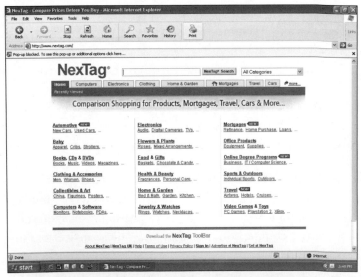

Figure 11.4. If you're offering your products at extremely competitive prices, consider advertising on a price-comparison website, such as Nextag.com.

Many price-comparison websites are advertiser based, which means that as the online merchant, you need to pay to be included. Depending on what you're selling and the prices you're charging, participating in these sites can generate traffic to your website, as well as sales. Unless you're offering something truly unique or more common items at a very low price point, however, this might not be the best marketing approach because you typically pay for impressions and click-throughs, whether or not you make the sale. After all, Web surfers use these sites to find the lowest price for what they're looking to purchase. Why would they click on the listing for your website if you're not offering the most competitive price?

Just the facts

- Registering your online business's URL with popular Internet search engines and Web directories enables Web surfers to locate your site.

- Taking advantage of website optimization will ensure that your site receives prominent placement on the search engines.

- Utilizing search marketing or keyword-based advertising is an extremely cost-effective way to kick-start your website's advertising and promotion.

- Using the search engines can be one of the least expensive and most powerful methods for generating traffic to your site.

- Advertising on a search engine gives you the opportunity to target a general Web-surfing audience or reach people with very specific interests.

PART V

Improving and Analyzing Your Site

GET THE SCOOP ON...
The pros and cons of Web browser plug-ins ▪
Utilizing Flash animations ▪ Using Java applets,
Shockwave, and other graphic technologies ▪
Understanding cookies

Making Your Site Look and Sound Great

Chapter 12

Throughout this book, I've stressed the importance of having a professional-looking website. Why? Because this concept is important! Creating a visually appealing and easy-to-navigate site doesn't necessarily mean incorporating a lot of flashy graphic effects, audio, and other technologies, but you should use these technologies if they're appropriate and can help you more effectively communicate your message to your site's visitors.

Using text, photos, and simple graphics throughout your website will allow you to convey key points about your company and the product or service you're offering. If flashier design elements and visual eye candy distract visitors, confuse them, make your site too busy or complex, or take away from the messages you're attempting to convey, avoid using them. Keeping your site simple, straightforward, visually appealing, and easy to navigate will be far more beneficial than creating a site that's loaded with bells and whistles.

271

During the website-design processes, you'll need to determine what graphic and animation elements you want incorporated into your site, then determine if those elements add or detract for your overall marketing message. Also, determine what the site is being designed to achieve. Next, you must consider download times for the visitor. Each new element you ad to your site, whether it's a graphic, animation, or streaming audio clip, for example, takes time to load. If a Web page takes too long to load, a Web surfer will quickly lose interest and navigate elsewhere.

Adding cool graphic effects, nice pictures, and eye-popping animations might be beneficial to your website, but if you overuse these technologies and they slow down your site, they could become detrimental.

Web browser plug-ins

The most popular Web browsers from Microsoft, Netscape, and Firefox are expandable and upgradeable using plug-ins. These are add-on programs Web surfers can download, usually for free, to enhance their Web-surfing capabilities.

From this chapter, you'll learn about some of the popular Web browser plug-ins. If someone has the RealPlayer plug-in from Real Networks (www.real.com) or Microsoft's Windows Media Player (www.microsoft.com), for example, they can listen to streaming audio or watch streaming video that's being broadcast from websites. (*Streaming* audio or video refers to broadcasts of audio, as if you were listening to the radio, or broadcasts of live-action video/TV footage over the Web.) Thus, if you decide to offer video or audio on your site, anyone with the RealPlayer

 Bright Idea

Before using technology in your website that requires plug-ins, make sure they're compatible with the popular browsers that your visitors will be using. To learn more about plug-ins endorsed by Netscape for its browser, visit http://browser.netscape.com/ns8/community/plugin.jsp. For details about Microsoft Explorer, visit http://support.microsoft.com/ie6.

Bright Idea

One quick and easy way to add streaming audio to your website is to use the tools provided by www.mp3soundstream.com. To easily add streaming video to your site, check out the tools offered by www.instantvideocreator.com.

or Windows Media Player plug-in, for example, will be able to hear the audio and see your video content automatically. Some of the popular Web browser plug-ins you can take advantage of to create rich multimedia content are discussed here.

Macromedia Flash

When it comes to adding eye-catching animation to your website, the most widely used application to create these animations is Macromedia's Flash MX ($499; www.macromedia.com). This is a commercially available software application that enables you to design fancy animated effects that compress to become extremely small graphic files. This translates into ultra-quick load times for Web surfers.

Flash takes some time to learn, but the results can be very impressive. The Macromedia Studio MX application suite ($899) offers a wide range of website-development tools for creating professional-looking sites using Flash.

Your site can deliver effective Macromedia Flash experiences across desktops and devices equipped with Macromedia Flash Player, a free Web browser download that's already installed on more than 97 percent of the Internet-enabled personal computers and Web-surfing devices—that's 600 million computers. The Flash Player plug-in is installed by more than two million new Web surfers everyday.

For more information about this technology and how website designers and e-commerce business operators are using it, download *The Flash Platform White Paper* (www.macromedia. com/platform/whitepapers/platform_overview.pdf), a free, 32-page document.

Bright Idea

One of the easiest ways to add pizzazz to your website easily is to incorporate colorful and detailed photographs, such as product shots. Instead of just taking a generic-looking shot, add some creativity to your photos. Become proficient with using a photo-editing program, such as Adobe Photoshop CS2 or Photoshop Elements, and you'll be able to make your photos jump off the page visually. Every website operator definitely should have a version of Photoshop in their software library.

Adobe Acrobat and Reader

Most Web surfers have access to color inkjet printers or black-and-white laser printers. If you have a traditional printed product brochure that you use as a powerful sales tool, you can convert the brochure to an electronic file in the Adobe Portable Document Format (PDF) and offer it on your site to anyone with the Adobe Reader plug-in (www.adobe.com/prodindex/acrobat).

To create a PDF file, you'll need to use Adobe's Acrobat application, which is a commercially available software package (available from Adobe at www.adobe.com). Web surfers can then read PDF files created using this software by downloading the free Adobe Reader or Adobe eBook Reader. These are extremely common Web browser plug-ins, which an ever-growing number of Web surfers and computer users already have.

Using the Reader plug-in, visitors can quickly download your PDF files and view them on their computer screens or print them in the exact format in which they were originally created. In other words, your printed brochure can be transferred electronically to Web surfers and used as a powerful sales tool in conjunction with your website.

Acrobat lets you convert any document (created electronically or scanned into a computer) into a PDF file, with its original appearance preserved. You can then distribute it for viewing and printing on any system.

Adobe PDF is the standard for electronic document distribution worldwide. PDF is a universal file format that preserves all of the fonts, formatting, colors, and graphics of any source document, regardless of the application and platform used to create it. PDF files are also compact.

According to Adobe, PDF also offers the following benefits:

- PDF files can be published and distributed anywhere: in print, attached to e-mail, on corporate servers, posted on websites, or on CD-ROM. They're also compatible with many PDAs and some Smartphones.

- Adobe has distributed more than half a billion copies of Adobe Reader since its 1993 introduction.

- Compact PDF files are smaller than their source files and download a page at a time for fast display on the Web.

- Using Adobe Acrobat software, bookmarks, cross-document links, Web links, live forms, security options, sound, and video can be added to PDF files for enhanced online viewing.

RealNetworks' RealPlayer

RealNetworks (www.real.com) lets you "broadcast" audio and video over the Internet. This company develops and markets software products and services to help PC users send and receive audio, video, and other multimedia services using the Web.

 Moneysaver

Acrobat Reader, Flash Player, RealPlayer, Shockwave, and QuickTime are free, easy-to-download browser plug-ins that can be freely distributed by anyone.

RealPlayer and Microsoft's Windows Media Player are the most popular applications for playing real-time or streaming media on the Web. These plug-ins work with any speed Internet connection, although surfers with a broadband or DSL connection will better benefit from the multimedia streaming capabilities of these applications.

> **66** RealNetworks, Inc. is the leading creator of digital media services and software, including the award-winning Rhapsody Internet jukebox service and RealPlayer, the first product to integrate finding, organizing, buying, playing, and managing digital audio and video in a single product. **99**
>
> —RealNetworks, Inc.

Apple's QuickTime

Like RealPlayer or Windows Media Player, QuickTime is another popular way for Web surfers to view streaming audio and video via the Internet. Applications developed by Apple Computer allow website designers to easily and inexpensively incorporate streaming video and audio into their websites.

According to Apple Computer, the developer of this format, "At its simplest, QuickTime is software that allows Mac and Windows users to play back audio and video on their computers. But taking a deeper look, QuickTime is many things: a file format, an environment for media authoring, and a suite of applications." These applications include the following:

- **QuickTime Player**—A free download for playing back audio and video files.
- **QuickTime Pro**—A commercially available software package for flexible multimedia authoring.
- **Browser plug-ins**—for viewing media within a Web page.
- **PictureViewer**—for working with still images. (Windows only; Preview is available on Mac OS X.)

Bright Idea

To discover how to incorporate QuickTime video into your website, read the tutorials offered by QuickTime's creators by going to www.apple.com/quicktime.

- **QuickTime Streaming Server**—Open-source streaming server for delivering streaming media files on the Internet in real time.

- **Darwin Streaming Server**—for delivering streaming media with Linux, Solaris, and Windows.

- **QuickTime Broadcaster**—for delivering live events on the Internet (free download).

- **MPEG-2 Playback Component**—for playing back MPEG-2 content (requires separate purchase).

Apple reports, "When you distribute your media in QuickTime, you automatically gain access to a massive platform. Available for Windows and Mac, QuickTime 6 was downloaded more than 350 million times. Moreover, 98 percent of those downloads were from PC users, at a rate of over 10 million per month. QuickTime offers a mature platform with thousands of professional and consumer authoring applications."

Shockwave

According to Macromedia, Shockwave lets you view interactive Web content such as games, business presentations, entertainment, and advertisements from your Web browser. It's similar to Flash in that it allows you to create animated content, but in this case, when you use Shockwave, the content can be interactive.

Shockwave (www.macromedia.com/shockwave) has been incorporated into thousands of websites. It's readily available, and easy to download and distribute. Shockwave attracts visitors, engages them, and brings them back often.

As of mid-2005, more than 390 million Web users have installed Macromedia Shockwave Player for use with their browsers. These people have access to some of the best the Web has to offer, including dazzling 3-D games and entertainment, interactive product demonstrations, and online learning applications. Shockwave Player displays Web content created by Macromedia Director software ($399; www.macromedia.com/software/director). You can download a free, 30-day trial version of the Director software from the company's website. The Shockwave Player is a free download/Web browser plug-in that's available to anyone.

Chatting within your site

Online chat rooms enable you to transform a basic website into a virtual interactive community. Using this technology, companies can communicate in real-time with their customers to answer sales questions or provide technical support on a one-on-one basis.

Through a chat room, customers can also communicate with each other in real-time. Depending on the type of online-based business you're seeking to establish, adding chat capabilities to your website could be used as a way to encourage visitors to keep returning to your site. Chat rooms can be used for virtual meetings, live training, conferencing, distance learning, moderated events, and social chat.

Some ISPs and website-design software applications offer chat-room functionality; but for website designers, this is typically an add-on application. Chat applications can also be custom-programmed into a site using Java, PHP, and/or CGI scripts, but this requires programming knowledge.

For a monthly fee, many companies host chat services for existing websites, including the following:

Live2Support	www.live2support.com
Everywhere Chat	www.everywherechat.com/addchat.htm
Bold Chat Plus	www.boldchatplus.com/features.jsp
Free Java Chat	www.freejavachat.com
Hotscripts	www.Hotscripts.com

Beware! Not everyone uses plug-ins

The problem with designing a website that requires someone to have special plug-ins is that not everyone has or wants these Web browser add-ons.

Although millions of Web surfers—especially those with high-speed connections and the latest version of the popular Web browsers—already have the most popular plug-ins, requiring less-savvy visitors to have them when they visit your site might discourage them from spending time exploring your site and receiving whatever sales or promotional messages you're attempting to convey.

One popular option for online businesses who want to address the needs of all visitors is to create two versions of their website—one that features Flash animations and requires plug-ins and one version that's created using just HTML programming, which all browsers can display properly. The first time the visitor comes to your site, they can either choose which version of the site they wish to view, or the site can be programmed to detect plug-ins automatically and display the appropriate content.

The Internet is an extremely unique marketing tool. You have at your disposal the ability to communicate in many ways, using the printed word, full-color photos, and graphics (like you'd see in a newspaper or magazine, on a billboard, or within a printed product brochure). Also at your disposal are animated graphics, video, and audio (like you'd see on television or hear on the radio). Unlike any other form of media, however, these communication methods can be combined in whatever way you see fit to capture your visitor's attention and sell your product.

 Bright Idea

Consider using hyperlinks throughout your Web pages. This enables visitors to your site to roam, explore, and gather the information they're interested in, all at their own pace.

What's more, the Internet is interactive. You're not limited to a 30- or 60-second time period to get your sales pitch across, nor are you confined to a specific-size print ad to convey your messages.

It's your job to offer an online environment that provides the information your visitors are looking for using the best possible communication tools. You must decide whether you can convey your message best using text, still graphics (such as line art and logos), photographs, animated graphics, audio clips, video clips, or a combination of these elements.

Using Java applets and other graphic technologies

Most text- and graphic-based Web pages that don't contain anything fancy are created using only *HyperText Markup Language (HTML)* programming. HTML is a page-description language that determines the position of Web-page elements on the actual page. In order to make the Internet more interactive and give webmasters the opportunity to add functionality to their sites, an actual programming language for the Web, called Java, was created by Sun Microsystems.

> **❝** Java is a programming language expressly designed for use in the distributed environment of the Internet. It was designed to have the 'look and feel' of the C++ language, but it is simpler to use than C++ and enforces a completely [object-oriented] view of programming. **❞**
>
> —Whatis.com

Most Web pages that incorporate Java applications, called applets, do so to add special features to their site. Whereas someone with no programming knowledge can create a website using a software package that automatically produces HTML programming based on a point-and-click, drag-and-drop user interface, adding Java applets to a Web page is a bit trickier for someone

who doesn't know the programming language. Many websites, however, offer hundreds of free, prewritten Java applets that you can download and incorporate into your site. This requires only minimal knowledge of Java, unless you choose to customize the applets you download.

To find prewritten freeware or shareware Java applets you can add to your Web page, using any search engine, enter the search phrase "Java applet." A few sites that offer free Java applets for download include the following:

Java Boutique	http://javaboutique.internet.com
Freeware Java.com	www.freewarejava.com
Java.Sun.com	www.java.sun.com/applets/index.html

The official website for Sun Microsystems (www.java.sun.com/openstudio/guide.html), the creators of Java, is an excellent resource for learning more about this programming language and how you can use Java on your website. On this site you'll find informative FAQs, tutorials, downloadable applets, and hundreds of links to other relevant sites.

According to Sun's website, "Adding applets to your site is much like adding images. The page on which you wish to present the applet needs to reference the location of the applet code. Applet code filenames end with the *.class* extension. You must also have the xxx.class file located in the same directory as the HTML file which is calling it."

Programming using Java is a bit more complicated than HTML, but the capabilities of this language are far greater. If you're interested in incorporating Java applets into your site, it's a good idea to familiarize yourself with this programming language first or to hire a freelance programmer who knows how to add Java applications into a website seamlessly.

How do Java applets benefit your site? Some of the common Java applets for websites include the following:

▪ Hit counters
▪ Clocks

- Animated ticker displays (for displaying custom text messages)
- Animated LED signs
- Text animation and special effects
- Interactive games
- The ability to add search capabilities to your site
- Password protection for your site (or parts of it)
- The ability to collect information or take quick polls
- A real-time calculator
- Display of a "slide show" of images

Should your site use cookies?

There's been a lot of hype about how companies using the Internet to conduct business are using cookies as a way to invade people's privacy. Much of this hype is based on a misconception about what cookies actually do and what they're capable of. In reality, a legitimate online business can use cookies to make visitors' experiences on their website less troublesome, especially if they return to the site often.

Whatis.com (www.whatis.com) describes a *cookie* as "A special file that a website puts on your hard disk so that it can remember something about you at a later time. Typically, a cookie records your preferences when using a particular site. Using the Web's Hypertext Transfer Protocol (HTTP), each request for a

> 66 A cookie is a piece of information sent to a browser by a Web server. The browser then returns that information to the Web server. This is how some Web pages "remember" your previous visits; for example, an e-commerce site might use a cookie to remember which items you've placed in your online shopping cart. Cookies can also store user preference information, log-in data, etc. 99
>
> —Verio.Com

Bright Idea

Novice Web surfers have often heard a lot of negative information about cookies and how they're used to capture and disseminate private information about them. Web surfers, however don't have to fear cookies. A cookie is just text, not a spyware program or a virus. If you'll be using cookies on your website to capture information, explain how they're used by publishing a Privacy Statement on your site.

Web page is independent of all other requests. For this reason, the Web-page server has no memory of what pages it has sent to a user previously or anything about your previous visits. A cookie is a mechanism that allows the server to store its own file about a user on the user's computer. The file [may be] stored in a subdirectory of the browser directory (for example, as a subdirectory under the Netscape directory). The cookie subdirectory will contain a cookie file for each website you've been to that uses cookies. Cookies can be used to customize the pages sent to you based on your browser type or other information you may have provided the website. Web users must agree to let cookies be saved for them, but, in general, it helps websites to serve users better."

For someone interested in learning more about cookies, David Whalen's *The Unofficial Cookie FAQ* (www.cookiecentral.com/faq), an electronic document not affiliated with Wiley's *Unofficial Guides,* is a useful resource. This document states, "Cookies are a very useful tool in maintaining state variables on the Web. Since HTTP is a 'stateless' (non-persistent) protocol, it is impossible to differentiate between visits to a website, unless the server can somehow 'mark' a visitor. This is done by storing a piece of information in the visitor's browser. Cookies can store database information, custom page settings, or just about anything that would make a site customizable. An analogy I like to use is that cookies are very much like a laundry 'claim-check' of sorts. You drop something off, and get a ticket. When you return with the ticket, you get that same something back. A cookie is simply an HTTP header that consists of a text-only string that gets entered into the memory of a browser. This string contains the domain, path, lifetime, and value of a variable that a website sets. If the lifetime of this variable is longer than the time the user spends at that site, then this string is saved to file for future reference."

There are many reasons a given site would want to use cookies. These range from the ability to personalize information, or to help with online sales/services, or simply for the purposes of tracking popular links or demographics. Cookies also provide programmers with a quick and convenient means of keeping site content fresh and relevant to the user's interests.

One of the most popular features of Amazon.com (www.amazon.com) is the "1-Click Ordering" feature. After you enter your personal information once (such as name, address, phone number, e-mail address, and credit-card information), you can then return to the site anytime and Amazon.com knows exactly who you are, your buying history on the site, and what your preferences are. Now, when you find a book you want to order, you simply click the mouse on the 1-Click Ordering icon, and that book will be automatically shipped to you. There's no need for visitors to keep having to fill out electronic order forms each time they place an order.

Many of the search engines/information portals also use cookies to allow visitors to customize their main pages. Once someone fills out the online questionnaire for My Yahoo!, for example, each subsequent time they visit Yahoo!, the service will display customized news, weather, stock market and sports reports, entertainment news, and local lottery numbers, and display only personalized information the visitor specifically requested.

 Watch Out!

Many Web surfers don't truly understand what cookies are all about. As a result, they have set their Web-browser software to ignore cookies and avoid accepting them. When a user does this, any uses your website has involving cookies won't work.

Bright Idea

Based on the type of online business you're looking to establish, if you're planning to have customers return to your site often or place multiple orders over time, using cookies is one way to make their visits to your site easier and make ordering more convenient.

Paying attention to download times

One of the best ways to determine which Internet technologies and features you want to incorporate into your website is to spend time surfing the Net and see how other companies are using these technologies to their advantage. Adding these technologies might make your site look absolutely fantastic, but for those Web surfers who will visit your site using a dial-up connection, the fancy eye candy can dramatically slow down their surfing experience.

The more "cool" stuff you add to your site, the longer it will take for your site to download. For surfers using a DSL or broadband connection, download times aren't as big of an issue. As an online business owner, you need to determine whether the majority of your visitors are savvy Web surfers with high-speed connections, or whether they're primarily using a dial-up connection to reach your website. This information alone can help you determine what types of fancy bells and whistles to add to your website.

When it comes to e-commerce and keeping people's attention on the Web, long download times are an absolute no-no! If someone has to wait more than 20 seconds for a Web page to load, chances are they won't have the patience to wait and will surf elsewhere. Optimize your site to achieve the fastest possible downloading time.

Photographs and graphics with lots of color fields, and particularly colors that blend and fade into one another, are best served by using graphic images saved in the popular JPEG format. If, on the other hand, your image has flat color fields, it will compress well in the GIF format.

Bright Idea

Many e-commerce websites use product photos to demonstrate to a customer exactly what they'll be purchasing, since they can't physically touch or see the item itself. Some companies, however, are very creative in how they used graphics to sell their products. For example, Life Is Good (www.LifeIsGood.com) is a trendy clothing company that uses graphic images, not photographs, to showcase its products in a unique way on its website.

The best way to determine the download time of your site is to connect to the Internet using a dial-up connection, a DLS connection, and then a broadband connection.

Next, grab a stopwatch. From a search engine, time exactly how long it takes for your site to download once you enter the URL into your browser software. Between tests, be sure to clear your "Internet Temporary Files" subdirectory on your hard drive so that your later download times won't be misleadingly fast.

Take note of what graphic images or aspects of your site take the longest to load, and see what you can do to speed things up. You might consider reducing the size of your graphic images, reducing the number of animations on each page, and deleting all unnecessary graphics.

Website optimization is a service many professional website designers and even some ISPs offer. Your site will be evaluated and then sped up using various types of compression technology. These services will also ensure that you have no dead links on your site and that your meta tags are being used properly.

Web Site Optimization (www.websiteoptimization.com), Site Report Card (http://sitereportcard.com), and Net Mechanic (http://netmechanic.com) are examples of companies that offer this type of service.

Test browser compatibility

As you test your website before making it available to the public, make sure it's totally compatible with all of the popular Web browsers—Microsoft Internet Explorer, Netscape Navigator, Firefox, and AOL's browser.

The best way to do this is to load each of these browsers into your computer and then surf around your website using them. Pay careful attention to the formatting of your site. Make sure it looks the same with each browser. You might find subtle compatibility differences, especially when it comes to fonts, colors, and overall page layout.

Also, pay attention to the graphics resolution your Web browser displays. If you have a higher-end computer, it's most likely capable of displaying higher-resolution graphics. Those same graphics will look very different to someone using a less-advanced graphics card and monitor (viewing your site at 800 × 600 resolution, as opposed to 1024 × 768, for example). The most common graphic resolutions used by average Web surfers are 800 × 600 (for people using low-end computers) or 1024 × 768 (for Web surfers using more powerful computers). The following website will help you better understand how to adjust your website to display properly at the most commonly used graphic resolutions: www.boutell.com/newfaq/creating/resolution.html.

Giving visitors something of value

The purpose of any online-based business is to sell products directly over the Web. The goal of a business is, of course, to make money. As you've probably figured out by now, the Internet is like no other sales tool/advertising medium in existence because of its interactive and information-on-demand nature.

 Bright Idea

As an online business operator, it's important to become familiar with all of the popular browser programs surfers will use to access your website. To learn about the Firefox Web browser and available plug-ins, visit www.firefox.com. As of mid-2005, Firefox was being used by more than 65 million Web surfers. This award-winning browser supports almost all of the same plug-ins as Explorer and Navigator.

By offering something Web surfers are interested in, you'll most likely be able to generate traffic to your site; the trick, however, is to keep them there long enough so that you can sell them your product. Using the various Web technologies described in this chapter can help you create a website that's visually appealing, highly engaging, interactive, and exciting.

Although the look, layout/design, and user interface of your site are all important, the other key ingredient of a successful site is providing information that your visitors want.

Only by providing information that's unique, informative, timely, and considered valuable to your visitors will they be encouraged to stay on your site, explore it, and then return to it often. Thus, it's important to regularly update the content and even the look of your site. As you determine ways to keep the content of your site fresh, keep trying to make your site more of a valuable information resource, where someone can go for accurate and timely information about your product.

Depending on the type of online business you'll be creating, consider offering something of value on your site for free. Many e-commerce sites that sell software packages, for example, offer free 30-day trial versions of their software. Companies that sell products online but ship them to customers via a traditional courier sometimes offer free shipping or some type of value-added incentive for shopping online.

Shoppers love receiving free gifts! In Chapter 16, you'll read about Louisdog.com and how that website offers free gifts to its frequent shoppers as an incentive to keep people coming back.

 Bright Idea

To make your customers more comfortable shopping online from your site, it's an excellent strategy to offer a 30-day trial. This means they can return the product, with no questions asked, within 30 days for a full refund. This is one way to build credibility among new customers because you're taking some of the risk out of making a purchase.

Bright Idea

Throughout this book, hundreds of URLs are listed where you can go for additional information about specific topics. As part of your research as you gear up to launch an online business, spend time visiting these and other sites to learn about the e-commerce industry and the potential capabilities of your website.

Offering free information in the form of a newsletter or "how-to" articles/tutorials is also a viable option. Using your website to offer something that visitors to your site perceive as valuable (whether it's information or something tangible) will help keep their attention and help you build consumer confidence. Contests (with prizes) and money-saving promotions (such as holiday sales) also work well.

Combining valuable and informative content with a sales pitch for your product and the ability to place orders securely online are important elements of a successful e-commerce site. Using the various Internet technologies described in this chapter to help you convey your information can help you transform a basic website into a powerful marketing and sales tool.

Think before you act

Before you spend countless hours (and dollars) adding a bunch of really cool features to your website in order to improve its "look," consider the following:

- Who is your target audience? Unless you're catering to the relatively small group of highly computer-literate, Internet-savvy Web surfers, think twice about incorporating technology into your site that might be difficult for average visitors to figure out. Also be careful of technologies the average user might not have the necessary browser plug-ins to use.

- Does the Web technology you plan to incorporate into your site help sell your product? Does it serve a definite purpose, or is it there just to make your site look flashy?

- Does the Web technology or graphics incorporated into your site slow down downloading time dramatically? What is the average download time of your site for someone surfing the Web using a dial-up connection?

- What can you do to better optimize your site and improve download times? When it comes to surfing the Web, speed is critical!

As you plan and ultimately create your site, stay focused on conveying your message and achieving your goal of generating business and orders. Although it's vital that your site have a professional appearance, don't get caught up in all of the exciting technologies at your disposal and incorporate them into your site simply to add pizzazz. Use only the technologies you need to achieve your ultimate goals.

Look to the future . . . wait, it's already here!

In addition to the website-design technologies described in this book, there are countless others now in development. As more and more people tap the power of high-speed Internet connections, the demand for rich, interactive content grows. New technologies and tools to provide this innovative content are always being created.

For example, as this book was being written, eBay.com announced plans to launch a service called ProStores (www. prostores.com/product-information.shtml) that's similar to the e-commerce turnkey solution offered by Yahoo! Stores. (See Chapters 4 and 14 for details.)

As a website designer and online business operator, one of your many jobs will be to keep your finger on the pulse of these new technologies and to determine how they can help your online business grow and become more profitable.

These days, people don't just surf the Web from their desktop computers while at home or at work. Internet cafés have sprung up across America, plus public Internet access is readily

Bright Idea

If you're using a turnkey solution to design and host your e-commerce website, make sure it's fully compatible with the technologies described in this chapter so that you can add animations, streaming audio or video, PDF files, and other rich content to your website now or in the future.

available in schools and libraries. Furthermore, thanks to Wi-Fi (wireless Internet technology), coffee shops, hotels, airports, libraries and bookstores, for example, provide Wi-Fi hot spots for people looking to surf the Web wirelessly using their laptop computers and wireless PDAs.

Virtually all of the new home video game systems from Nintendo, Sony, and Microsoft (including consoles that connect to a traditional television set and the handheld systems) can now connect to the World Wide Web.

Millions of people also now surf the Web using their cellular phones, Smartphones, or wireless PDAs (personal digital assistants). These handheld devices offer smaller, but full-color screens. As a result, some forward-thinking online business operators have begun creating specialized websites and content that cater to cell phone, Smartphone, and wireless PDA users who enjoy surfing the Web from these handheld devices.

The speed at which cell phone wireless networks allow surfers to explore the Web is quickly improving, thanks in part to the new 3G wireless networks. We've recently seen companies, such as Sprint PCS, begin offering streaming audio and video directly to Web-enabled cell phones.

New technology continues to bring more and more Web surfers online, thus broadening your potential customer base as an online business operator. As your company grows, it's important to keep up with these latest technologies to ensure that you're able to provide your (potential) customers with the products and services they're looking for, exactly when and where they're wanted and needed.

Bright Idea

If a large graphic, in terms of file size (such as a product shot), is absolutely necessary, consider using a small thumbnail image on your main Web pages and let the visitors click on the image if they want to see a slower-loading, but larger and more detailed image.

Just the facts

- Use the fancy features described in this chapter only if they'll help your site achieve its objective—to sell your product.

- The most popular Web browsers, from Microsoft, Netscape, and Firefox, are expandable and upgradeable using plug-ins. These are add-on programs Web surfers can download, usually for free, to enhance their Web-surfing capabilities.

- Java was created by Sun Microsystems. Using Java, you can create and use special applets in your site.

- When it comes to incorporating animation and visual effects into your site, Flash, from Macromedia, is definitely the way to go.

- Long download times can easily cause you to lose people's attention on the Web.

- By offering something Web surfers are interested in, you'll most likely be able to generate traffic to your site.

GET THE SCOOP ON...
Final steps ▪ How visitors see your site ▪
Soliciting feedback ▪ Updating your site

Analyzing Your Site

Chapter 13

O kay, you're nearing the end of the planning, design, and website-creation phase. You're almost ready to open for business by publishing your site and going online. At this point, you should be preparing to launch your promotional and marketing efforts for your site, keeping in mind that these efforts might take several weeks to kick in.

Before going online, however, it's important to review your site carefully to determine that everything is how it should be and that it conveys a highly professional image. Visitors to your site should find all of the content informative, easy to find, and valuable. At the same time, the site should help to build your company, product, or service's brand and overall image, and it should make visitors feel comfortable with making a purchase online (if your online business is set up for e-commerce).

Use the following last-minute checklist to make sure you've dealt appropriately with many of the details regarding the creation of your site.

Pre-grand opening checklist

Take advantage of the following actions *before* opening your site to the public. The order in which you tackle each of these tasks isn't important, as long as they're all completed before your site goes live.

❑ Use a spell checker and have the site proofread by multiple people who have a flair for writing to ensure that the entire site contains no spelling, punctuation, or grammatical errors.

❑ Review the actual content of your site to ensure that all information is factually correct. This includes checking product numbers, making sure that all photos and artwork correspond to the proper product descriptions, and verifying that all prices are listed correctly.

❑ Check all links within your site to ensure that they lead visitors to the appropriate locations. It's extremely unprofessional for your site to have *dead links*—that is, links to Web pages or sites that are not operational. If your visitor clicks a dead link, they'll receive an annoying error message.

❑ Review the online order forms/shopping-cart features of your site to be certain you'll be obtaining all the information you need from customers to process their orders.

❑ Make sure your company's phone number, fax number, mailing address, and e-mail address appear prominently within the site, and that all of this information is listed correctly.

❑ Using several different-speed Internet connections (including a dial-up connection, DSL, and broadband), visit your site several times and check the download time for each page. If download times are long, determine ways to reduce them whenever possible (using GIF/JPEG file-compression utilities, for example). Web pages that take more than 20 seconds to download lose more than 50 percent of their potential visitors.

❑ Try accessing your site using different versions of the popular Internet browsers, including Microsoft Internet Explorer, Netscape Navigator, AOL's browser, and Firefox. The site should look consistent using all of these browser programs. Make sure you've used a Web-safe color palette and that all colors and graphics appear as they should using each browser program. How this is done is described in greater detail within Chapter 4.

❑ Pretend you're a shopper and place a number of sample orders. For example, place an order for a single product, and then for multiple products. Enter a separate "ship-to" and "bill-to" address for each. Experiment with all of the various options, in different combinations, to ensure that everything works properly.

❑ Make sure the text on your site is written in easy-to-understand language and will appeal to people with extremely short attention spans. Be sure to limit the length of your text. Keep word counts below 800 words per page.

❑ Find a group of people not directly involved with the creation of the website to test it before it actually goes online. These people should not necessarily be highly computer literate; you want to make sure they find it easy to navigate through the site. Pay careful attention to the feedback these people offer. Be sure you communicate to your testers exactly what the purpose of your site is and what it's supposed to offer. This will help them determine whether what you've created lives up to the overall objective of the site.

❑ Ask your site's testers specific questions about the site's content, the ease of navigation, the layout and design of the site, and the look of the site (such as the text and background colors, or the fonts and typestyles used). Do they feel anything is missing from the site? Ask specific questions to generate feedback that will be useful for improving the site before it actually goes online.

Watch Out!

Be sure to use plenty of white space, graphics, and different type sizes to create visually appealing pages on your website. The actual text should be displayed in an easy-to-read font and a good-size typestyle (no smaller than 10-point type for the main text).

❑ Make sure your site has a "Search" feature, which allows a visitor to find the information they're looking for quickly by entering a keyword, search phrase, product name, or product number.

❑ Give your testers specific assignments while they're online and measure how long it takes them to accomplish those assignments. For example, ask them to find a specific product on your site, place an order for that product, and then request it to be shipped as a gift to someone else. Are average Web surfers able to do this with ease?

❑ Make sure you have ample inventory in place and that you have your "shipping department" ready to process orders. This includes ensuring that you understand how to process credit-card orders using your merchant account (or PayPal).

❑ Obviously, once your site is ready to go online, register it with all of the major search engines. Nearly 85 percent of the visitors to most websites find their destinations using a search engine. You can create and launch a keyword-based ad campaign on the search engines in less than 30 minutes, using Googles AdWords or Yahoo! Search Marketing.

Make sure you have your site's testers document (in writing) all of the problems they encounter. This will help you fix the problems quickly. Also, provide them with a questionnaire that addresses specific issues you're concerned with.

If you find your testers are having problems placing orders or finding specific information on your site, or if they seem to be losing interest in your site quickly, consider revamping before going online. Remember that old saying, "You only get one chance to make a first impression." If you go online and the people who visit your site early aren't impressed, don't count on them ever returning. Don't be so anxious to go online that you put off fixing the major problems with your site and addressing the criticisms your testers offer.

Determining how your site is perceived

Now that the site is actually ready to go online, using feedback from your testers, make sure the site actually lives up to your goals. When someone visits your site, will they believe they're dealing with a highly professional and reputable company? Will they feel comfortable placing orders online? Does your site offer them information they want and are looking for?

In addition to using testers, there arc many website traffic tracking services and software packages you can use to determine exactly who is visiting your site, where they came from, what they did while surfing your site, and so forth. WebTrends Corporation (www.webtrends.com), for example, is one of many companies offering software packages designed to track and analyze website traffic information. Many of the turnkey services described in this book—including those from Yahoo!, GoDaddy.com, Clickincome.com, and eBay—offer traffic tracking and analysis as part of their suite of site-management applications and programs.

By analyzing traffic to your site, you'll discover who's actually visiting and why. This will enable you to better target your actual visitors (potential customers and customers) as opposed to the

 Bright Idea

One way to find potential "testers" for your site is to contact some existing customers and offer them an incentive to visit your site. Consider offering them a substantial discount on their online purchases, holding a contest with a prize, or giving them something of value for their time and honest feedback.

people you initially perceived would be your customers when you were first planning your site. An article on Builder.com suggests

Gathering this information lets you develop, expand, and refine your content. If you discover that your audience is very different from what you originally anticipated, you can adjust your site's content, design, style, product line, and features to recapture the audience you originally sought or to satisfy the audience you've actually attracted. You can convince potential advertisers that your users are people who will be willing and able to buy their products. The more information you can supply—raw data, specific trends, and detailed facts—the more you can advertise to vertical markets.

> 66 The three most common motivations for analyzing Web traffic are business development, increasing marketing and advertising sales, and technical resource and capacity planning. 99
>
> —"Why Collect Statistics?" published on Builder.com (www.builder.com)

If you'll be selling advertising space on your site, you must be able to provide the advertiser with statistics about how much traffic each page of your site receives, when the peak times are, and who the primary audience is. If your site becomes very busy, it's important to track traffic to ensure that your servers (or the ISP you're using) can handle the traffic and that visitors can access your site whenever they choose—even during peak periods. Having insufficient bandwidth or capacity will result in the loss of customers.

Soliciting comments and feedback from visitors

Even after your site goes online, it is and will always be a work in progress. Because you and anyone working for you will be extremely close to your business emotionally, it's easy for you to lose track of what's really happening on your site in terms of how people perceive your online-based business.

It's important to constantly seek out feedback from people not directly associated with the operation of your business—ideally, members of your target market. Actively soliciting comments, ideas, and suggestions relating to your site (and offering a reward for people who share their thoughts) is one way to conduct market research that will provide valuable insight into what people really think of your site.

On your site, develop a short survey asking questions such as what visitors liked about the site, what problems they experienced while exploring the site, and what could be added to improve the site. In exchange for this feedback, offer free shipping, a discount on the visitor's next order, or something else of value.

Another more obvious approach is to focus on the people's actions. Examine what parts of your site are visited the most and which areas of your site are receiving less traffic. If you receive complaints that a product offered on your site was misrepresented, for example, consider rewriting the product description in order to make it more accurate. Perhaps you're in need of more detailed product photos.

If someone calls your business on the phone to place an order, but mentions that they first visited your website, while taking the phone order, ask why the person chose to call instead of placing their order online. Listen carefully to the response, and don't be afraid to ask a follow-up question, if necessary. Your goal is to find out whether the Web visitors trust your site enough to place orders directly on it, and if not, why not.

 Bright Idea

If you receive positive feedback from customers, post it directly on your site for others to read, but don't attribute it without permission. Some people are very touchy about having their praise for a product posted. Many companies use just the first name and city/state of their customer when quoting them.

Finally, learn from other people's mistakes. As you surf the Web looking at other sites, take detailed notes when you visit a site that simply doesn't work, and be sure to do things differently on your site. In addition, Chapters 15 and 16 offer interviews with e-commerce experts offering advice on pitfalls to avoid as you launch your online business.

Keeping your site's content fresh

Repeat business is one of the ways you'll generate long-term revenue. Thus, in addition to offering top-notch customer service, providing personalized attention to customers when it's needed, and making visitors to your site feel welcome, it's important to encourage them to return to your site often.

One of the best ways to keep people coming back is to constantly update the content of your site. Depending on the type of business you're operating, this might mean including information on new products, posting news-related announcements about your industry, holding weekly contests, and so forth. In addition, consider giving your site a major design overhaul at least once or twice a year.

No matter how successful your online-based business becomes, always think about new features, services, types of information, or content you can add that will increase the overall value of the site, make it easier to use, and make it more enjoyable for the visitors.

If you visit any retail store or department store, you'll notice that displays change regularly. This is to ensure that customers keep coming back to see what's new. Changing the look and

 Watch Out!

One of the worst long-term mistakes you can make as an online business operator is to simply leave your website's content the same. Look for opportunities to change or update your site in creative ways. If it's appropriate, offer special content, sales, or promotions focused around upcoming holidays.

content of your site will have the same impact on customers, encouraging them to return.

Just the facts

- Visitors to your site should find the content informative, easy to find, and intuitive, and they should feel comfortable making a purchase online.

- Before going online, review the checklist in this chapter to make sure your site is 100 percent error-free and user-friendly.

- Try accessing your site using different browsers.

- Find a group of people not directly involved with the creation of your website to test it before it goes online.

- Constantly seek out feedback from people not directly associated with the operation of your business—ideally, members of your target market.

- Once your online business is open to the public, you'll want to analyze your traffic and fine-tune the site's content and design on an ongoing basis.

PART VI

The Experts Speak

GET THE SCOOP ON...
Launching auctions in minutes ▪ Testing demand
for your product(s) ▪ Creating an eBay Store ▪
Secrets for earning auction profits ▪ eBay's
ProStores

Doing Business the eBay Way

Chapter 14

With more than 45 million active registered users in the U.S. alone (135.5 million worldwide) and an average of 29 million auctions taking place at any given moment, eBay has become the Internet's hub for individuals and businesses interested in buying and selling virtually anything through online-based auctions.

When it was established in 1995 as "AuctionWeb," this online service quickly made e-commerce something virtually anyone could participate in quickly, cheaply, and easily, with no start-up costs or programming required. Since then, eBay has continued to expand and improve upon its array of auction-based services.

Recently, it also began offering ProStores (www.prostores.com), a turnkey e-commerce solution for online business operators that's similar to the offerings of Yahoo! Store.

For individuals and small businesses interested in auctions, eBay offers an inexpensive, one-stop shop

Bright Idea

Get free advice from eBay experts! For useful tips and strategies about launching and operating your online business venture, eBay offers a free newsletter. To subscribe, visit www.prostores.com/prostores-newsletter-form.shtml.

to quickly start earning online revenues. For those who get hooked on eBay, one can establish an eBay Store to sell almost any type of (legal) product using a combination of auction and "Buy It Now" techniques with a virtual storefront that's totally personalized with your company's branding. With an eBay Store you can also accept checks, money transfers, or credit cards as payment for goods sold, all within the eBay online environment.

As a precursor to launching your own e-commerce website or as an alternative or additional revenue stream, eBay offers the opportunity for people to buy and sell virtually anything online. You'll soon discover, however, that simply starting an eBay membership and putting items up for bid at auction isn't a guarantee for success or profits. Although many people consider buying and selling items on eBay to be their part-time or even full-time job, there are secrets you need to learn in order to truly profit from this online auction bonanza, the popularity of which has quickly spread across America and throughout the Internet-surfing world.

eBay auctions 101

For individuals looking to sell a small number of new or used items on eBay.com, simply setting up an account and posting a few auction listings might be enough to get your items sold, especially if your auction listings are well-written, are descriptive, and are accompanied by one or more product photos. (The more pictures you include, the better!) Generating a real profit on eBay, however, is a bit more challenging, due in part to the intense competition from other sellers.

There are many things to consider when setting yourself up as an eBay seller and creating your eBay account. For example, your user name (like a website domain name) says a lot about who you are. What's more important than your user name, however, is your feedback rating (and related feedback score). This ranking demonstrates to other eBay members exactly how credible you are because it's based on the experiences other members have had doing business with you.

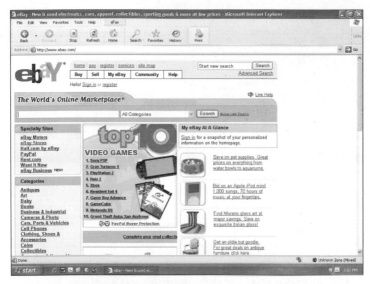

Figure 14.1. From eBay.com's main Web page, you can find and bid on millions of auction items or place your own items up for auction.

The reason for eBay's user-feedback system is clear. Unfortunately, although eBay can be a wonderful sales tool, the marketplace is not without its share of fraudulent activity. In some cases, for example, people have listed auctions and collected money for items that don't exist or that are purposely misrepresented (such as an item being described as a brand new, expensive designer handbag or watch with a retail price of hundreds of dollars, when really it is a cheap knockoff worth much less than the advertised price). These people use confidential P.O. Box addresses and untraceable e-mail addresses that make it very difficult for eBay or officials to track them down.

To create a sense of trust for their marketplace, eBay developed the feedback system. When someone gets burned on eBay, the buyer can post negative feedback for that seller. The more negative feedback someone receives, the lower the seller's feedback score goes.

> 66 Every day, more than 3.5 million new items are put up for auction on eBay.com. More than $1,000 worth of merchandise is sold every second. 99
>
> —eBay.com

As a seller on eBay, if you can effectively demonstrate that what you're selling is legitimate, it really is as described, it's something that's in demand by others, and you're offering it at a fair opening bid price, chances are you'll find people on eBay eager to bid on your products.

Even if you're selling just one item, when you become an eBay seller, you'll be conducting business online, which means you have to convey a highly professional image and attitude. Offering top-notch customer service and responding to questions from bidders in a timely manner is critical.

Reasons to use eBay

There are many ways to use eBay as a powerful tool if you're an owner of an established online or traditional business. You can do the following:

- Sell overstock, returned but saleable, or closeout items sitting in your inventory.

- Test interest for new products.

- Offer a sampling of your products via auction in hopes of generating traffic to your website and boosting awareness of what you're offering.

- Generate easier sales on eBay by selling original, hand-crafted, or exclusive items at auction that don't compete with the thousands of sellers offering more common products.

As you decide what to offer on eBay, there are several things to consider. First, you want to choose the right product(s) to sell. Ideally, you want to offer items that are profitable and that can be easily described using text and photos.

Suggested retail prices have little relevance on eBay. Thus, it's important to determine what items that are similar to yours actually sell on a regular basis on eBay and how much they typically sell for. In addition to simply monitoring other auctions, there are a variety of research tools available to help you figure out or accurately predict what an item will most likely sell for at auction.

> **66** More than 430,000 people in the United States have transformed buying and selling items on eBay into a part-time or full-time job. **99**
>
> —eBay.com

For those who are serious about selling items on eBay, Clickincome.com (www.clickincome.com) offers a powerful auction analysis tool exclusively to its registered customers, called Auction Analysis Pro. This software allows you to perform statistical research on eBay sales data instantly and make well-educated selling decisions.

Create effective product listings

Creating effective product listings on eBay is a skill that must be constantly fine-tuned. Your product descriptions need to be totally accurate, extremely detailed, and easy to understand. They also need to be sales-oriented and help you convey credibility to bidders. The use of product photos is also extremely important, as is the type(s) of listings you actually create.

Bright Idea

If you're new to eBay, start off by participating in a variety of auctions as a buyer to see how the whole process works. Try bidding on a handful of items offered by individuals as well as eBay Store merchants. Next, try selling a few items on eBay.

When you start listing items on eBay, you'll quickly discover that you have many options. Knowing which options to use and how to use them is important because each option costs extra and can dramatically increase your eBay listing fees. (eBay generates its revenue by charging listing fees for every item being put up for auction or being sold on its service.)

Although you want to keep your listing fees as low as possible (to ensure higher profits), to successfully sell your items, you need your listings to stand out.

How you'll accept payment from winning bidders is also an important factor to consider. Because eBay owns PayPal (www.paypal.com), this is often a preferred method of payment when using this service. As a seller, setting up a PayPal account (which is separate from your eBay account) enables you to accept major credit cards without a merchant account, plus it enables you to accept electronic check payments and electronic money transfers for your goods.

Of course, you can also accept personal checks, money orders, or cashier's checks, or set up your own credit-card merchant account in order to accept payments from your eBay bidders.

As you become well acquainted with how eBay works, you'll most likely discover ways you can use this service to help boost revenue and traffic for your existing e-commerce website or use the service to learn the basic fundamentals of running an online business before starting your own website.

eBay offers extensive online technical support in the form of "how-to" articles and tutorials to help anyone get started as a buyer or seller on the service.

Your feedback will make or break your reputation

If you want people to do business with you on eBay, it's critical to have a respectable feedback score and ratings. This demonstrates how reputable you are and how well you've dealt with your customers in the past.

According to the eBay.com website, "Feedback ratings are used to determine each member's feedback score. A positive rating adds one (1) to the score, a negative rating decreases it by one (1), and a neutral rating has no impact. The higher the feedback score, the more positive ratings the eBay member has received from other members. However, a member can increase or decrease another member's score by only one (1), no matter how many transactions they share." Thus, someone with a feedback score in the hundreds or thousands has been selling products successfully on eBay for a while and is considered reputable in the eBay community.

In conjunction with every item you put up for auction on eBay, part of your listing will include a link to your eBay profile. This profile displays basic information about you, including details about the feedback you've received. Feedback that other members leave about you automatically becomes a permanent addition to your profile.

To ensure that you receive positive feedback from the people you do business with on eBay, you can do multiple things:

- Make sure that what you're selling is exactly as described.
- Respond to all questions from eBay members promptly.
- Once an auction for an item you're selling ends, get in contact with the high bidder immediately and ship the product promptly once payment is received.

Watch Out!

Always be 100 percent truthful in your auction listings. If you attempt to deceive potential bidders, you'll wind up receiving negative feedback, costing potential revenue, and damaging your online reputation as a seller. For example, describing an item as "Brand New!" tends to mean unopened and in the original packaging, not "slightly used" with no original packaging.

- Make the buyer's experience as pleasant and easy as possible.
- After you've concluded your business transaction successfully, request that the buyer leave positive feedback for you.

Strategies for listing items for an eBay auction

Once you've set up your eBay account, placing an item up for auction takes just minutes. First, sign on to the eBay.com website using your unique username and password. From the site's home page, click on the "Sell" icon at the top of the screen, and then click on "Sell Your Item."

You'll be given the option to sell your item at auction or to sell it for a fixed price. Later in this chapter, you'll learn more about the different pricing options eBay auctions use.

As you begin creating your auction listings, carefully follow the prompts on the screen. Make sure that you accurately and completely provide the information you're promoted for.

Selecting your auction's category

Step one involves selecting the category under which your item will be listed. There are many categories to choose from. The onscreen "Browse Categories" feature will help you define the appropriate eBay category for what you're selling. Depending on the item, you could choose (for an additional fee) to list your item under a second category. As you'll discover, there are literally hundreds of narrowly defined categories to choose from.

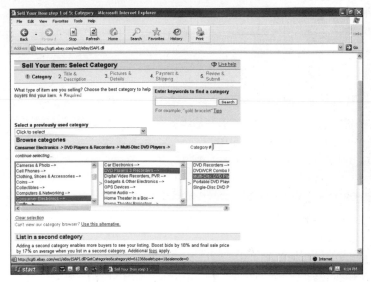

Figure 14.2. Listing an item for auction is an easy process that takes only a few minutes once your eBay account is set up. Simply fill out the onscreen questionnaire as completely as possible, choosing the listing options you want to use.

Giving your auction a title

Next, you'll be prompted to create the main title ("Item Title") for your auction listing. This title can be 55 characters long. The Item Title is what will initially catch the attention of potential bidders, so use catchy wording and your creativity to help ensure that your listing stands out.

For an additional fee, you can add a 55-character subtitle to your listing. When creating your title and subtitle, use descriptive words. For example, if the item is brand new and still in its

 Bright Idea

When creating an eBay auction listing, use your Title, Subtitle, Description, and Photo(s) to generate as much attention as possible. This will reduce the need for more costly add-ons, such as a listing with a border or bold typestyle.

original packaging, this is important to convey to bidders. Also, be sure to list the specific product name, product number, size, and color, if applicable. From the Item Title, people should know exactly what they'll be bidding on.

Create a detailed item description

The next step is to create a detailed "Item Description." Here, you can use full paragraphs of text, in a variety of fonts, type-styles, and sizes, to convey your sales message and describe exactly what you're selling. You can also format the text to look visually pleasing on the screen and incorporate graphics. As you create your description, accuracy and detail are extremely important. This is your chance to sell your item to bidders and make them want it! The description also needs to help set your listing apart from countless others.

Understanding eBay's pricing options

Every auction begins with a "Starting Price." This is the initial bid amount that you, the seller, get to set. The amount you list here should be the lowest you're willing to sell the item for. From the bidder's perspective, however, a low starting price will generate interest faster. Setting no minimum bid is also possible and could quickly generate interest among bidders, but you run the risk of losing money on the sale if the bidding doesn't reach your desired level. If your minimum bid is offered, you are obligated to sell the item for the highest bid price when the auction officially ends, even if it's your minimum bid price. If you

 Watch Out!

Although no confirmable statistics are available, reports and user complaints show that that some transactions on eBay are fraudulent. This means that the seller (who is in no way affiliated with eBay.com) has somehow misrepresented what they're offering to the public or is using the eBay service to somehow commit fraud or perpetuate a scam.

did not list a minimum bid, you're obligated to sell the product for whatever the highest bid is at the end of the action.

For an additional fee, as the seller, you can also set a "Reserve Price" for the item(s) you're selling on eBay. According to the eBay.com website, "A reserve price is the lowest price at which you are willing to sell your item. If a bidder does not meet that price, you're *not* obligated to sell your item. You set your reserve price, as well as a starting price, when you list your item.

"The reserve price is not disclosed to bidders, but they will be told that your auction has a reserve price and whether or not the reserve has been met."

> 66 In 2004, more than $2.2 billion in collectibles merchandise was sold on eBay.com. 99
> —*Entrepreneur* magazine (May 2005)

You, as the seller, can set a "Buy It Now" price when placing your listing. This is a price that you're willing to sell the item for immediately. If you're lucky enough to find a bidder who wants to purchase your item immediately and not wait around for the auction to end in order to see whether they're the high bidder, they can offer you the "Buy It Now" price. The first bidder willing to pay the "Buy It Now" price wins the auction. There's an additional fee to register a "Buy It Now" price with your listing.

Auctions have a duration that the seller sets

The next decision you'll need to make when creating a new auction listing is the duration of the auction. The duration can be 1, 3, 5, 7, or 10 days. (A 10-day listing costs extra.)

According to Clickincome.com, which offers the Auction Analysis Pro service (www.clickincome.com), the day you start and end your auction can impact your success selling it. Statistics show you could have significantly better luck getting higher bids if the auction ends on either a weekday or weekend, depending on what you're selling. Furthermore, the actual time of day (or night) the auction ends could impact bidding. Only by doing statistical research can an eBay seller determine the best duration for their auction, as well as the potentially most profitable start and end day and time.

Pictures speak louder than words

Although offering a detailed and accurate text-based description is important, actual photographs of the product(s) you're selling are extremely powerful sales tools. Your photos should be detailed, be clear, and really showcase the most appealing visual aspects of your product. Consider using photos that showcase your item(s) from multiple angles. Close-up photos that show specific areas of the product can also be useful to bidders. The first photo you place within your listing is free. There is a small fee to add each additional photo. As the seller, you'll need to supply the photo(s) and upload them to eBay in conjunction with your listings.

For additional fees, you can "super-size" the photos with your listings, which means that they'll appear larger than standard photos when seen by bidders. There are a variety of other things you can do to your listings (for additional fees) to help them stand out. Listings can be displayed in bold, contain a border, or be highlighted, plus they can have a hit counter displayed, for example. Listings can also receive prominent placement on the eBay site, or be displayed within eBay's more prominent Gallery.

To appeal to a broader audience, it's also possible to offer add-on services, such as express shipping or gift wrapping. How you use the add-on features will definitely impact bidding and your profit. The add-on services increase the price of your listings, however, thus lowering your profit margin.

Accepting payment from buyers

One of the final steps in placing an item up for auction on eBay is to determine the payment method(s) you'll accept from the

Bright Idea

eBay.com is the world's most popular online auction site and a major success story in the e-commerce industry. You can use eBay to test your online business idea and help determine whether there's a market for what you intend to sell. You can do this by listing a sampling of your items on the eBay site and offering them at auction.

high bidder. You can accept PayPal, check, money order, cashier's check, or a major credit card (if you have your own merchant account). You must also determine where you're willing to ship the item to (within the U.S. or anywhere in the world), plus how it will be shipped and whether you'll charge extra for shipping. The eBay service can help you calculate shipping charges for the United States Postal Service or UPS. You must also decide whether you'll charge sales tax for the item(s) sold. Guidelines for whether you need to charge sales tax and how much to charge is offered on the eBay site to sellers.

Part of your listing can disclose your return policy for the item, if any, as well as special payment instructions for the high bidder. You can also block certain eBay members from bidding on your item(s), based on their past history or feedback score, for example.

Once you've completed the eBay listing process, you'll have the opportunity to preview and edit your listing before it goes live. You can click on the "Submit Listing" icon to actually start the auction and publish your listing.

After your auction goes live, it's a good strategy to monitor it, plus to pay attention to the "My eBay" area so that you can determine whether you've received any messages or questions from bidders. When the auction comes to an end, take the appropriate actions quickly in order to conclude your business and generate the highest possible feedback.

The process of listing items for auction on eBay might seem daunting at first; however, once you've been through the

Bright Idea

If you get good at selling your own items on eBay, consider earning additional profits by becoming an eBay Trading Assistant and helping others sell their products. To discover how, visit this website: http://pages.ebay.com/trading assistants/becoming-trading-assistant.html.

process a few times and have experienced a few successful auctions, creating high-impact listings becomes fast and easy.

Creating individual listings for your items is ideal if you're only occasionally selling items or you have only a few items to sell. More serious eBay sellers should consider launching an eBay Store.

eBay spin-off businesses generate huge profits

While millions of people continue to earn money selling their own items on eBay, entrepreneurs have found ways to earn profits by assisting sellers.

eBay Trading Assistants, for example, are independent entrepreneurs (authorized by eBay) to help sellers successfully sell items on eBay in exchange for a sales commission. There are also a handful of retail franchises that have storefronts where people can drop off items they wish to sell on eBay. For a pre-set fee or a commission, all of the details relating to selling that item will then be handled on behalf of the seller. Most UPS Stores, for example, offer this service.

Establishing an eBay store

For some online business entrepreneurs, conducting dozens of auctions simultaneously is their ideal way to do business and generate maximum revenue (as opposed to creating their own e-commerce website). If you're one of these people, a variety of tools are available to help you transform a hodgepodge of auction listings into a cohesive online presence on eBay. There are also a handful of third-party tools to help you manage your auctions, reach the most bidders, and ultimately generate the highest possible revenues.

According to the eBay website, "An eBay Store is an online selling platform tied to eBay, the World's Online Marketplace. You can build you own eBay Store, create custom categories to merchandise your Store, cross-sell and up-sell all of your items, and use your own logo and HTML to provide information about you, your Store, and your policies."

Up-selling or cross-selling are common sales terms that refer to enticing customers to buy related items at the time a purchase is being made. For example, if someone is purchasing a blue shirt from your website, an up-sell might be to show them a matching pair of pants they might be interested in and perhaps offering them an instant discount on those pants.

For online business operators, up-selling can be done automatically (if a website is programmed correctly) and this can generate extra revenue. You can up-sell related products, accessories, and other products a customer might also be interested in. As someone clicks on "Buy" for a specific item, a message appears saying "People who have purchased this item have also purchased (insert item)." Amazon.com, for example, does an excellent job up-selling and cross-selling its products.

For a monthly fee, starting at $15.95, you can open an eBay Store (http://stores.ebay.com). By customizing your store with creative listings, your company logo, and artwork (using templates provided), you can create a unique online presence within the eBay environment where you can have many auctions happening

 Moneysaver

Need a company logo to help define your business's brand or image? You could hire a local graphic artist or point your Web browser to an online-based company, such as LogoWorks (www.logoworks.com), which offers logo-design services for under $300.

Bright Idea

eBay offers several options for selling items online. You can create a single auction listing on eBay, create and manage an eBay Store (which is ideal for managing many auctions simultaneously), or create an online business using the company's ProStores turnkey solution for e-commerce websites. Choose which option is most suitable for you based on your goals and objectives.

simultaneously. In essence, eBay Store allows you to utilize the powerful eBay auction functionality, but create and manage your own online business with its own domain name and identity.

The eBay Store service helps you handle all aspects of managing your online business, including promotions, inventory tracking, and accounting. Like many of the turnkey e-commerce solutions, such as Yahoo! Store, eBay Store is online-based, easy-to-use, and extremely customizable. The difference between Yahoo! Store and eBay Store, however, is that eBay Store follows an auction-based sales model.

No programming knowledge is required to open and manage an eBay Store, although customized HTML programming can be incorporated, if you want. Depending on the complexity of the online store you're looking to create, eBay Stores offers several programs—"Basic" ($15.95 per month), "Featured" ($49.95 per month), and "Anchor Store" ($499.95 per month).

Because the concept behind opening an eBay Store is that you'll be running many auctions simultaneously, the service allows you to categorize your auctions, grouping them together any way you see fit. For example, if you're selling consumer electronics, you could have categories such as TVs, DVD Players, Video Games, Cameras, and so on. Plus, each auction listing will be customized with your business name and logo, in a professional-looking format that will help set you apart from your competition. You can also cross-sell and up-sell your auction items.

Like any e-commerce website, your eBay Store will have its own unique domain name and URL (www.YourStoreName.com), but can also be accessed through the main eBay service, when someone uses keyword searches to find what they're looking for, for example.

To help manage your eBay Store's finances, the service is fully compatible with Intuit's QuickBooks Pro, Premier, and Enterprise editions finance software, plus it has its own built-in bookkeeping functionality.

Although eBay Store operators have access to a wide range of online-based marketing, advertising, and promotional opportunities and tools through eBay, the company also supports co-op advertising in traditional media, which can be used to broaden awareness for your business.

> 66 Creating an eBay Store offered us the functionality, flexibility, and customization we needed to successfully launch and manage our business, without having to design and host our own online auction service. In addition to the online functionality, with eBay, we have a built-in customer base of over 100 million registered users. 99
>
> — Melissa Rich, Interschola

One major benefit to hosting an eBay Store, either as a stand-alone business or in conjunction with a more traditional e-commerce website, is that you can cross-promote your store on eBay in order to reach eBay's vast membership. By successfully utilizing eBay's keyword-based search engine, for example, you'll drive bidders to your store who wouldn't otherwise know it existed.

An eBay store is scalable

Although plenty of small businesses use eBay Stores to success-fully manage a large number of simultaneous online auctions, many companies use eBay Store on an even bigger scale.

Interschola (www.interschola.com), for example, is one such company that has found a niche on eBay.

According to founder Melissa Rich, "Interschola is a ser-vice business established to help K–12 schools sell their surplus education goods to other school institutions nationwide and to a wider global audience in an online auction environment."

Rich, who held executive-level positions at Intel, Excite.com, Classroom Connect, Chemical Bank, and Sony Corporation of America prior to launching Interschola, made an early decision to use an eBay Store to host all of the company's online-based auctions rather than build a proprietary auction platform.

Interschola is just one example of how eBay Stores is being used by a small but fast-growing company to reach a niche mar-ket comprised of public- and private-school administrators.

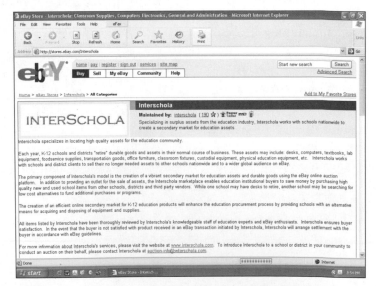

Figure 14.3. Interschola (www. interschola.com) is just one example of a specialized, vertical-market company that uses the eBay Store platform.

eBay ProStores: another turnkey e-commerce solution

If the business model of using online auctions doesn't work for you and establishing an eBay Store won't help you achieve your business objectives, eBay now offers a powerful, yet inexpensive turnkey e-commerce solution, called eBay ProStores (www. ProStores.com). For details about this relatively new service, see Chapter 4.

Just the facts

- Millions of people use eBay.com everyday to buy and sell all sorts of products. If you're interested in testing out the viability of selling products on the Web, listing a few items with eBay for auction is an ideal way to get started.

- There are several benefits to using eBay to sell your products even if you already have an independent e-commerce website or traditional brick-and-mortar business. For example, you can use eBay to sell overstock, returned but saleable, or closeout items sitting in your inventory. You can test new product ideas. You can offer a sampling of your products via auction in hopes of generating traffic to your website and boosting awareness of what you're offering.

- Some online business ventures find the auction format is ideal for selling their products and generating the highest possible revenues. If this is the case for you, opening an eBay Store will give you a unique identity and brand, but also allow you to use all of eBay's functionality as you conduct and manage online auctions.

- As an alternative to running an online business using online auctions, eBay ProStores offers a more traditional way to create, launch, and manage an e-commerce website.

GET THE SCOOP ON...
E-commerce industry expert interviews ▪ Trends
for the future ▪ E-commerce tips and strategies ▪
Insider advice

E-commerce Industry Experts Share Their Knowledge and Secrets

Many companies have lost a fortune attempting to launch some type of online business. As you should have learned already from this book and by conducting your own research, there are many potential pitfalls in the e-commerce industry. A failed venture could be due to poor planning; lack of funding; bad management; an inadequate business plan; unrealistic expectations; insufficient advertising, marketing, and promotions; or a lack of understanding of how e-commerce actually works.

Instead of trying to reinvent the wheel as you attempt to launch your own online business venture, this chapter and the next offer you the opportunity to tap the knowledge of several experts in various aspects of e-commerce. These people have already successfully done what you're attempting to do.

Chapter 15

Moneysaver

A turnkey solution such as Yahoo! Store or eBay ProStores is useful if you don't want to deal with an Internet Service Provider, higher-priced website development and maintenance software, and separate services to handle website-management and traffic-reporting tasks.

Each of the experts interviewed in this chapter share his or her advice and firsthand knowledge of how e-commerce works and how you, too, can benefit from the products or services their companies offer.

As you read this chapter, hopefully some of the advice will seem obvious to you. If that's the case, you're already becoming knowledgeable about e-commerce, which means you're well on your way to being prepared to launch your own online business venture.

Obviously there are no set rules when it comes to e-commerce. In fact, there are many ways of operating highly successful online businesses that are totally different from what the people interviewed in this chapter describe. There are also countless other products and services not mentioned in these interviews (or in this book, for that matter) that can be useful tools for helping you launch a successful online business.

Whether or not you choose to follow the precise advice of these experts is, of course, up to you. However, because all of these people are involved with products or services that have helped many start-up online businesses succeed, it's in your best interest at least to consider what these experts have to say before attempting to launch your own venture.

Each person interviewed in this chapter works for a company that provides e-commerce solutions to entrepreneurs, like you. All have achieved success and have discovered countless secrets and strategies for effectively using their company's products or services to help you too achieve success.

The people interviewed in this chapter include the following:

Sandy Bendremer, Cofounder

Company: Galaxy Internet Services

Website: www.gis.net

Topic: Choosing an ISP to host your site.

Rich Riley, Vice President/General Manager, Yahoo! Small Business

Jimmy Duvall, Senior Product Manager, Yahoo! Merchant Solutions

Company: Yahoo!

Websites: http://smallbusiness.yahoo.com

http://smallbusiness.yahoo.com/merchant

http://searchmarketing.yahoo.com

http://shopping.yahoo.com

Topic: Tips and strategies for best utilizing Yahoo! Store as your e-commerce turnkey solution, plus utilizing the other marketing and advertising services Yahoo! offers to online business operators.

Troy Stevens, General Manager

Jeff Vikari, Executive Director

Company: Clickincome.com

Website: www.Clickincome.com

Topics: The importance of having mentors when entering this industry.

Barry Schnitt, Spokesperson

Company: Google

Website: www.AdWords.com

Topic: Strategies the online business operator can use to best utilize the Google AdWords service to drive traffic to a website.

Sandy Bendremer, Cofounder, Galaxy Internet Services

Website: www.gis.net

Sandy Bendremer is the cofounder of Galaxy Internet Services, a fast-growing, full-service Internet Service Provider and Web-hosting service based in Newton, Massachusetts. The company was founded in 1995.

Galaxy Internet Services offers dial-up and broadband Internet access, along with voice-over-IP services to individuals and small- to medium-size companies, plus offers Web-hosting and colocation services to companies of all sizes located throughout the country.

Galaxy Internet Services also offers Website development and programming, plus a full range of technical support services. One of the company's latest offerings is a set of online development tools people with little or no programming experience can use to quickly develop a website.

Jason Rich: What's the difference between an ISP and a Web-hosting service?

Sandy Bendremer: "An Internet Service Provider or ISP typically offers Internet access as well as Web-hosting services. There are, however, companies that establish themselves exclusively as Web-hosting companies. These companies purchase connectivity from an ISP and then resell Web-hosting services to clients. An ISP requires a far more substantial technological infrastructure to support dial-up and broadband Web access, leased-line access, and other methods of connecting to the Internet."

Rich: When looking for an ISP/Web-hosting service, what should someone consider?

Bendremer: "Look at the entire package being offered, in terms of how it can accommodate the needs of your online-based business. Typically, Web-hosting services are offered as package deals. Look at things like the amount of storage space on the Web server being provided, what type of technical support the company will provide, and what additional services are offered that you may require. Additional services may include consulting and/or website-development tools.

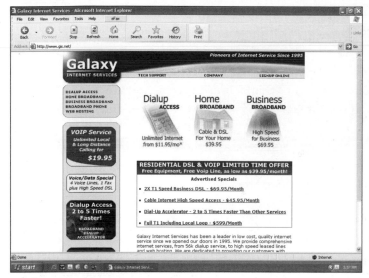

Figure 15.1. Galaxy Internet Services (www.gis.net) is a full-service, extremely reliable ISP and Web-hosting service.

"In terms of storage space on a Web server, few sites are larger than 10 or 20 megabytes. If you're creating an e-commerce site, you'll want to make sure the ISP/Web-hosting service offers shopping carts, secure online credit-card processing, the ability to handle inquiry forms, and CGI programs that can be incorporated

 Bright Idea

If you're using a turnkey solution or off-the-shelf website-development software package that uses precreated, professionally designed Web-page templates, be sure to customize the template you use. Incorporate your own graphics, photos, and text to ensure that your site is unique. Using templates can cut website-development time, but it's important that your site look truly customized. Just plugging your company name and products into a predefined template without really customizing it will probably look generic and convey a lack of professionalism.

into your site to add functionality. This will allow you to easily use off-the-shelf website-development tools, like Microsoft FrontPage or osCommerce, for example."

Rich: What are CGI programs and how are they used?

Bendremer: "CGI programs reside on the Web server and can be used to extend the functionality of websites hosted on that server. These programs allow you to do things like secure credit-card processing transactions, accept and process online-based forms completed by visitors to your site, and add website hit counters. One of the more complex CGI programs involves shopping-cart applications, which are important to e-commerce sites."

Rich: After asking what services are offered by an ISP/Web-hosting service, what should a perspective client do next?

Bendremer: "Actually visit other websites hosted by the ISP/Web-hosting service. Make sure your business fits into the business model the ISP/Web-hosting service is capable of servicing."

Rich: What should it cost to sign up with an ISP/Web-hosting service and get a site online?

Bendremer: "Web hosting is certainly the commodity of the new millennium. The costs can be as low as $10 per month, or even be free, or it can go up into the thousands of dollars per month range, depending on what's being offered. You need to look at the capabilities of the provider and how your business is going to operate within those capabilities, particularly if you have a high-volume website that will be transferring a lot of data via the Internet.

"Most of the time, when you see a price quoted for Web-hosting services, you'll see an asterisk indicating the price is based on a predefined amount of server storage space and the amount of data you can transfer. The main costs to the Web-hosting service involve storing your data and delivering it out over the Internet. The ISP/Web-hosting service's bandwidth is important. You want to ensure that the service has adequate bandwidth to manage the traffic that will be coming to your site. Finally, make sure you're signing up with a service that's stable and won't disappear overnight."

Rich: Can you describe the differences among "shared hosting," "dedicated hosting," "unmanaged hosting," and "managed hosting"?

Bendremer: "Shared hosting is when your website sits on a server along with other websites. Your individual site looks unique and can have its own unique URL, but you are subject to some restrictions on what you can do with the server and what applications are available. Since the server is shared, you need to be careful that there are sufficient resources for your applications and that other companies' applications won't cause yours to slow down.

"Dedicated hosting is when you have a whole server dedicated to your website. Usually this allows you to run any application, such as your own CGIs, databases, chat rooms, shopping carts, etc. Unlike a shared server, dedicated hosting ensures that all of the server's resources are dedicated to your website.

"Unmanaged hosting is when you have a dedicated server, provided by the hosting company or by you, colocated at the hosting company's location. The hosting company does not provide any management services for the server, however. Any repairs, upgrades, operating system patches, software fixes, etc. are your sole responsibility. Many things can be managed remotely, but you may need to physically access the system to perform repairs or simply do a reboot. Many colocation facilities offer 'remote hands' services, however, that can help, but the hourly cost of these services can be very expensive.

"Managed hosting is when the hosting company performs all of the typical management functions required to keep your server running smoothly. This would typically include hardware repairs, operating system patches and upgrades, data backup, etc. Customers should understand their requirements and check with the hosting company to make sure there aren't any hidden costs in keeping their server running over time."

Rich: If someone will be hiring a Web-hosting service to also help create their site, what else should they look for when evaluating the company?

Bendremer: "The service should be able to develop Web pages from scratch using HTML and other programming languages, like Java. They should also be proficient using tools like Flash and Photoshop. What you don't want is someone who will simply modify some precreated templates. You also want Web-page developers who have artistic abilities to ensure your site will look professional and be visually appealing. The site's designer should be fully able to program back-end capabilities into your site, be able to create shopping-cart applications and links to databases as needed. This last level of service is usually the most expensive."

Rich: What's actually required to be able to handle secure financial transactions, such as credit-card processing, online?

Bendremer: "First, a secure Web server is required. Finding an ISP/Web-hosting service that offers this technology should be very simple. In addition to being able to receive data securely from customers, make sure the ISP/Web-hosting service you choose is able to keep that information totally secure once it's actually received. SSL is the standard security protocol. The people visiting your site also need to be using a secure Web browser that supports SSL, such as the browsers available from Microsoft and Netscape."

Rich: How can someone ensure that they'll receive the technical support services needed from their ISP/Web-hosting service?

Bendremer: "You want to make sure the technical support staff will be accessible. The biggest complaint people have with smaller Web-hosting services is the lack of support that's offered, or the limited hours when technical support services are available. You need to be able to get problems fixed and your questions answered 24 hours a day, 7 days a week.

"The other problem people run into is that their ISP/Web-hosting service charges a low monthly fee for the basic service, but then nickel-and-dimes their clients if they need support or

Watch Out!

Although it's helpful to keep an eye on new Web technologies, exercise caution when incorporating them into your site. There is always a lag from the time a new technology is introduced to its widespread use. You don't want to invest a lot of money in features that only a fraction of your visitors can take advantage of.

require simple things done to their site in terms of maintenance or updating. These additional fees can add up quickly and make it very difficult to develop and maintain your Internet presence the way you want to.

"Also, if you call a technical support phone number and you're put on hold for 10 to 15 minutes or longer, you should wonder if the company is adequately staffed. You also want to ensure that the people who ultimately do answer the phone will have the technical expertise to actually solve your problem or answer your questions. If you call the technical support phone number and the person who answers the phone can't answer your question or solve your problem, you need to know what happens next. Does the company have the resources to help you, and will they expend those resources as needed?"

Rich: What questions or problems will an ISP/Web-hosting service not address?

Bendremer: "Most Web-hosting services won't address questions involving website development, programming, or search-engine optimization, for example, unless you're specifically paying them for these additional services, which is often billed by the hour."

Rich: What are some of the biggest problems people run into if they choose the wrong ISP/Web-hosting service?

Bendremer: "People often choose a service based on cost, not based on their actual needs. One common problem is the service doesn't have enough bandwidth to accommodate the number of visitors to a site or the server can't transfer the amount of data needed. This means people can't access your site or can't get the information they need from it. If the Web-hosting service you choose is hosting too many other companies that require band-width, the speed of your site may suffer.

"I recommend asking for a list of other websites the ISP/Web-hosting service hosts, and trying to access those sites repeatedly at various times of the day and night, particularly during peak times."

Rich: There are local companies as well as much larger national companies offering Web-hosting services. Does it matter which one someone hires to host their site?

Bendremer: "Most of the time, it really doesn't matter, as long as the company you hire to host your site offers the services and technical features you need to operate your online-based business or e-commerce site. What really matters is how the service you choose is actually connected to the Internet's backbone. Your host service doesn't have to be a 'tier-one' Internet provider, as long as they're well-connected to a 'tier-one' backbone.

"Most ISPs and Web-hosting services can support any type of Web content, such as streaming audio and video, but if your site requires a high level of resources, make sure the service you choose has the necessary server capacity in place before signing up with them. Look at who the service's other customers are. Are they in the same league as you?

"The barrier to entry for a basic Web-hosting service is very low, so make sure the company you choose has a good reputation and will be around for years to come. Many of the smaller services can and sometimes do disappear overnight because they can't compete in this highly competitive Web-hosting industry. When dealing with any business you're going to depend on, check references, do research, and ask questions. Never sign a long-term contract or prepay for any hosting services unless there's a real cost advantage. Especially if you're dealing with a small hosting service, think twice about prepaying for services, no matter what the cost savings."

Rich: As a start-up company, does it make sense to develop a site from scratch by hiring programmers who know HTML, Flash,

and Java, or it is okay to rely on a commercial software package, such as Microsoft FrontPage, to create and help manage a site?

Bendremer: "That all depends on your budget, experience level, and what you're trying to accomplish. Using an off-the-shelf tool allows you to quickly and easily build a highly functional website. If you start to do things beyond what straight HTML is capable of, however, you may need to hire a programmer to create the online applications or website features you need and want. This, of course, requires more of a financial investment. Building complex interactive forms or e-commerce features into your site from scratch will really start to tax the capabilities of most off-the-shelf programs, especially the cheaper ones."

Rich: What are some of the mistakes you've seen people make when creating their website and getting it online?

Bendremer: "Many people launch a website, online business, or e-commerce site without having realistic expectations about what's involved in actually creating and managing the site, as well as what they can expect from it once it's online. I recommend speaking with as many people as possible who have experienced the process of creating a website and putting it online before going through this experience yourself.

"The biggest disasters happen when you start rushing into things without proper planning and research. Before creating and programming a website, for example, spend time designing it on paper, perhaps using storyboards. Know exactly what you want the site to do, what content you want to make available, and how you want to present the content. Do this planning before actually starting to develop and/or program the site. You want to take an organized approach to this process in order to save yourself time, money, and frustration. I suggest looking at many other websites and tapping them for ideas—without stealing copyrighted materials, of course. Once you define exactly what you want, a programmer or professional Web-page designer will be able to create it much easier and faster."

Moneysaver

If you have the budget available to you, by all means consider making use of a graphic artist. You might well be able to handle the graphics yourself, however, and produce an uncluttered and attractive site at a much lower expense.

Rich: What other potential pitfalls should someone watch out for when creating a website and putting it online?

Bendremer: "It's very easy to create a basic website that looks nice and conveys information. It's much more difficult to create a truly interactive site that's useful and provides a service to your customers. If you surf the Web, only 1 in 100 sites will truly offer an engaging and interactive experience that allows the visitor to do exactly what he or she needs to do. Make sure your expectations for your site are realistic. Don't expect miraculous results the first days or weeks you're online. Look at website design as a long, ongoing, and somewhat tedious process. Make sure your site isn't so blatantly commercial that people become offended or annoyed to the point they want to leave."

Rich: What types of features should companies try to incorporate into their websites?

Bendremer: "Once you're familiar with what the Internet can do, pinpoint existing business processes that might traditionally be done over the phone or in person with your customers, and develop ways these processes can be done online in a way that helps the customer. For example, if your business currently accepts the majority of its orders from people who call your toll-free phone number, offering online ordering capabilities not only speeds up the ordering process for consumers, but in the long run will save your company money and resources.

"If you can give online customers access to your product databases and other information, this too, can be exceptionally helpful. Amazon.com, for example, not only gives users the ability to search through a database of hundreds of thousands of book titles and order any of those books; the system will also automatically make additional book recommendations based on criteria the user selects, such as a particular subject matter or author. Amazon.com will also e-mail users when additional books in their area of interest become available, and that's something more traditional retail bookstores won't do."

Rich: There are so many Web technologies available, such as streaming audio and video. Which of these technologies should a start-up online business consider incorporating into its site?

Bendremer: "I recommend catering your website to the lowest common denominator of users. Look at what features the popular Web browsers, such as Microsoft Explorer, Netscape, and Firefox, can deliver natively, without add-ons, and design your site around those features. Some add-ons, such as Flash Player, Acrobat Reader, and RealPlayer, for example, have become commonplace, especially among surfers with high-speed connections to the Internet.

"I also strongly recommend against developing a site where the download times are too significant to keep the visitor's attention. Internet surfers have the shortest attention spans imaginable. If someone gets tired of waiting, the Back or Home icon on their browser is always only a millisecond away. Always test your site using a standard dial-up Internet connection to see how the rest of the world will see your site. In my opinion, a 20-second waiting time for a page to download is too long for most sites."

Rich: What are some of the other considerations a start-up business should think about when choosing a Web-hosting service?

 Moneysaver

Instead of keeping an inventory of the products you sell, you can find wholesalers willing to drop-ship items directly to your customers from their warehouse. For a list of wholesale product suppliers who will drop-ship on behalf of their customers (who are online business operators), point your Web browser to www.dropshipper.clicksitebuilder.com. By using these wholesalers, you'll be able to quickly build up your catalog of products for your online business, without having to invest a lot of money in inventory.

Bendremer: "If you'll be operating a high-volume site requiring very specific types of services, one option is to purchase your own Web server, which has become pretty cheap these days, and locate your service with your provider. This is called 'colocation.' The provider will sell you space on an equipment rack and will maintain your server for you. The benefit is that you won't have to adhere to any restrictions imposed by the Web-hosting service regarding the use of their servers. If you're using colocation services, you'll typically be billed based on the amount of bandwidth your site requires. This has become a very common practice, even among very large Fortune 500 companies with an Internet presence who aren't themselves Internet Service Providers."

Rich: Is it necessary to choose an ISP/Web-hosting service that's geographically located near your company?

Bendremer: "Unless you're using colocation services where you might need hands-on access to your Web-server hardware, there's absolutely no need to be in the same geographic area as your Web-hosting service. All of your website maintenance and programming can be done on your own computer, located anywhere, and transferred to your Web server using a standard Internet connection."

Rich Riley, Vice President/General Manager, Yahoo! Small Business

Jimmy Duvall, Senior Product Manager, Yahoo! Merchant Solutions

Websites: http://smallbusiness.yahoo.com
http://smallbusiness.yahoo.com/merchant
http://searchmarketing.yahoo.com
http://shopping.yahoo.com

Everyone knows Yahoo! (www.yahoo.com) as one of the world's leading search engines and Internet portals. Over the years, however, the company has diversified in order to offer a wide range of online-based services. As the division names suggest, Yahoo!

Small Business and Yahoo! Merchant Solutions were created to offer online business entrepreneurs the services and resources they need to create and manage their online presence.

The Yahoo! Store service is an integral part of what Yahoo! Small Business offers, which is an all-in-one turnkey solution for e-commerce website owners and operators. If your business doesn't require e-commerce applications, such as a shopping cart and credit-card processing, the Yahoo! Sites service could provide the website-development tools and hosting services you're looking for at an affordable price.

By combining easy-to-use website-design tools with hosting services, technical support, and a wide range of tools for managing, marketing, advertising, and promoting an online business, Yahoo! Small Business is one of the world's most popular and affordable turnkey solutions available.

The company reports that one out of every eight online businesses in existence operates using the Yahoo! Store platform. This translates to more than 30,000 merchants currently using the Yahoo! Store platform.

Jason Rich: Could you begin by talking about how Yahoo! Store is a leader in its category?

Rich Riley: "Through our platform, we handle billions of dollars in sales for our merchants. We believe we are the leading provider of e-commerce to small business, by far. We're also a leading provider of e-mail and other services a small business can use to establish their online presence. Only a small number of businesses actually sell online, so we also offer Yahoo! Site for those existing businesses that just want or need an online presence."

 Bright Idea

When it comes to choosing a turnkey solution with which to operate your online business, go with a company you know, respect, and that has experience. Yahoo! Store (from Yahoo! Small Business), for example, was the first e-commerce solution offered to businesses on the Web. It was launched in the summer of 1995.

Rich: How does Yahoo! help small-business and online business operators achieve success?

Riley: "Over the past few years, we have been working hard to improve our product to make it easy for someone to establish their online presence. Yahoo! SiteBuilder is an online-based application for designing websites that's very easy to use and extremely flexible. We now offer several hundred different templates someone can use to begin designing their site. We also integrate our Yahoo! Search Marketing and Yahoo! Shopping services into Yahoo! Store, making it easy to promote and market an online business and drive traffic to your site.

"Yahoo! Small Business is the world's most popular resource for small-business operators. We offer thousands of informative articles and a wide range of tools to help people learn the basics of e-commerce."

Rich: For Yahoo! Store, who is your target audience?

Riley: "Any aspiring online merchant is part of our target. Anyone with an established offline business who wants to add an online component to their operations is also part of our target. Many established online merchants have also graduated to our platform because of its scalability, stability, and reliability."

Jimmy Duvall: "Yahoo! Store offers a robust platform that's secure, which is very appealing to established online merchants looking for better tools to design and manage their e-commerce websites. We also bring a tremendous level of professionalism and experience to the table."

Rich: Realistically, what's involved in launching an e-commerce website using Yahoo! Store?

Duvall: "We have Yahoo! Store packages that start at $39.95 per month. Going beyond that, a start-up online business will need to gather their catalog of products, purchase inventory, obtain a merchant account, and develop the core elements of their business. These costs will vary greatly, based on the type of business. Many merchants don't calculate into their initial budget all of the costs associated with getting started. There's also an investment

Bright Idea

Personal products (such as lingerie) tend to sell well online because people can shop in the privacy of their own homes.

that needs to be made in advertising and marketing. We try to help our new merchants become as prepared as possible before actually opening for business."

Rich: Based on your vast experience, what types of products have you seen sell very well on the Web?

Duvall: "I can't say that any one type of product sells better than another. Anything that can be sold at retail or through a mail-order catalog can potentially sell well online. It's incredible what certain folks can sell online when they use creativity and successfully reach a niche market. Items that you can't readily find at a traditional retail store tend to sell well online."

Riley: "We've seen everything from websites dedicated to selling refrigerator magnets (see the interview with Chris Gwynn, founder/CEO of Fridgedoor.com in Chapter 16), to toy train sets for children, and a successful site that sells nothing but pet-ferret supplies. Online businesses that target a niche market tend to do well."

Rich: In terms of computer experience and business experience, how much is really needed to launch a successful business using Yahoo! Stores?

Riley: "You don't need a lot of computer experience. We work very closely with a number of extremely talented website designers and developers who can help someone build their Yahoo! Store. People should not let their level of technical sophistication be a determining factor when deciding whether or not to open an online business. What is important is to have a solid business concept and a strong understanding of marketing. You need to understand who your customers are, know what they need, and know how to reach them effectively."

Duvall: "We provide a comprehensive selection of tools for designing, building, and managing an e-commerce website. These tools are scalable, so you can take it to whatever level you wish. If you don't have the technical know-how to do something, you can hire a professional programmer who is familiar with the Yahoo! Store platform to assist you."

Rich: Is it important for an online business operator to maintain their own inventory, or is it okay to develop a drop-shipping relationship with suppliers?

Duvall: "We find most of our merchants manage their own inventory. This gives them greater control over how quickly orders get processed, for example."

Rich: What types of experts or professional help should an online business operator hire to assist them?

Duvall: "I'd recommend hiring a talented and experienced website designer and programmer to assist you in initially designing the look, organization, and functionality of your e-commerce site. You need to strike a balance between the visual elements of your site and the structural elements that actually make it operate correctly. A graphic designer alone typically can't handle the technical aspects of a website. How the site is organized and the interface that allows the surfer to easily navigate throughout the site to find exactly what they're looking for is what a website designer or programmer can help you do. For this, you need to find someone with experience who understands how e-commerce works in the real world."

Rich: Is it possible for someone to incorporate streaming audio or video into their e-commerce site designed using the Yahoo! Store platform?

Duvall: "We are completely open to all third-party media. Our building tools allow the merchant to use whatever Web-based technologies they wish. We've seen a lot of our merchants successfully using Flash, for example, to really highlight certain aspects of what they're selling. Our platform is very expandable, but it's also very easy to use. All of the templates in the SiteBuilder toolset are completely customizable. The merchant can also create their own, unique templates from scratch."

Rich: What are some basic website-design tips you can offer to start-up online businesses?

Duvall: "Before you start programming your site, it's important to really think through your business and determine what functionality you want your site to have. You then need to determine how you want your site laid out so that items can be easily found by visitors with the least number of clicks possible. Really think through the structure of the site and how you'll be organizing and categorizing items and information. It's also important to keep a personal aspect to the site, allowing customers to contact you, via e-mail."

Rich: What other website-design tips can you offer?

Duvall: "As you're designing your site, incorporate clear and crisp, high-resolution images of your products. The product photos need to show detail, such as the front and back, or a top and bottom view of each item. Pay attention to the backgrounds used in your product shots. Everything needs to be visually appealing. Don't allow your backgrounds to be distracting. Always use neutral backgrounds in your photos.

"When it comes to writing product descriptions, be extremely detailed. Finally, the site's visitors need to be able to quickly find the items they're looking for, access your shopping cart, and make their purchases, which is why the overall design and organization of your site is important. Having an online search feature to help someone find what they're looking for is also important."

Riley: "We've found that Web surfers like to know about the companies they're doing business with. Offering an 'About Us' area on your site is important. This area should tell people about your company and the people running it. It should convey your company's story and help build confidence amongst visitors."

Bright Idea

Some turnkey solutions for online businesses are customized to sell very specific types of products or services. Choose your solution based on the objectives of your company. eProfitFactory.com is another example of a company that sells inexpensive, turnkey online businesses, complete with precreated website designs and drop-shippable inventory. To earn profits, you simply need to market your site. The drawback is that you're not offering anything new or unique, which makes driving traffic to your site more challenging.

Rich: How important is it for an online merchant to offer value-added content?

Duvall: "We think it's very beneficial. Web surfers are always looking for the full experience when they visit a site. Our toolset allows for unlimited flexibility in terms of the content you add to your site. Our goal is to help you define what that content should be as you create and design your site. Any extra services or information you can offer on your site will differentiate your company and make it more of a resource to your buying community. A company's e-commerce site should really represent, promote, and help build their overall brand."

Rich: Please explain what a "cross-sell engine" is and how this can be successfully incorporated into an e-commerce website.

Duvall: "When someone decides to purchase an item from your website, the site will automatically recommend several other related items that same customer might be interested in. A good cross-sell engine will allow the merchant to offer a discount for additional items someone purchases. For example, if someone chooses a specific pair of pants, a cross-sell engine will automatically recommend a matching shirt and could offer a 10 percent discount on that additional product. Perhaps someone is buying a cell phone from your site. A cross-sell engine could then recommend two or three useful phone accessories to go along with that specific model phone.

"This type of merchandising capability, which is built into the Yahoo! Store platform, can dramatically increase your revenue.

As you structure your site, it's important to carefully think through your site's design and organization, so you can offer related items together. Give people incentives to make purchases. Use discounts or incentives, for example, to help encourage the purchase of multiple products as a result of a cross-sell or up-sell."

Rich: Can you talk about the importance of marketing when launching a start-up online business?

Duvall: "Marketing your website is extremely important. All businesses require marketing. When you're online, you need a way to get your name out there. Yahoo! Search Marketing and Yahoo! Shopping are services you can use to help kick-start your marketing efforts. The technology behind Yahoo! Store will not create a viable business for you. It's only the toolbox for creating the business. You have to understand how business works and make sure your business idea and business model are viable. No matter how much technology you throw at a business, there's no replacement for having a core understanding of business and marketing fundamentals. The mentality that 'If you build it they will come' doesn't hold true for e-commerce unless you truly understand what you're trying to do."

Rich: How important is online security to online business operators?

Duvall: "Online security is something that Yahoo! takes extremely seriously. We are certified by third parties and all of the credit-card agencies to offer secure credit-card transactions. Security is something that every online business operator needs to take into consideration. We offer very robust security solutions for e-commerce."

Rich: What type of technical support do you offer when someone signs up for Yahoo! Stores?

Duvall: "For the first 30 days, we offer an unlimited concierge telephone consulting service to help our new merchants get up and running. We also offer a comprehensive, 300-page eBook to help people get started using our platform. After that, we offer unlimited telephone-based technical support, 24 hours per day,

7 days per week. For our larger merchants, we have a team of dedicated account managers.

"The concierge service is designed to help merchants set up all aspects of their online business venture. We get into topics like order fulfillment and acquiring a merchant account, in addition to offering website design and organization strategies. After the initial 30 days of concierge service, we believe the typical merchant will have the knowledge they need to operate their business."

Rich: What is the relationship between Yahoo! Store, which is the website design and management platform, and Yahoo! Shopping, which is the online shopping area of Yahoo! that's open to the general public?

Duvall: "Any of our Yahoo! Store merchants can participate in Yahoo! Shopping for an additional, but discounted, fee. We offer a 20 percent discount off of Yahoo! Shopping's services. What we offer is seamless integration between your website and Yahoo! Shopping, to ensure that your item listings are accurate, timely, and properly categorized. Yahoo! Shopping is a comprehensive shopping destination that allows consumers to do research about products and perform product comparisons. It also allows buyers to view ratings of participating merchants, based on feedback from previous customers."

Rich: What is Yahoo! Search Marketing, and how can it be used to promote an online business?

Duvall: "Yahoo! Search Marketing is an add-on service that allows you to decide exactly how you'll spend your advertising dollars to reach your target customers using keywords and our Yahoo! search engine. We then allow you to carefully track your customers and those who view your advertising. Yahoo! Store's merchants automatically receive a $100 Yahoo! Search Marketing credit, so they can test out the service and experiment using keyword-based advertising.

"More and more consumers are using search engines to find what they're looking for online. This is the primary reason why search marketing or keyword-based advertising works so well. For the merchant, the results from using this type of advertising are extremely easy to track, so you can instantly see the results. There's also a very low cost of entry and no large initial outlay of advertising dollars. This type of advertising also allows you to target very specific audiences in a cost-effective way."

Riley: "While search marketing is an important advertising vehicle for almost any online merchant, your very first step should be to register your site with the search engines and to focus on search-engine optimization. There are methods for building and organizing each Web page on your site to vastly improve search-engine rankings, beyond the use of meta tags. We teach people how to do this when they use the Yahoo! Store platform. In terms of the Yahoo! search engine, simply by using the Yahoo! Store platform, your site will automatically be optimized for our search engine. Your Web-page keywords and descriptions, along with the descriptive text within your site, all contribute to how well your site is optimized for the search engines."

Jeff Vikari, Executive Director, Clickincome.com

Troy Stevens, General Manager, Clickincome.com

Website: www.Clickincome.com

In Chapter 4, you learned about the various tools and resources available to help you design, build, and maintain your website with off-the-shelf software (such as Microsoft FrontPage or osCommerce) and complete turnkey solutions that are available to e-commerce-based business operators.

Like many companies, Clickincome.com offers bundled turnkey solutions designed for the e-business beginner, plus advanced solutions for the established online business owner and operator.

Clickincome.com is a certified development partner with eBay. The company also offers ClickClub, a catalog of thousands of drop-shippable products any merchant can easily begin selling on their own site, without having to maintain an inventory.

These ClickClub products can be the primary offerings of a start-up online business or used to round out your online catalog, which targets a niche audience by selling very specialized or unique goods in addition to the ClickClub items being offered on your site.

Although the actual website-development tools offered by Clickincome.com are similar albeit less powerful and robust than offerings from Yahoo! Store or eBay ProStores, this service offers one-on-one education, plus telephone and online mentoring to its merchants for an additional fee.

Clickincome.com offers an easy and inexpensive starting point for someone with no previous e-commerce or business experience.

The company was established in 2000 as a sister company to World Net Services Inc., which launched in 1995 as an ISP and high-end Web hosting and development, content management and provisioning, e-commerce, and sales and sales-lead management solution. Another sister company to Clickincome.com, called Aria Financial Corporation, assists numerous online and offline merchants in obtaining credit-card processing merchant accounts.

 Bright Idea

Aside from Clickincome.com, other companies offer complete, turnkey solutions for online businesses, complete with precreated websites and drop-shippable inventory, so research your options, then choose the one that makes the most sense for your specific business. DropShipStores2Go.com (www.dropshipstores2go.com), for example, offers inexpensive turnkey solutions for opening a pet-supply, gift-basket, crafts and home décor, or kitchen-accessories e-commerce website. The drawback is that you're not offering unique products or services. Thus, the success of your business will depend on your marketing and advertising efforts and your ability to compete head-on with traditional retailers, plus others who have bought into the same online business opportunity as you.

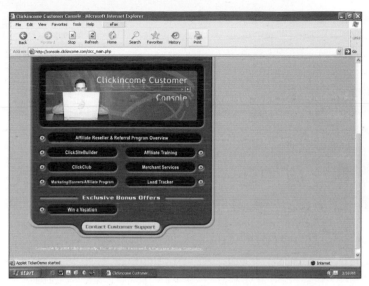

Figure 15.2. From ClickIncome.com's website, online business operators can access this easy-to-use control panel to help them create and manage their websites.

Jason Rich: What's one thing that potential online business owners need to understand before getting involved with this type of venture?

Jeff Vikari: "The first thing people need to understand when they start an online business is that they're becoming the CEO of their own company and will be expected to act like a CEO in terms of the decisions they make and the actions they take.

"A lot of online business operators don't consider themselves to be CEOs, and their businesses suffer. People need to think like a CEO and function like a CEO when running an online business. We teach people how to do that.

"The biggest misconception people have is that the Internet is magic. It's the gold-rush mentality. People believe that if they invest a few thousand dollars into their online business, profits will simply start shooting out of their computer automatically. That's obviously not the case. People need to follow many of the same steps they'd take if they were to start a traditional brick-and-mortar business. The cost of starting an online-based business, however, is significantly lower."

Rich: Once someone launches their online business, what advice can you offer in terms of how it should be marketed, promoted, and advertised?

Stevens: "Every business needs to be handled totally differently, depending on what's being sold and who it's being sold to. There's no cookie-cutter approach. Initially, I recommend trying a few different advertising techniques, for example, to see what works best. With each technique, you'll need to fine-tune your approach as you go. The first step, however, is to identify what needs to be done and to determine what it'll take to be successful. You'll also need to really get to you know your products, so you can determine the best way to promote and sell them. Then, focus in on getting to know your customers. All this has to happen before you launch your business and start advertising it.

"One major tip I can offer in terms of advertising is not to put your entire budget into one advertising vehicle, such as search-engine marketing or banner advertising. Diversify.

"You need to remember that your online business can't be everything to everyone. You're not going to be the next online Wal-Mart. Wal-Mart is already online themselves. Find your niche. Niche marketing is a lot more powerful than general marketing. I always recommend selling the benefits of your product, not the features."

Vikari: I recommend taking a passion, hobby, or interest and transforming it into an online business venture. You also need to understand that even in the online world, basic business principles apply. You need to create a website that targets a specific demographic, discover how to best reach that market, offer those people something they want or need, and then offer it at a price they're willing to pay."

Rich: You mentioned the importance of fine-tuning your web-site and marketing approach. Could you elaborate?

Vikari: "One of the biggest advantages of an online business is that you can make changes and fine-tune your site or your adver-tising messages almost instantly, based on the results you receive. Thus, it becomes extremely important to track the impact of your advertising, as well as the effectiveness of your site's design. You want to draw a visitor into your site within the first 10 seconds of their visit. You need to engage them in a short period of time and get them to commit to something, even if it's just getting them to commit to visiting another page of your website.

"It's always a good idea to offer people incentives to make a purchase or to take an action. You can use discounts, special offers, free gifts, or other marketing techniques to make this happen. A wide range of traffic-monitoring and analysis tools exist to help with this process."

Rich: Is there any other advice you can offer to start-up online business operators?

Vikari: "Get a mentor. Find someone who has done this before and seek out their guidance. In terms of a mentor, find someone who is a teacher and who has e-commerce experience. Ideally you want a mentor who knows about website design, business, and marketing. Mentoring works because it can respond to your indi-vidual needs. Having up-to-date technology at your disposal is important, but you also need the right knowledge to be success-ful. Basic and advanced e-business mentoring is one of the key things that Clickincome.com offers. Our 30- to 60-minute, one-on-one mentoring sessions are highly educational. These sessions

 Bright Idea

As you're deciding which turnkey solution to use for your business, take a close look at sample websites from other companies that were created using the tools offered by each of the turnkey solutions you're considering. Here are URLs for several online businesses created and managed using Clickincome.com's ser-vices: www.artandcharity.com and www.menshoenet.com.

Bright Idea

Visit the Clickincome.com website (www.clickincome.com) to subscribe to *eShopTalk,* a free online newsletter for online business operators.

are much more elaborate than simply receiving technical support to get a specific question answered.

Barry Schnitt, Spokesperson, Google AdWords

Website: www.AdWords.com

Google (www.google.com) is one of the world's most popular Internet search engines. In conjunction with its search engine, the company offers the AdWords service, and has become a pioneer in search marketing and keyword advertising—an inexpensive, fast, and easy way to drive traffic to a website.

For website operators and online business owners looking to generate revenue by displaying AdWords ads from other companies, Google offers the AdSense service (www.google.com/adsense).

In this interview, Barry Schnitt, a spokesperson for Google, discusses the AdWords service and offers strategies for how it can best be utilized to drive traffic to a website.

Jason Rich: How would you describe Google's AdWords service?
Barry Schnitt: "It's an auction-based advertising program that enables business operators to deliver relevant ads targeted to specific search results or Web content. Our AdWords program provides advertisers with a cost-effective way to deliver ads to customers across Google sites and through the Google Network."

Rich: How does AdWords compare to similar services, such as Yahoo! Search Marketing? What sets the two services apart?
Schnitt: "Relevance is the key differentiator between the programs. AdWords, for example, includes click-through rate in the auction formula for ranking ads. That is, with AdWords, you need to be relevant, not just paying more, for your ad to show. In

addition, AdWords offers a discounter that automatically monitors competition and lowers cost-per-click to one cent above theirs. Also, AdWords requires only a $5 start-up fee and no monthly minimums. We've put together an informative Web page that describes more of the differences between AdWords and its competitors. The URL is https://adwords.google.com/select/comparison.html."

Rich: How can a start-up online business best utilize AdWords?

Schnitt: "AdWords can be a great way for a new business to test products, services, and promotions. It also provides reach around the world and across the Internet, through our partner network of search and content sites. As a result, a new business can raise awareness about their company."

Rich: How quickly can someone get started and see the benefits of using AdWords?

Schnitt: "An account can be created in less than 15 minutes. Once the campaign is finished, ads go live instantly and an advertiser can start to see results in moments."

Rich: What are some of the common pitfalls you see online business operators make when they first start using AdWords? What's the best way to overcome these challenges?

Schnitt: "The most common mistake is not putting time into the campaign. Google offers many tools to automate a number of processes for the advertiser. However, decisions and changes still need to be made by the online business operator.

"Advertisers get as much out of AdWords as they put in. Test different ideas, such as the use of different keywords and ad text. Optimize based on the results and start the process over again. In the end, you'll get the most out of your advertising dollar."

 Watch Out!

Beware of turnkey solutions for online casinos, online sports books, or gambling websites. At the time this book was being written, there were new laws being proposed that could dramatically hinder an online casino's ability to do business in the U.S.

Rich: What are some strategies for getting the best results from AdWords?

Schnitt: "We've created a Web page which offers detailed tips and strategies for best utilizing our AdWords service. The URL is https://adwords.google.com/select/tips.html."

Rich: What strategies can you offer for setting a cost-per-click figure and daily budget when using AdWords?

Schnitt: "Based on the keywords you enter, the AdWords system will automatically calculate a suggested maximum CPC (cost-per-click), then show you the clicks and costs-per-day that would result. You can accept that CPC or enter your own. When creating a campaign, click on the 'View Traffic Estimator' icon for a closer look at positioning and costs for individual keywords.

"You can also make changes to your maximum CPC and see the effect those changes would have on your ad's average position, clicks, and cost. The best way to find out what to bid and budget is to test and track your results. Ultimately, you need to determine what a click is actually worth to your business. A click represents someone viewing your ad and then visiting your website."

Rich: How can someone ensure that they choose the best keywords for their online business?

Schnitt: "Google offers a Keyword Tool that can help advertisers find useful alternate keywords which they may not have considered. In addition, we recommend thinking like a potential customer. What words would your customers use to characterize your business, products, or service? How would they search online to find it? In other words, what search word or phrase would someone type into a search engine? The answers to these questions will help you compile a list of great keywords."

Rich: An AdWords ad is comprised of a headline, two lines of text (35 characters per line), and the displayed URL. What tips can you offer for creating a high-impact AdWords ad?

Schnitt: "There are a few simple things advertisers can do to create compelling and effective ads. First, place keywords in the headline of the ad. Second, state a clear benefit to the viewer. Third, incorporate a strong call to action into the ad's wording."

Rich: How has "search marketing" or "keyword advertising" evolved over the past few years? How will it change in the next one to two years?

Schnitt: "Search marketing has evolved from a direct-response vehicle for the very tech savvy to an increasingly flexible marketing platform for anyone with a business. In the future, the market will continue to expand and vendors will offer advertisers additional tools and options for managing, targeting, tracking, and pricing their campaigns."

Rich: Should AdWords represent an online business's entire advertising and marketing strategy?

Schnitt: "Businesses and their goals vary widely. We feel that Google AdWords can be a part of any marketing strategy, but the overall plan depends on the business. This holds true for any type of advertising, marketing, or promotional activities."

Rich: What are some of the best success stories you've seen in terms of small online businesses using AdWords?

Schnitt: "We've seen literally thousands of success stories. Some especially compelling stories have been compiled and put on the following Web page: https://adwords.google.com/select/success.html."

Rich: What is Google's AdSense service and how does it relate to AdWords?

Schnitt: "Google AdSense (www.google.com/adsense) is a fast and easy way for website publishers of all sizes to display relevant Google ads on their website's content pages and earn money. Because the ads are related to what visitors are looking for, or matched to the characteristics and interests of the visitors the content attracts, publishers have a way to both monetize and enhance their content pages. It's also a way for website publishers to provide Google Web and site search to their visitors and to earn money by displaying Google ads on the search results pages."

Just the facts

- Choose an ISP that offers not just the technology, but the technical support resources you need, when you need them.

- To find an ISP or Web-hosting service, look beyond your geographic area because all of your website design and maintenance can be done from any computer that's connected to the Internet.

- Find an ISP/Web-hosting service that has experience working with online businesses like yours. Make sure it has the proper security in place and that bandwidth won't be an issue. Also, make sure the company has been around for a while and won't disappear overnight.

- For many online businesses, a turnkey solution such as Yahoo! Store offers the flexibility, reliability, and expandability that's needed to create and manage an e-commerce website.

- If you're new to e-commerce, work with a company that offers mentoring or find yourself a mentor who can guide you through the processes of launching a successful online business.

- Google's AdWords offers an inexpensive and fast way to drive traffic to a website or promote a product, service, company, or brand.

GET THE SCOOP ON...
In-depth interviews with successful online
entrepreneurs ■ Firsthand experiences ■ How
to overcome mistakes ■ The road to success
in cyberspace

Successful E-commerce Entrepreneurs Speak Out

Chapter 16

Throughout this book, you've read about the many steps involved in coming up with an idea for an e-commerce website, designing your site, and launching an advertising and marketing campaign. We've also looked at what's involved in managing the day-to-day operations of your online business venture.

By this point, hopefully, you realize that although there are incredible opportunities for success in cyberspace, striking it rich by launching an online business isn't something that will happen quickly. It's going to take a great business idea, hard work, careful planning, and a significant investment of time and money.

Even if you've already gathered all of the resources necessary to create and launch your business, there are still potential pitfalls, many of which have already been discussed in this book. Before you proceed further in establishing your online-based business, take a look at several entrepreneurs who have already achieved success in cyberspace.

By reading these interviews, you'll discover that people from all walks of life are currently operating successful online businesses. There are no barriers based on age, race, sex, religion, or geographic region. If you have access to the Web and a great business idea, you too can become a successful online business operator, even with little or no programming knowledge.

From a handful of people who are successfully operating an online business, in this chapter, you'll get a firsthand perspective of what it takes to achieve success, as well as what dangers to watch out for. You'll also get a taste of what the e-commerce industry is really like. The entrepreneurs interviewed in this chapter are the following:

- Taeyoung Oh, Founder/CEO, Louisdog.com
- Jeremy Alicandri, Founder/Owner, SimplyCheap.com
- Carole Jane Rossi, Founder/Owner, JOriginals.com
- Christian Girts, Founder/Owner, AnglersVice.com
- Scott Meyer, Founder, OnlyOneCreations.com
- Chris Gwynn, Founder/CEO, Fridgedoor.com

The online business opportunities available to entrepreneurs are extremely diverse. Although the advice the people interviewed in this chapter offer worked for them, not everything discussed here may be applicable to your situation. Remember to keep in mind the special circumstances you face—the type of

 Bright Idea

If you know people already involved in e-commerce, consider asking them about their own experiences. They might have tips you can apply to your own business.

Moneysaver

One advantage of online catalogs is that you can quickly revise your product list, prices, and so forth. Traditional catalogs have to be printed and then distributed (usually by mail). Printing and distributing catalogs can be costly, but updating an online catalog is fast and comparably less expensive.

business you plan to launch, how you plan to promote it, and how you will manage operations.

In addition, there are no definitive right or wrong ways of doing things when it comes to operating an online business. Thus, you might not agree with everything the people interviewed here have to say, and that's fine. The purpose of this chapter is simply to give you an idea of the types of businesses that can be successful in cyberspace and to explain how these people were able to make their online business ventures successful.

Taeyoung Oh, Founder/CEO, Louisdog.com

Capitalizing on peoples' love for their pets, Louisdog.com has established an internationally known brand of high-end, luxury dog furniture, accessories, toys, and fashions. With products ranging from handcrafted cashmere sweaters for dogs to dog beds and carriers, Louisdog.com is a one-stop shop for anyone who truly wants to pamper that pooch.

Louisdog.com is based in Seoul, Korea, and was founded in August 2000 by both Taeyoung Oh, a Cornell University graduate, and Bella Baek, a School of Visual Arts graduate. Prior to starting this business, Taeyoung Oh had only three months of experience working at an IT company. He quickly hired professionals who were capable of creating an e-commerce website to assist him in launching the online aspect of his business, while initially working on a relatively small budget.

Louisdog.com is an excellent example of how someone with a great idea for high-end niche products, but limited resources, can launch and grow a successful and highly profitable online business.

Figure 16.1. Louisdog.com targets a specialized market of upscale dog owners, offering them high-end furniture, clothing, and accessories for their pets. The exclusive dog bed design shown here is a bestseller for the company.

Jason Rich: What resources did you have available when you started Louisdog.com?

Taeyoung Oh: "I simply had an idea for a product line and I knew the niche customer base it would appeal to. I wanted to target upscale dog owners with high-end products for their pet that couldn't readily be purchased from their local pet store.

"In terms of finances, Bella Baek, cofounder and Chief Designer of Louisdog, and I only had $2,000 to invest when we launched the business. My partner and I used my parents' house as our office. We had only one personal computer, which we used at night, because at the time, we had jobs during the day. About half of our initial budget was dedicated to creating our Web page. It took us about one month to go from the idea phase to getting our business online and having our initial products manufactured on a small scale."

Rich: When choosing a niche market for your business, you chose the fast-growing luxury pet market. Would you elaborate on your decision?

Oh: "I saw an opportunity to develop a full product line of luxury dog products and distribute them through upscale retail chains worldwide, as well as on the Internet. Our sales are now increasing at a significant growth rate, especially in Europe.

"Right now, most of our sales revenue comes from the European market, especially the UK, France, Benelux, and Germany. In addition to our website, Louisdog products are currently being sold at premium department stores throughout Europe, like Harrods and Debenhams.

"The second biggest market for Louisdog is the U.S. Orders that are placed on our website by consumers and retailers; then all shipments are delivered directly from our warehouse in Korea by DHL."

Rich: Describe some of your unique products.

Oh: "At first, our pet furniture line was our top priority. However, we soon realized that the pet furniture market was limited, due to each product's physical size and price point. Manufacturing and shipping was expensive. One of our classic dog sofas, for example, sells for $350 (U.S.). It was easy to attract people's interest, but it was initially hard to turn that interest into sales. Our furniture did, however, play a major role in promoting Louisdog as a popular and premium brand.

"From our initial experience, we discovered that we needed to also produce items that are smaller, plus easier to sell and ship, at a relatively low price, compared to our high-end pet furniture.

Watch Out!

Pay close attention to the technology you'll need for your particular business. For example, if you'll rely on a large number of photos to display your products, it's imperative to use a host that can easily handle photo downloading.

"We soon began exploring the pet-carrier market. Thanks to several Hollywood movies, such as *Legally Blonde,* demand for premium pet carriers was skyrocketing in the U.S., as well as throughout the world. In 2002, Louisdog successfully added a pet-carrier line.

"Recently, our dog-apparel line has been added, and it has become more successful than our pet-furniture and carrier lines. We also produce and manufacture pet toys, accessories, and other accompanying items like mats and rugs. In fall 2005, we added a collection of collars and leashes."

Rich: By creating a high-end product line with international appeal, how are you catering to each country you market your products in?

Oh: "Right now, we manage three different websites which cater to customers in different regions. These sites are in Korean, English, and Dutch. We're currently developing sites in Chinese, Japanese, and German. Our entire team was educated in countries like China, Germany, France, Japan, and the UK, so we're able to successfully manage these websites internally."

Rich: What do you think it takes to successfully run an online business in today's marketplace?

Oh: "Your items have to be unique! For a small online retailer to be successful, you have to keep finding unique items that are not readily available at retail or even online from other websites. Ideally, you want to manufacture your own unique products that people can't find anywhere else. It is almost impossible to compete with giant online retailers if you're selling common products, especially when it comes to competing based on price."

Rich: When you initially created your website, did you use a turnkey e-commerce application or package, such as Yahoo! Stores?

Oh: "No. Our website was developed using a Linux program. I hired someone to create and design the website for us. In terms of maintaining the website, we quickly discovered that to achieve success, having an easy-to-use and visually pleasing user interface is critical.

"It's also important to have a stable e-commerce process and shopping cart, plus ways to communicate directly with your website's visitors. Once you've developed a user interface that works, don't make frequent changes to it. Updating the website's content is important, but the interface should remain consistent."

Rich: Did you incorporate any streaming audio or video components into your website to improve its look?

Oh: "No. We did incorporate a small amount of Flash programming, however. We primarily used text and photos, with a simple, yet visually appealing, Web-page design.

Rich: You've achieved a lot of success reaching your niche target customer base. What are some of the ways you continue to market, advertise, and promote Louisdog.com?

Oh: "Keyword advertising on Google, for example, works extremely well for us. We discovered, however, that banner advertising was totally ineffective.

"In terms of online promotions, we continuously target our present and past customers with special offers. To those who purchase Louisdog products directly from our website, we give a free gift, such as a pillow, blanket, toy, or an extra cushion. Since we have our own manufacturing facility, it is not difficult or costly to make those small items. Our customers love the presents. Based on what a customer orders online, they can choose a free gift with each order.

"Before launching a new promotion on a global scale, we typically test it out on one of our regional websites first."

Rich: What else do you do online to attract visitors, build customer loyalty, and generate repeat business?

Oh: "Online communities, chat rooms, and message boards are very popular in Korea, just as they are worldwide. We've created our own online community as part of our website. Web surfers are required to register in order to gain access. This allows us to gather names, addresses, e-mail addresses, and other pertinent information about our customers and potential customers.

"This online community offers us an excellent way to communicate directly with customers and prospects in an informal way. We constantly post new designs for products and offer previews of what we'll be offering in the near future, plus we offer a behind-the-scenes look at our company and its staff using text and photos.

"Our customers are also encouraged to post photos of their own dogs using our products, which become valuable testimonials. The photos and comments posted by customers show prospects what our products look like in real life.

"Through this online community, we're able to get valuable feedback to improve our products, plus build customer loyalty and provide excellent customer service. Communication has to be bilateral, not unilateral, with your prospects and customers. Through our message boards and direct customer contact, we strive to fix any customer complaints immediately and favorably."

Rich: Have you found it difficult convincing customers to purchase your expensive, high-end products online using a major credit card?

Oh: "No. E-commerce has become part of everyday life. We do not use a toll-free phone number for customers to contact us. All customer communication is done through e-mail or through our website. In addition to accepting major credit cards, we recently began accepting payments via PayPal, which has proven to be a welcome alternative for customers interested in making purchases."

Rich: Is there any other advice you can offer to someone interested in starting their own online business?

Oh: "First, find an item or product line that's truly unique. Then, determine the best ways to reach your niche target audience to tell them about your website along with your products.

"Having the right products is critical, but being able to successfully reach your customers will determine how successful your online business becomes.

"Invest a lot of time and hard work into your start-up business. If you're not good at website design, hire someone who is. Your website must look professional and be visually appealing, plus offer what the visitors are looking for."

Jeremy Alicandri, Founder/Owner, SimplyCheap.com

When most teenagers decide to get a job in order to supplement their weekly allowances, they turn to mowing lawns, getting an after-school retail job, or delivering newspapers. At age 16, however, Long Island, New York, native Jeremy Alicandri took a more high-tech approach.

With just $800 in start-up capital, which he raised by selling a birthday gift he received, Jeremy began purchasing and then reselling closeout consumer electronics on eBay.com.

Upon quickly discovering his business idea could become a profitable one, in 1999, he launched a stand-alone e-commerce site, called SimplyCheap.com. He continues to use Yahoo! Store as his turnkey solution for creating and managing his online business. Previously, he'd been operating a website for his school district, so he had some self-taught experience as a webmaster, but no business experience.

With the goal of selling closeout consumer electronics to price-minded consumers, Jeremy saw his business grow dramatically. By 2005, SimplyCheap.com's annual revenues exceeded $2.7 million. Running the business has become a full-time job for Jeremy, who now has seven full-time employees working for him.

Figure 16.2. SimplyCheap.com utilizes the Yahoo! Store platform to successfully offer a wide range of consumer electronics to its consumers at discounted prices.

Jason Rich: What was involved in launching SimplyCheap.com once you had experience selling products on eBay?

Jeremy Alicandri: "It took about $800 and just over one month for me to create my website using Yahoo! Store, to obtain my merchant account to accept credit cards, and to get my phone numbers in place. I already had some experience programming websites in HTML, so I had a good understanding of the Internet. In the first six months, I did something like $200,000 in revenue."

Rich: How important was the timing when you first launched SimplyCheap.com back in 1999?

Alicandri: "If I had launched SimplyCheap.com two years earlier than I did, I would be a multimillionaire right now. If I had launched the company two years later than I did, it never would have made a profit, due to the intense competition. Starting a *profitable* business online has become difficult. Simply launching an online-based business, however, has never been easier.

Bright Idea

Be aware of the difference between online advertising and more traditional ads. If someone sees your URL in a newspaper ad, for example, they'll have to log onto the Internet and type your address to access your site. If, however, you have an ad on an Internet site, a visitor can just click on the ad and be connected to your site.

"To be successful is difficult, due to the intense competition. It's hard to find a product that's truly unique. If you're selling products that are readily available on the Internet, dealing with the competition is going to be a huge challenge. Don't expect to make a profit overnight. Never overextend yourself in terms of what you spend on advertising and be sure to monitor the results of every advertising, marketing, and promotional effort you try."

Rich: How did you come up with the company name, SimplyCheap.com?

Alicandri: "I came up with about 100 different names for my company, which I actually liked better. The problem was, when I tried to register the domain names, they were all taken. I finally typed in SimplyCheap. The name made sense based on what I was trying to do, which was sell inexpensive, closeout consumer electronics and office-technology products. I thought there was a good market for consumer electronics. At the time, it was easy to be competitive selling these items because I was primarily competing with brick-and-mortar stores. This was back in 1999. I also had a strong familiarity and interest in consumer electronics."

Rich: Who is your target customer?

Alicandri: "Unlike many successful online businesses in operation today, my target customer is rather broad. Anyone can purchase consumer electronics because they appeal to many types of people. I see my primary target audience, however, as the savvy Internet shopper who knows how to surf the Web to find bargains. My audience is someone who knows how to use price-comparison websites. They're interested in finding the absolute lowest price for what they're looking to purchase."

Bright Idea

Although you don't need much specialized skill to start your own online business, any experience you have can give you a competitive advantage. For example, computer and design skills can help you design your site, and marketing skills can help you understand how to establish your brand effectively.

Rich: Now that you have a ton of competition online, what sets SimplyCheap.com apart?

Alicandri: "We continue to offer low prices, well-known, brand-name merchandise, and focus a lot of effort on providing top-notch customer service. We also offer a wide range of products. I don't think there's any single factor that sets us apart. It's a combination of factors. Because of what we're selling, we don't get a lot of repeat business, but we do receive a lot of referrals. There's not a lot of loyalty among Internet consumers."

Rich: When you were first launching your business, what were some of the unexpected obstacles you encountered?

Alicandri: "The biggest thing was dealing with the high level of lost income due to credit-card fraud. It continues to be a major issue and not something the merchant-account providers prepare you to deal with. Initially, I lost a lot of money as a result of credit-card chargebacks. One of the ways I've dealt with this is to teach myself all of the laws pertaining to a merchant's rights. We then established very specific order-taking policies and developed a multilayered approach to filtering our incoming orders to weed out the fraudulent ones. Statistically, we're doing a lot better at dealing with credit-card fraud than others. More recently, the challenge has been dealing with the incredible level of competition and being able to differentiate SimplyCheap.com from the competition."

Rich: Why did you choose Yahoo! Store as your turnkey solution? Are you pleased with the services that Yahoo! provides?

Alicandri: "I did a little bit of research back in 1999. I went with Yahoo! Store because of their well-known reputation and the functionality they offered. Later on, I did a lot of research to see if there were any better alternatives for SimplyCheap.com, but I didn't find anything better, which is why I've stayed with Yahoo! Store.

"This service is the most established e-commerce platform in the world. One in eight online stores is hosted and created using Yahoo! Store. There's also a lot of third-party support for this platform. I also like the integration between Yahoo! Store and the Yahoo! Shopping area. The back-end store-building features are also very easy to use. Like all of the turnkey solutions, Yahoo! Stores does have limitations, but we've been able to work around and overcome them."

Rich: From a website-design standpoint, what tips and strategies can you offer to help someone succeed?

Alicandri: "You need to think about how the customer will find your product(s) on your site. The visitor needs to be able to navigate around your website with ease. The visitor needs to be able to figure out where they are on the site and instinctively know where they need to go next. Also, make sure you make the pricing of your products very clear. It's also important to clearly post all of your policies, such as your return policy, and offer very accurate and detailed descriptions of your products.

"It's very easy for an online business operator to cut corners when it comes to creating detailed product descriptions, but these are very important. The customer needs to know exactly what they're buying and have no uncertainty in their mind. Using clear photos of your products is also very important."

Rich: On an ongoing basis, what type of marketing and promotion do you do for SimplyCheap.com?

Alicandri: "About 15 percent of our revenue is spent on marketing, promotions, and advertising. We do many different things to advertise and promote the company. We send out a monthly e-mail to our customers. We advertise with many of the third-party shopping sites. We also use banner ads and do extensive keyword advertising with both Yahoo! and Google. We've also developed an affiliate marketing program.

Watch Out!

Having a great idea isn't enough to be successful. You have to be realistic about all aspects of your online business, including how much capital you need to produce your product or deliver your service.

"In the past, what's worked the best for us is advertising on the third-party shopping sites, where surfers can go to quickly find the lowest price for what they're looking to purchase, then link to the merchant's website to place their order. All of these companies, however, have dramatically increased their cost-per-click rate, so our success rate with these services has deceased a bit. I strongly believe in the third-party shopping and price-comparison sites, but there's a lot of competition these days. They don't work unless you're offering the absolute lowest price for the products you're selling. People using those sites are looking for the most legitimate merchant with the lowest prices.

"All of the merchants are typically buying from the same distributors, which means the company offering the lowest price is making the least amount of profit. If you don't use those sites correctly, they can cost you a lot of money and not generate the results you're looking for. These sites definitely work better if you're offering a niche product and have less competition."

Rich: Out of all of the marketing, advertising, and promotional opportunities you've tried, what hasn't worked for you?

Alicandri: "Early on, we tried buying lists of e-mail addresses and using mass e-mail marketing, but that didn't work. Keep in mind, this is very different from sending e-mails to existing customers. We initially spent a lot of money on banner ads, but I wasn't impressed with those results, either. When I make a decision to spend money on advertising, I know there is risk involved, but I choose opportunities where the risk is in my favor. I try to calculate the risk involved."

Rich: Now that this is a full-time business for you and you have multiple employees, how do you spend most of your time?

Alicandri: "For me, this is a full-time, 40-plus-hour-per-week job. I spend a lot of my time doing administrative work and dealing with customer-service issues. I also work closely with our vendors and focus on making enhancements to the website.

"I pay attention to new technologies and decide what needs to be implemented and how. Recently, my challenge has been implementing ways to better automate our order processing. This has taken a lot of time. I am not someone who enjoys relaxing during my free time. I always need to be doing something that's productive. I think this is a personality trait that's helped my success."

Rich: What other advice can you offer to someone about to launch their own online business?

Alicandri: "Providing the best possible customer service is absolutely critical. It'll help you obtain repeat customers, increase word-of-mouth referrals, and decrease the number of credit-card chargebacks you receive. You need to be available via e-mail and telephone.

"When you make your policies clearly known on your website, managing your customer-service issues is that much easier. If you have a 14-day return policy, that needs to be clearly posted.

"Also, customers hate waiting to receive their order. Make sure you can process and ship orders quickly. If there's a delay, due to an item being backordered, you need to make the customer aware of this immediately. Also, never charge someone's credit card until you're ready to ship their order."

Rich: What new Internet-based technologies do you currently have your eye on and what would you like to incorporate into your website?

 Bright Idea

No matter how easy it is for your potential customers to order your product or service online, some people will still choose to place orders by phone or mail. So you'll need to offer good customer service in these more traditional areas as well.

Alicandri: "I've been looking at new product/photo display technology which allows merchants to display three-dimensional images of their products on the Web. In terms of advertising, there are a lot of new online-based opportunities available for reaching target markets. For example, Yahoo! offers what it calls Yahoo! Local for reaching customers in specific geographic regions."

Rich: What's the biggest mistake you've seen other online merchants make as they've launched their websites?

Alicandri: "Too many people launch their online business but don't have a good understanding of their products or their target market. They're also not prepared to deal with the unexpected challenges that arise, such as how to successfully deal with credit-card chargebacks, or they don't have the resources in place to maintain their business long enough to generate a profit, which could realistically take several months or longer."

Carole Jane Rossi, Founder/Owner, JOriginals.com

Three sisters, their mother, their grandmother, and their great-grandmother all shared a passion for knitting and crocheting. After years of crafting sweaters, scarves, ponchos, baby blankets, and a wide range of other items and then giving them as gifts to friends and family, Carole Jane Rossi came up with an idea. She decided to sell her creations at craft fairs and other festivals in and around Northford, Connecticut, where she lives.

By 2004, she'd established her company, J. Originals, and was earning a steady part-time income. With the help of her cousin, two sisters, and brother, she soon decided to expand her operation once again—this time, into cyberspace.

For Carole Jane Rossi, building J. Originals into a profitable part-time business has been a slow but steady process. First, she launched a website with no shopping-cart application and wasn't able to accept major credit cards. Anyone who wanted to place an order needed to call, fax, or use the traditional U.S. mail to send a check or money order.

As word about J. Originals spread, thanks to word of mouth and Carole's attendance at craft fairs (where she distributed business cards displaying her domain name), she soon signed up for a merchant account, allowing her to accept credit-card payments. Despite not having a shopping-cart application on her website, Carole immediately realized a dramatic boost in sales simply by accepting Visa and MasterCard.

Her cousin/webmaster then set out to add online ordering to the JOriginals.com website, allowing the site to become a fully functional online business. Having done this, Carole has transformed her love of knitting and crocheting into a profitable online business venture that continues to grow.

She recently caught the attention of the producers at *Martha Stewart Living* and is looking forward to soon retiring from her "real-life" job and dedicating all of her time and efforts to becoming an online entrepreneur and crafter.

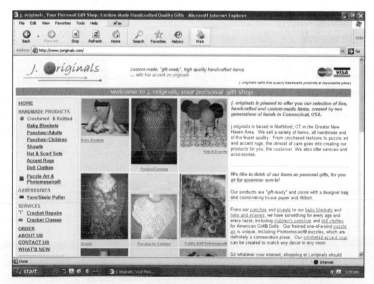

Figure 16.3. JOriginals.com allowed its founders to transform a hobby into a profitable online business venture. All of the items sold on this site are handcrafted and unique.

Jason Rich: What gave you the idea to launch JOriginals.com?

Carole Jane Rossi: "I, along with my sisters, learned how to crochet and knit as little girls. It's something that's always been a part of our lives. This all started as a passion and a hobby. I was giving so many of my items as gifts and received so many compliments, I saw an opportunity. I decided to launch the business. Each of my sisters and my brother has the middle initial 'J,' so we came up with the name 'J. Originals.'

"At the time we started the website, I had no computer experience. I decided to try selling my knit baby blankets on eBay, but I was competing against literally hundreds of other people selling their handmade knit baby blankets. I thought having my own website would allow me to achieve better success selling my items.

"My cousin knew about creating websites, so I recruited her to help me create the site, using photos of my products. For me, this was definitely the way to go, as opposed to using eBay. The JOriginals.com website was created from scratch.

"In terms of my time, I now dedicate about three days and two or three evenings per week to the business. This includes knitting time."

Rich: What type of financial investment did you initially make in your online business?

Rossi: "I was very fortunate in that my cousin created my website for free. This saved me a fortune in start-up costs. I had a discussion with my husband, and we used $1,000 of our savings to get the business started.

"I tried to do as much of the initial work as I could myself and discovered ways to save money. I printed my own business

 Moneysaver

Once you've established an online presence and a list of existing customers, you'll be able to market to them much more cheaply and effectively than you could with traditional tools. E-mail marketing is faster and cheaper than its print-mail counterpart.

cards on my computer, for example. As I made money, I invested it back into the business."

Rich: What lessons have you learned about running an online business?

Rossi: "You need to start small and slowly grow your business. I started with something very basic. I purchased a bunch of mannequins from stores going out of business and then bought photo equipment, so I could create professional-looking photos of my items to display on the website.

"At first, I didn't accept credit cards because I didn't have the money to establish a merchant account. I also didn't have a shopping-cart application tied into the website, which we quickly discovered was holding us back in terms of generating sales based on the level of traffic that was visiting the JOriginals.com website.

"If you don't have a lot of money to advertise and promote your online business, make sure you focus on search-engine optimization so people can find your website easily, especially if you have a lot of competition. Word of mouth and distributing my business cards at craft fairs and festivals has also driven a lot of traffic to my website. I haven't yet actually paid for any online advertising.

"The biggest lesson I've learned is that you have to work hard and be patient. Try to stay focused and make launching and operating your online business a fun project for yourself."

Rich: What surprised you the most once you became an online business operator?

Rossi: "I don't deal with rejection very well. For a while, the website didn't generate any orders whatsoever, and I took that as rejection, since I had worked so hard on establishing the business. It took me almost a year to earn the money so I could have a merchant account and ultimately boost sales. My family offered me a lot of moral support during this phase.

"Attending shows and fairs to show off my items in person definitely helped my business grow. Generating word of mouth generated positive results. Simply wearing my products when I go out also generates interest. I have sold a lot of product literally right off of my back."

Rich: How did you go about applying for and getting a merchant account?

Rossi: "I started by going to my local bank. They couldn't help me, but they gave me a referral to Global Payments [www.globalpaymentsinc.com]. I wound up meeting with a really nice and understanding woman at Global Payments, who helped me establish the merchant account quickly and for very little money. I can now accept credit cards online, as well as in person when I attend craft fairs. My upfront cost for the merchant account was about $200."

Rich: What have you done to differentiate yourself from other people selling their knitted items on the Internet?

Rossi: "I offer an array of different products, like baby blankets, hats, scarves, ponchos, and shawls. We've also created a very professional-looking website. I recently invented an item for knitters, called a 'Yarn Puller,' which I am currently seeking a U.S. Patent for. I'm selling this product on the website. It's a unique item that's only available from JOriginals.com."

Christian Girts, Founder/Owner, AnglersVice.com

Christian Girts was a successful businessman with a pressure-filled career on Wall Street. After dealing with the stresses of that job for a decade, he walked away and soon discovered how to transform his 20-year-long passion for fly-fishing into a profitable online business venture that he could operate from his home in San Francisco, California.

After some careful planning, Angler's Vice (www.anglersvice.com), a fly-fishing gear and supply company, was born. It's now a frequented website by fly-fishing hobbyists throughout the world.

Having achieved success operating this venture, Christian soon began planning a spin-off company, called BassBoyz.com, which targets the much larger and fast-growing bass-fishing hobbyist market.

Not only has Christian been able to create a profitable online business based around his longtime hobby, he's also discovered a very niche market that he is able to reach successfully and cater to through both traditional and online advertising techniques, most notably through the use of Yahoo!'s Search Marketing service (http://searchmarketing.yahoo.com).

Figure 16.4. To create this professional-looking website, the company's founder takes all of his own product photos, using a digital photography studio he built in his basement.

Jason Rich: How did you decide to go from working on Wall Street to launching an online business?
Christian Girts: "When I decided I'd start my own business, I knew it would have something to do with fly-fishing. I initially looked into opening a traditional brick-and-mortar retail store, but felt the investment in real estate and the hassle of staffing wasn't what I wanted to deal with. I spoke with several people who were successful online business entrepreneurs and was

Watch Out!

As mentioned repeatedly in this book, always keep in mind the technology your customers have. For example, although faster technologies exist, many Web surfers still have dial-up Internet connections as opposed to DSL or broadband. You need to design your website so that it's convenient for everyone to visit.

soon sold on the idea of being able to launch this type of business with low overhead."

Rich: Who is your target market for Anglersvice.com?

Girts: "Part of the reason why I went after the fly-fishing market first is because the average hobbyist earns over $100,000 per year, is between their mid-30s and mid-60s, and they have an above-average level of education. They also spend at least $600 per year on fly-fishing equipment.

"Fly-fishing is a very low-growth industry, and there's a lot of competition in it. We currently sell rods and reels, sunglasses, fishing gear, accessories, and a massive assortment of fly-fishing flies, fly-tying materials, and tools. We also sell how-to books and videos.

"My new business, BassBoyz.com, will cater to a much larger potential customer base. The bass-fishing market is 100 times larger than the fly-fishing market and growing rapidly at a rate of 15 to 20 percent per year."

Rich: With such a large selection of items, do you inventory everything or have you arranged for products to be drop-shipped by your vendors and wholesalers?

Girts: "We warehouse everything in my 700-square-foot basement at home. This allows us to ensure that all orders are processed within 24 hours or less. Fast order processing and superior customer service have been a critical element in our success. This, along with a large selection of merchandise, sets us apart from our competition. Being an experienced fly-fisherman, I know exactly how to cater to this market."

Rich: Do you have any employees?

Girts: "I have a part-time, paid college intern who helps me out during peak periods or when I want to take time off to go fishing. Otherwise, I run the business myself. At an absolute minimum, I spend four hours per day working on the business, maintaining the website, processing orders, and dealing with customer issues. Because the business is located in my basement, it never really closes. I often work up to 15 hours per day. It's easily a 40-hour-per-week, full-time job, but I can make my own hours."

Rich: Aside from fast order processing and offering superior customer service, what do you do to differentiate yourself from your competition?

Girts: "I have created my own in-house digital photo studio, complete with lighting and backdrops, and have become proficient using Photoshop [www.adobe.com/products/photoshop/main. html] to fine-tune the product photos used on my website.

"All of the product photos on the website are created by me. Because I am a fly-fisherman myself, I know what my customers are looking for. I am able to take custom photos that show off the features of the products that I know my customers will be most interested in. The product photos available from the various manufacturers didn't meet my needs."

Rich: Knowing that you have to reach a very niche target market, how have you accomplished this?

Girts: "On a monthly basis, I use a combination of traditional, direct mailings to our existing customers and potential customers who appear on specialized mailing lists which I purchase. I send out a mailing, which advertises specials along with a monthly newsletter. I also utilize print advertising in fly-fishing magazines, and use some of the more popular online marketing tools, like the Yahoo! Search Marketing service.

"Initially, when I launched the business, I invested a lot more on traditional magazine print advertising, but this is an area I plan to scale back on. In the first six months of operation, I learned a lot about how to successfully market the business.

"After trying several similar services that are available for online marketing, I now exclusively use Yahoo!'s Search Marketing services. I've also utilized search-engine-optimization techniques.

"Online marketing can get very expensive if you're not careful. I wound up using Yahoo!'s Search Marketing services because it's cost-effective and their customer service is excellent. My representative from the company also enjoys fly-fishing as a hobby, so he truly understands the niche market I'm trying to reach. As a result, his recommendations have generated excellent results in terms of boosting new traffic to the website based on search-engine marketing, using a fine-tuned list of about 400 keywords.

"There are a lot things you can do on your own when it comes to utilizing search marketing. I strongly recommend that you spend a little extra money upfront, however, and align yourself with a customer service rep from the service, like Yahoo! Search Marketing, you choose to work with. They can actually save you a lot of time and money, plus generate much better results than you can do on your own with limited knowledge and experience. The initial money you spend upfront for the personalized service will quickly become the best advertising and promotional money you spend.

"In a typical month, I spend between $2,500 to $3,000 on advertising and promotions, which right now is a significant percentage of our sales. A large portion of that is for expensive print ads, which are being scaled back."

Rich: When you first launched the business, what were some of the unexpected challenges you encountered?

Girts: "On the technology side, there weren't a lot of hiccups. It took me longer than expected to really fine-tune the website and develop the right product assortment. There was also a large learning curve, because I had no background in graphic design or website design.

"To operate the website, I use a powerful, full-featured, e-commerce platform from Ibex Solutions [www.arcticibex.com]. They've been extremely helpful in creating and hosting the actual website. I have been extremely pleased with the overall product and the personalized service this company has offered. I think it's a really slick platform that requires absolutely no programming knowledge on my part.

"For me, the biggest challenge was selecting the right selection of products to offer on the website. I found that some distributors and wholesalers didn't want to sell to online businesses because they wanted to protect their traditional retailers and dealers."

Rich: What type of initial financial investment did you make in the company to get it off the ground?

Girts: "Not including inventory costs, I invested about $5,000 to get the website designed and launched. I left my full-time job in September and had the website operational by November."

Rich: What's one feature or design element of your website that you've discovered has generated the most revenue?

Girts: "The ArticIbex e-commerce platform I use automatically tracks what a customer is purchasing and makes recommendations to the customer in real time about other products that might be of interest. When someone selects a specific item, a message will appear that states, 'People who have purchased this item have also purchased this item,' and an item name, photo, and description are automatically displayed. This feature alone has generated a tremendous amount of additional sales."

Rich: What other advice can you offer to new online business operators?

Girts: "There's a lot of competition out there. You need to realize that. I have learned to avoid using drop-shippers and maintain my own inventory. If you use a drop-shipper, you're giving up product control. That can hurt your business. Make sure you do some research about the suppliers you choose to work with.

Ensure that inventory will be available to you when you need it and that your suppliers have no qualms working with an online merchant.

"In terms of obtaining a merchant account, choose a well-known and established company that has a solid reputation and that utilizes all of the latest security bells and whistles. Your customers need to feel confident in your company, in the products you're offering, and in the security of their online transactions."

Scott Meyer, Founder, OnlyOneCreations.com

Since childhood, Scott Meyer has been what he calls a "crafting hobbyist" using woods, metals, and plastics to create his one-of-a-kind artwork. Earlier in his life, he worked as a tool-and-die maker. He later changed careers and worked full-time as a computer network engineer.

Using the skills, experience, and knowledge he's acquired over a lifetime, Scott now works full-time operating a handful of small businesses that have allowed him to transform his hobby into a profit-making venture.

As a craftsman and artist, Scott Meyer has launched a website to sell his handcrafted, one-of-a-kind fountain pens and fine writing instruments. His target consumers are upscale pen collectors and affluent businesspeople.

Each of his pens is handmade using a variety of materials ranging from gold and platinum to titanium, rubber, acrylics, and other exotic materials. Many are commissioned specifically by a customer and ordered online from the OnlyOneCreations.com website.

Based in Caledonia, Michigan, Scott is a perfect example of someone who has transformed his hobby and passion into a profitable online business venture, albeit on a relatively small scale that targets a very niche market. He operates a website he's created from scratch using his self-taught programming knowledge.

Figure 16.5. OnlyOneCreations.com has allowed founder Scott Meyer to develop a successful business targeting a specialized market (comprised of pen collectors) with his one-of-a-kind fine-writing instruments, which he creates by hand.

Jason Rich: How did you get started creating fountain pens and fine writing instruments?

Scott Meyer: "As a child, I built model steam engines as a hobby. I was also extremely interested in crafting using exotic materials. Later in life, I developed an interest in fine writing instruments and decided to begin creating them from scratch as a hobby. Fine writing instruments make excellent gifts and are in high demand by affluent collectors. The art of writing a handwritten note can be much more effective than writing an e-mail, for example. I create one-of-a-kind writing instruments that are works of art unto themselves and allow people to better enjoy the art of writing."

Rich: How did you come up with the name OnlyOneCreations. com?

Meyer: "The concept behind my fine writing instruments is that each of them is a one-of-a-kind work of art. I wanted to communicate this in the name of my company and in the domain name for my online business. I am not selling mass-produced products."

Rich: How and when did you launch OnlyOneCreations.com?

Meyer: "I launched the online aspect of the business in late 2003. Initially, I hired a professional Web designer to create my website. While she was a skilled Web-page designer, she didn't understand how to create e-commerce websites, nor did she truly understand my business, so I wound up having to recreate the website myself from scratch using HTML and other higher-level programming languages, which I taught myself.

"I am currently working on another website which is osCommerce-based [www.oscommerce.com]. This is a popular, heavily supported, open-source, e-commerce business solution that's not as turnkey as Yahoo! Store, for example, but it's highly customizable if you know some website-design basics."

Rich: How much did you initially invest in the launch of your online business and how long did the process take?

Meyer: "I spent about $700 to hire the website designer to initially create my site. That wasn't money well spent. In terms of launching the entire business, I invested about $3,000, which included purchasing materials to create the writing instruments.

"From the time I came up with the idea to do this to the time OnlyOneCreations.com went online, it took about six months. A lot of that time was spent educating myself about e-commerce and website creation."

Rich: Since launching OnlyOneCreations.com, has it been as successful as you'd hoped?

Meyer: "Honestly, no. Only recently have I begun utilizing traditional, but highly targeted, print advertising to promote the website in conjunction with utilizing search-engine-optimization techniques and other inexpensive online-based advertising and promotional opportunities, such as link exchanges. I quickly discovered that driving a niche-target customer to a website is more challenging than I originally expected.

"Until recently, I relied on word of mouth and referrals. One promotional opportunity which has worked well is donating items to charities for use in traditional auctions or giveaways. In exchange for the donation, the charity promotes my company.

"Early on, I tried using banner ads to promote the site, but they simply didn't work."

Rich: What advice can you offer to an online business operator in terms of successfully marketing their new venture?

Meyer: "Teach yourself search-engine optimization and take advantage of the free opportunities to promote your website that the search engines offer. Search-engine optimization takes time and effort, but it's well worth the investment if you want to inexpensively drive traffic to your website. You can hire a consultant or a company to help you with search-engine optimization, but it's much cheaper to do it yourself once you learn how.

"I recently began running one-sixth-of-a-page traditional print ads in *Pen World,* which is a very specialized publication targeted specifically to pen collectors. The print ads have been very successful in terms of reaching my target audience and driving traffic to the website."

Rich: From a website-design standpoint, what design techniques have you discovered are important?

Meyer: "Your website must quickly establish a sense of trust between your customer and you, the business operator. If you can't develop that trust, the visitors won't be transformed into customers. On my website, I have a 'Meet The Artist' page as well as an 'FAQ' page, plus detailed pages about the different types of fine writing instruments I create. By reading these pages, the visitor gets to know more about me as an artist."

Rich: How much time do you spend working each week?

Meyer: "Between OnlyOneCreations.com and my other businesses, I wind up working between 80 and 90 hours per week, but a lot of that time is spent actually crafting the handmade writing instruments. A single fountain pen, for example, might take me anywhere from one to three days to complete, depending on the materials I'm using and the complexity of the design that's been commissioned by the client. This is a full-time job, but it's also my passion."

Chris Gwynn, Founder/CEO, Fridgedoor.com

Fridgedoor.com (www.fridgedoor.com) is one of the Web's many e-commerce success stories. When company founder Chris Gwynn began searching for an online business opportunity, he wanted a product to sell that would be of interest to a niche market, fun to work with, easy to ship, and one that customers could decide to purchase easily based on seeing a picture.

After considering various products and doing research on various industries, Gwynn decided to sell refrigerator magnets on the Web. After all, he thought, everyone has a refrigerator, and many people enjoy decorating their kitchen's largest appliance with cute magnets. Fridgedoor.com also caters to a growing collector's market.

The concept for Fridgedoor.com first began taking shape in May 1997. Gwynn had spent more than a decade working for large companies in the online business industry. During his career, he experienced five massive layoffs (several of which he survived) within the companies he was working for, and he wanted to find a career opportunity that offered greater stability and control. He decided to launch an online business, at first as a project in his spare time to supplement his income.

These days, Fridgedoor.com is Gwynn's full-time job. He currently has several part-time employees who assist with online marketing and order fulfillment. Based on the growing success of his company, he has begun expanding into other collectible markets by launching spin-off businesses.

Figure 16.6. Since it was founded in 1997, Fridgedoor.com has created a successful and ever-growing online business selling inexpensive refrigerator magnets to collectors.

Jason Rich: After you came up with the idea to sell refrigerator magnets online, what steps did you take to make your business idea a reality?

Chris Gwynn: "One of my previous employers was AT&T. I was a product manager for a service they were developing designed to help small businesses build their own website. While working on that project, I learned about all of the services out there, and chose Yahoo! Store to develop my e-commerce site with. I believe Yahoo! Store offers the greatest ease of use and the most power. Their service is also competitively priced. I had taken some HTML programming courses, but I don't consider myself a programmer or website designer.

"I took advantage of Yahoo! Store's introductory offer, and for $100 created a ministore selling 20 different magnets. I wanted to see if this was a viable business before making a large investment of time and finances. The research I did beforehand on the magnet industry showed that it could be viable. Nobody was selling magnets on the Web. I created the online ministore in May 1997. After I discovered this type of business had potential, I spent most of my spare time that summer actually creating a complete e-commerce site/online store for Fridgedoor.com. I had to contact many different manufacturers of magnets to acquire inventory, create the website, and develop a marketing plan.

"It was in September 1997 that I actually launched Fridgedoor.com as a full-scale online business with over 500 items. Currently, I offer over 1,500 different magnet items, all of which I keep in inventory."

Rich: When you first decided to sell refrigerator magnets online, did you do a lot of research about the magnet industry?

Gwynn: "I had seen a chain of retail stores that sold nothing but refrigerator magnets. The stores are located primarily in high-rent tourist areas, and they seemed to be earning money. I realized that if a chain of retail stores could survive selling nothing but magnets, an online-based store could be successful as well. I did my own research to determine the size of the market and learned about the major manufacturers and distributors of refrigerator magnets. I determined that the overall magnet market is pretty small, but it was big enough for me to create an online store and be successful at it."

Rich: Where is your business based?

Gwynn: "Fridgedoor.com is based in my home in Quincy, Massachusetts. My basement is my warehouse, and several spare rooms in my house are used as offices."

Rich: What type of initial financial investment was made in the company?

Gwynn: "I invested my own money. I'd rather not give an exact figure in terms of my investment, but it was over $20,000. Getting a website actually created and online is only a small part of the time and financial investment necessary to operate a successful online business. The costs of inventory, computer equipment, and marketing are all substantial. I had to purchase a rather sophisticated mail-order-management software package, called

Mail Order Manager from Dydacomp Development Corporation, which represented an over $2,000 investment in software alone. This software is used to automate almost every aspect of the business's operation, from order fulfillment to inventory management. The software isn't 100 percent ideal, but it's the best software I could find to meet the needs of my business."

Rich: What is one of the most important lessons you've learned since starting Fridgedoor.com?

Gwynn: "I discovered it's critical to control the entire order-fulfillment process. This means having your inventory on hand instead of having products drop-shipped. When an order comes in, you need to immediately send the customer an e-mail acknowledging the order. That order then needs to be processed promptly, with the merchant being in total control of the package's look and content. When the order is sent, a second e-mail needs to be sent to the customer providing the shipment's tracking number, if applicable. I buy my inventory from over 50 different suppliers, so having products drop-shipped, while it might look like an attractive business option on paper, really isn't viable for my business."

Rich: You mentioned making a substantial investment in the marketing of your company. What exactly did this entail?

Gwynn: "A lot of the advertising and marketing we tried early on was expensive and didn't work. I tried using paid banner ads and wound up wasting a lot of money. Our average order is about $20, so finding paid advertising opportunities that would pay for themselves was very difficult.

"I have since focused exclusively on guerilla marketing techniques to promote the business. I created an affiliate program that has worked extremely well. Fridgedoor.com is always looking for related sites to place a link back to us. In return, we will pay these sites 15 percent of all sales that are generated from their site's traffic. Payments are made quarterly by check, and are accompanied by a detailed traffic/revenue report. In addition, affiliates are provided with a URL to view the daily updates to their traffic/revenue report. This report is generated by an independent third party—our hosting provider, not us.

"For people who are interested in magnets or the characters featured on the magnets, such as Jeff Gordon or NASCAR magnets, one of the best ways to reach them is to develop relationships with the many small Jeff Gordon or NASCAR fan-operated websites, for example. I have someone working part-time doing nothing but contacting various fan websites about joining our affiliate program. We have over 400 affiliates, and that generates a good portion of our daily traffic.

"I also continue to spend a considerable amount of time keeping our site optimized for all of the Internet search engines. We've also had a lot of success in creating traffic for our site using online and offline public relations efforts . . . . Since we're part of Yahoo! Store, we benefit from traffic that Yahoo! generates for us, but we can't rely on this traffic to support our entire business."

Rich: How is marketing an online business different from marketing a traditional business?

Gwynn: "Based on my experience, a traditional business will typically spend about 2 to 20 percent of its gross revenue on marketing and advertising. To successfully promote an online business and generate enough traffic to the site to make it viable, it's necessary to spend upwards of 60 percent of gross revenue. Thus, if you don't have enough money set aside in your budget to market your online business properly, you should seriously reconsider launching it."

Rich: What are some of the lessons you've learned based on your experiences dealing with customers online?

Gwynn: "It's important to respond to people immediately, whether it's to fill an order or answer a question. Never fight with a customer. Give them what they want to make them happy. I try to provide our customers with as much information as possible about us as a company, our products, our shipping procedures, and whether or not our products are on backorder.

Bright Idea

By dividing your product line into convenient categories, such as type of product or price level, you make it easier for your potential customer to locate what they want quickly. For example, if you're selling DVDs, you could divide your inventory based on movie genre (horror, sci-fi, drama, comedy, and so on).

People really appreciate receiving e-mail that keeps them up-to-date on the status of their orders."

Rich: How do you deal with people who are afraid or hesitant to place credit-card orders online?

Gwynn: "On our website, we list our phone number and a fax number for placing orders. We don't, however, offer a toll-free number. I have found that some people feel more comfortable faxing their credit-card information when placing an order than they do placing it directly on the website. About 80 percent of our orders are placed online. The rest are either faxed in or placed by phone.

"On our site, we explain the online security we use; if someone is afraid to place an order online, however, there is nothing we can say to convince them it's safe. These people prefer actually speaking with a person. Being a small company, people don't necessarily know who we are, so I think it's more of a trust issue than an issue of online security. On our website, we have an 'Info' area that describes our company and contains a picture of us, so people can see the human beings behind the company."

Rich: How do you spend your time dealing with the day-to-day operations of your business?

Gwynn: "This is now a full-time job for me. I start working every weekday around 8:30 a.m. and keep working until around 6:00 p.m. If necessary, I'll also spend time working in the evenings and on weekends. About 50 percent of the man-hours spent operating the business are spent filling orders. A lot of my time is also spent on marketing."

Rich: What has been one of the biggest challenges in operating an online business?

Gwynn: "I think one of the most important lessons someone operating this type of business needs to learn is how to transform a visitor to your website into a paying customer who actually places an order. A huge part of this involves making people feel comfortable and welcome when they visit your site.

"I have learned that having a well-structured site is also important. People need to be able to find the items they're looking for as quickly as possible. I believe having a website design that's as clean and basic as possible is important. We use simple graphics and a basic layout, which makes it easier for a customer to navigate through our site."

Rich: What steps do you take to generate repeat business and build customer loyalty?

Gwynn: "In addition to offering top-notch customer service, we are constantly adding new items to the Fridgedoor.com site. We also change the featured item each week, and every month have some type of special offer. One of the most successful special offers we've run is to include free first-class-mail shipping on all orders over $25. On our home page, we also invite people to subscribe to our free monthly e-mail-based newsletter. Each month, we send out this newsletter, which describes new items and mentions our special promotions. This newsletter has been a very successful tool for generating repeat business."

Just the facts

- Although there are incredible opportunities for success in cyberspace, striking it rich by launching an online business isn't something that will happen quickly.

- It takes a much bigger financial investment than most people think to launch an online business and do it well, but it is still a smaller investment than opening a retail store or establishing a traditional mail-order business.

- When choosing a service to host your online business, don't rely on the marketing materials supplied by the service itself. It's important to do your own research to compare various services.

- It's critical to control the entire order-fulfillment process. This means having your inventory on hand instead of having products drop-shipped.

- To create a successful e-commerce website, you can create the site from scratch (programming it using HTML and other languages), use a complete turnkey solution (such as the one offered by Yahoo! Stores), or use a semi-turnkey package, such as osCommerce, which is extremely powerful, flexible, and well supported by third-party developers.

- To ensure that your product photos look their absolute best, consider taking your own digital photos and editing them using a software package such as Photoshop.

Glossary

The following are definitions for terms you'll want to know as you begin designing and managing your online business, as well as handling the online advertising, marketing, and promotional aspects of your business.

ad click   The user's action of clicking on an advertising-related file. A click does not guarantee that the user actually arrives at the requested (target) URL (a *click-through*). Ad clicks are nearly always greater than ad click-throughs. (Contrast to *ad transfer.*)

ad transfer (also ad *click-through*)   The successful arrival of a user at an advertiser's website, resulting from the user's click on an ad. (In some cases, because of technical difficulties, an ad click might not result in an ad transfer.)

ad view   The viewing of an online-based advertisement (equivalent to ad impression).

affiliate marketing   An advertising method based on the *cost-per-action (CPA)* or *cost-per-click (CPC)* payment method. Websites run advertisers' banners for free, but the websites then get paid on any sales or registrations that result from visitors who click on the banner. There are many third-party companies that manage affiliate marketing programs for websites.

animated ad   An ad that automatically changes in appearance. These ads are most frequently created using Flash, Shockwave, JavaScript, or Java.

bandwidth   This is the amount of data transmitted or received over a period of time. For example, a dial-up modem that works at 57,600 bps has twice the bandwidth (twice as fast) as a modem that works at 28,800 bps. From the standpoint of a website operator, the higher your bandwidth, the larger amount of traffic your site can handle at one time.

banner burnout   Occurs when a banner ad has been shown to the same Web surfer(s) so many times that the click-through rate drops dramatically. To avoid this, create multiple ads and rotate them regularly.

blog   A blog is an online-based digital diary, journal, or forum where anyone can write anything and make it available for the Web-surfing public in minutes. It incorporates basic text, graphics, and photos. A blog can be an excellent marketing and promotional tool for an online business operator.

click-through   When it comes to online display advertising, such as banner ads or button ads, if a Web surfer clicks on the ad in order to visit a website, that's a click-through. The *Click-Through Rate* is the percentage of people who see the ad and actually click on it. When conducting a banner ad campaign, for example, you want to strive for the highest Click-Through-Rate possible.

colocation   Some businesses choose to maintain their own Internet server to host their website. When a company uses their own server, but has it located and maintained by a Web-hosting company located off-site, this is called colocation.

cookie   A cookie can be used to identify Web surfers and potentially prepare customized Web pages for them. Information provided by the user (or about the user) can be saved in a cookie, which is sent to and stored by the surfer's browser. This information can be accessed and utilized by the website during subsequent visits.

cost-per-action   When paying for online advertising, often through an affiliate program, one way you'd be billed is based on a cost-per-action model. Each time a Web surfer does something specific, such as sign up for an electronic newsletter or takes an online survey, you'd pay the website that displayed your ad or link.

CPC (cost per click)   The fee an online advertiser pays every time a Web surfer clicks on their ad, link, or banner.

CPM (cost per *mille* [French for *thousand*])   CPM refers to the total cost of 1,000 visitor requests to view an ad. The CPM describes the advertiser's cost for making 1,000 impressions with its ad.

dead link   A link is a way for Web surfers to click on an icon, graphic, or line of text (a hyperlink) and be instantly transferred to a specific URL, Web page, or area within a Web page. A dead link occurs when the URL is not valid. This results in the Web surfer receiving an error as opposed to being able to access the desired Web page. From a website designer's standpoint, dead links should be avoided. They convey a lack of professionalism and are frustrating for the Web surfer when encountered.

dedicated hosting   A Web-hosting feature allowing a site to have its own server. This is more flexible than shared hosting, because the webmaster maintains full control over the back end of the server, including choice of the operating system used. Administration and maintenance of the server is handled by the hosting company.

drop-shipping   Instead of maintaining an inventory of items you wish to sell, some online business operators are able to develop a drop-shipping relationship with their wholesalers. This means that when one of your customers places an order, the actual items are shipped directly from your wholesaler to your customer.

expandable banner   A banner ad that expands into a larger, usually animated, display ad when initiated by the Web surfer.

Flash   This is popular animation creation software developed by Macromedia. Flash animations require little bandwidth, making them friendly to users with low or high-speed connections. To view a Flash animation, a Web surfer must have the appropriate plug-in installed with their browser.

floating ads   Display ads that appear and "float" over the content a surfer is looking at on the page.

GIF (Acronym for Graphic Interchange Format)   A standard format used to encode graphic images across different types of computers or computer software. For stylized images such as icons or logos, the GIF format is usually more compact than alternative encodings of the same image.

GIF89a   A GIF format that contains several separate GIF images that are presented sequentially by a Web browser; the sequence of images is usually used to create a visual animation (animated GIFs).

hit   A request for a document or other Web asset received by a Web server from a user's Web browser. Note that a hit is generated for each distinct file included in a Web document: a Web page containing a graphical navigation bar, an ad banner, and a company logo image would generate four hits to a Web server (the document plus the three images). Hits typically inflate the count of actual page requests by about 5 to 10 times; page requests inflate the number of unique users by about 4 times.

HyperText Markup Language (HTML)   This is a popular programming language for developing websites. Web pages are built with HTML tags or codes embedded in the text. HTML defines the page layout, fonts, and graphic elements, as well as the hypertext links to other documents.

impressions   The number of times an ad banner is requested by site visitors' browsers and hopefully actually viewed by the Web surfers. In an advertising contract, the number of "guaranteed impressions" refers to the minimum times an ad has the opportunity to be seen by visitors.

in-banner All text and graphic images stay within the actual size of the display ad.

JPEG This is a popular graphics format utilizing a special data compression technique. Photos and graphics that you want displayed in a high resolution, without a large file size, can be saved in this format and displayed on a Web page.

keyword A word or phrase that is entered into a search engine in an effort to get the search engine to return matching and relevant results. Search engines such as Google and Yahoo!, along with many websites, feature advertising based on keyword targeting.

merchant account Before your online business can begin accepting major credit cards as payment for purchases, you, as the business operator, must secure a merchant account from a bank, financial institution, or company that offers this type of service. A sign-up fee, monthly fee, and per-transaction fee typically applies. Yet, being able to accept credit cards from your e-commerce website is an absolute must. When shopping for a merchant account, look for companies offering the lowest rates and fees.

opt-in list While sending spam is considered to be an annoyance and can hurt the reputation of your company, sending marketing and advertising materials in the form of e-mail or an electronic newsletter to people who specifically request the information can be a viable and highly effective marketing tool. When someone signs up to be on your company's e-mail list (and receive your e-mails) or subscribes to your electronic newsletter, they're opting in.

page view Each time a Web surfer comes to your site and views one or more of the site's pages, this is referred to as a page view.

PayPal This is a service owned by eBay, which makes securely paying for online purchases without using a major credit card possible. It was originally created as a way for online auction buyers and sellers to transfer funds to each other online. e-commerce sites can now accept PayPal as an alternative (or in addition to) accepting credit cards through a merchant account. With PayPal, people can make purchases using funds from their checking account, debit card, or via a credit card.

PDF or **Portable Document Format**   This is a popular file format developed by Adobe Systems. It captures formatting information from a variety of applications, making it possible to send formatted documents and have them appear on the recipient's monitor or printer exactly as they were intended. To view a PDF file, Adobe Reader, a free application distributed by Adobe Systems, is required.

plug-in   A plug-in is a software application that gets added to a Web browser or used in conjunction with a browser to add functionality, such as the ability to display video or hear streaming audio. There are a handful of popular browser-plug ins that website designers can utilize, such as Flash, for creating animations.

pop-up ad   Ads that pop onto the screen, typically in a separate Web browser window, which appears over what the surfer is looking at.

search-engine optimization   The process of registering your website with the various search engines and using meta tags, keywords, and other techniques to ensure prominent placement.

search marketing   Website optimization, managing paid advertising solutions, content creation and optimization, submission to directories, and link-building campaigns are all advertising techniques that fall under the search-marketing category. Google's AdWords service is an excellent example of search marketing.

Secure Electronic Transaction Protocol (SET)   This is a programming and technology industry standard that ensures secure credit card processing via the Internet. As an online business operator, it's imperative that your business be able to process credit-card purchases securely using this or similar technology. Contact your merchant account provider or your Web-hosting service for details.

shopping cart A program that handles the e-commerce portion of a website. Shopping cart software allows users to browse for and purchase products online.

spam This is unsolicited and unwanted e-mail that gets sent to one or more recipients. Spam often contains an advertising message. Most Web surfers consider spam messages to be an annoyance. Spam is the equivalent to junk mail.

SSL (Secure Sockets Layer) A security protocol designed to protect confidential or sensitive information required to handle e-commerce transactions (like online credit-card purchases).

sticky content A website is considered to offer "sticky" content when surfers remain at that site longer than normal. Sticky content could be any "added-value" content, such as informative articles, free information, chat rooms, message boards, an online newsletter, contests, online games, surveys, and so on.

streaming To make a website more appealing, many companies choose to incorporate video and/or audio. The process of streaming video or audio via the Web allows surfers to view this content in real-time, without first having to download large media files.

target audience This is the group of people that fits the demographic you're trying to reach in order to sell your products or services. They're the people you believe will be the most interested in what you're selling. Your target audience can be defined by age, sex, race, income, geographic area, religion, special interests, occupation, or any other factor or factors.

traffic A measure of the volume of electronic files distributed to the volume of individual visitors to a website. Traffic has been measured in terms of *hits, page views, sessions,* or *unique users.*

turnkey Throughout this book, references are made to turnkey solutions for creating and managing an e-commerce website. These companies offer all of the tools and Web-hosting services needed to create, manage, and operate an online business venture. Yahoo! Store and eBay ProStores are examples of turnkey solutions offered to online business operators at a pre-set monthly fee.

URL (Uniform Resource Locator)   This is the address a browser uses to find and display Web content. For example, www. JasonRich.com. URLs are registered with a domain registrar.

unique users   The number of different individuals who visit a website within a specified period of time. The implicit redundancy (there is no such thing as a "non-unique user") arises from websites' past difficulty with (or indifference to) counting traffic or impressions as hits rather than as individual users. Website registration or user *cookies* are the standard methods for identifying unique users.

up-sell/cross-sell   When an online customer chooses an item to purchase, a well-designed e-commerce website will automatically display one or more additional items a customer might be interested in purchasing. This might be related accessories, similar items in a different color or style, an additional warrantee or something else that shopper would be interested in purchasing at that time as well. This process is called up-selling or cross-selling. A good example can be found at Amazon.com.

VoIP (Voice Over IP)   This technology allows people to make and receive local and long distance telephone calls using the Internet as opposed to traditional phone lines.

WHOIS   A central database which tracks all domain name/IP registrations. No matter which domain registrar you use to register your website, the information gets registered with WHOIS.

Resource Guide

The following are the most helpful Web addresses mentioned in this book (listed alphabetically).

1001 Fonts	www.1001fonts.com
1-Hit	www.1-hit.com
About.com	www.about.com
Act!	www.act.com
Adobe	www.adobe.com
Advertising Age	www.adage.com
AdWeek	www.adweek.com
AltaVista.com	www.altavista.com
Amazon	www.amazon.com
American Express	www.americanexpress.com
America Online	www.aol.com
America's Business Funding	www.businessfinance.com
Angler's Vice	www.anglersvice.com
Aria Financial Corp.	www.arianet.com
Ask Jeeves	www.ask.com
Bacons	www.bacons.com
Banner 123	www.banner123.com
BannerSwap	www.bannerswap.com
Better Business Bureau	www.bbb.org
BLOGOMONSTER	www.blogomonster.com

Bloggers.com	www.bloggers.com
Build Traffic	www.buildtraffic.com
Builder.com	www.builder.com
Burrelle's Media	www.burrellesluce.com
Canalys	www.canalys.com
Card Services International	www.cscicard.com
CheapClick	www.cheapclick.com
Cingular	www.cingular.com
Click4Click	www.click4click.com
Clickincome.com	www.clickincome.com
Clickz	www.clickz.com
Clip Art	www.clip-art.com
C|Net Builder	www.Builder.com
Comcast	www.comcast.com
Copyright Office	www.copyright.gov
Corel	www.corel.com
Credit Merchant Account	www.merchantaccount.net
Datexchanges	www.datexchanges.net
Dell Computer	www.dell.com
DHL	www.dhl.com
Direct PC	www.direcway.com
Dotster.com	www.dotster.com
EarthLink	www.earthlink.com
ECHO	www.echo-inc.com
eBay ProStores	www.prostores.com
eBay Stores	http://stores.ebay.com
eBay.com	www.ebay.com
eFax	www.efax.com
eLance	www.elance.com

Electronic Transfer, Inc.	www.paymentmall.com
Engine Seeker	www.engineseeker.com
eSiteBlast	www.esiteblast.com
Exchange-It	www.exchange-it.com
Federal Trade Commission	www.ftc.org
FedEx	www.fedex.com
Find-A-Host	http://findahost.smesource. com/hosting
Firefox	www.firefox.com
Folder Express	www.folderexpress.com
FontSite	www.fontsite.com
Fridgedoor.com	www.fridgedoor.com
Galaxy Internet Services	www.gis.net
Gateway Computer	www.gateway.com
Getz Color Graphics	www.getzcolor.com
Gif Wizard	www.gifwizard.com
GoDaddy.com	www.godaddy.com
Google	www.google.com
Google AdWords	www.adwords.com
Hello Direct	www.hellodirect.com
Home Office Direct	www.homeofficedirect.com
Host Index	www.hostindex.com
Host Review	www.hostreview.com
Host Search	www.hostsearch.com
HotBot.com	www.hotbot.com
Interschola	www.interschola.com
Jason Rich's website	www.jasonrich.com
Java Boutique	www.javaboutique.internet. com

JOriginals	www.joriginals.com
Juno	www.juno.com
Levenger	www.levenger.com
LinkShare	www.linkshare.com
Louis Dog	www.louisdog.com
LowerMyBills.com	www.lowermybills.com
LView Pro	www.lview.com
Lycos	www.lycos.com
Macromedia	www.macromedia.com
Merchant Account Company	www.merchantaccount.com
Merchant Express	www.merchantexpress.com
Merchant Warehouse	www.merchantwarehouse.com
Microsoft	www.microsoft.com
MSN	www.msn.com
NameStormers	www.namestormers.com
Net Mechanic	www.netmechanic.com
Netscape	www.netscape.com
Network Solutions	www.networksolutions.com
NetZero	www.netzero.com
NexTag	www.nextag.com
OfficeMax	www.officemax.com
Only One Creations	www.onlyonecreations.com
osCommerce	www.oscommerce.com
Palm	www.palm.com
PalmOne	www.palmone.com
Pasware	www.pasware.com
PayPal	www.paypal.com
Postmaster Direct	www.postmasterdirect.com
PR Place	www.prplace.com

Price Grabber	www.pricegrabber.com
PriceScan	www.pricescan.com
PriceWatch	www.pricewatch.com
Promotion Pro	www.promotionpro.biz
Publishing Perfection	www.publishingperfection. com
QuickBooks	www.quickbooks.com
Register.com	www.register.com
SCORE	www.score.org
Shopping.com	www.shopping.com
Shopzilla	www.shopzilla.com
SimplyCheap.com	www.simplycheap.com
Sprint PCS	www.sprintpcs.com
Stamps.com	www.stamps.com
Staples	www.staples.com
Submission Pro	www.submission-pro.com
Submit Express	www.submitexpress.com
Superior Bankcard	www.ezmerchantaccounts. com
T-Mobile	www.tmobile.com
TrafficRanking.com	www.trafficranking.com
UPS	www.ups.com
U.S. Patent & Trademark Office	www.uspto.gov
U.S. Postal Service	www.usps.com
Verizon Online	www.verizon.com
Vonage	www.vonage.com
W Promote	www.wpromote.com
Wacom	www.i3now.com

Web Promotion, Inc.	www.webpromotion.com
WhatIs.com	www.whatis.com
Wiley Publishing	www.wiley.com
Word Tracker	www.wordtracker.com
Xara	www.xara.com
Yahoo!	www.yahoo.com
Yahoo! Search Marketing	http://searchmarketing.yahoo.com
Yahoo! Web Hosting	http://smallbusiness.yahoo.com/webhosting/
Yahoo! Merchant Solutions	http://smallbusiness.yahoo.com/business_services/

You Sold It, Now Ship It

One of the first things you'll need to deal with after actually launching your website and opening for business is the process of shipping the items you sell to your new customers.

Although you can buy shipping materials at your local office-supply superstore (such as OfficeMax, Office Depot, or Staples), UPS Store, FedEx/Kinko's location, or even U.S. Post Office, you'll save a fortune if you buy your shipping supplies in bulk from a wholesaler.

In addition to shipping supplies, such as envelopes, boxes, labels, packing tape, Styrofoam peanuts, bubble wrap, invoices, and so on, you'll probably want to open accounts with popular shippers such as UPS, FedEx, and DHL, plus rent a postage machine.

Depending on what you're shipping and how fast you need it to get there, you have many options. Ideally, you'll want to give your customers a choice, allowing them to select their preferred shipping method (and ultimately bill the customer for shipping costs). Some shipping companies, such as UPS and FedEx, for example, will provide you with free shipping materials. Even the United States Post Office will provide free shipping materials for anything shipped via U.S. Priority or U.S. Overnight Express Mail.

Appendix C

No matter how you wind up shipping your items, keep in mind that you'll want to use a method that enables you to track your package(s) online using a tracking number supplied by the shipping company. Delivery confirmation, requiring the recipient's signature upon delivery, and insurance are other add-on services you should also consider.

As an online business owner, it's critically important to respond to new orders and ship them as quickly as possible, ideally within 24 to 48 hours.

When you receive a new order, immediately e-mail your new customer acknowledging the receipt of the order (and thank them for it). You'll then want to e-mail the customer again as soon as their order ships. In this second e-mail, provide the customer with pertinent shipping information about their order, such as the shipping method used, the package's tracking number, and anticipated delivery date.

The following are a handful of resources to help you set up your company's order-fulfillment and shipping department.

Shipping companies

- **Airborne/DHL**   800-CALL-DHL; www.DHL-USA.com
- **FedEx**   800-238-5355; www.FedEx.com
- **FedEx/Kinko's Stores**   800-254-6567; www.FedEx.com
- **UPS**   800-PICK-UPS; www.UPS.com
- **UPS Stores**   888-346-3623; www.upsstore.com
- **U.S. Post Office**   www.USPS.com

Postage machines and stamps

- **NeoPost**   800-NEO-POST; www.neopost.com
- **Pitney Bowes**   203-356-5000; www.pitneybowes.com
- **Stamps.com**   www.stamps.com
- **United States Post Office (Click 'N Ship)**   www.USPS.com

Shipping-supply companies

- **Boxes.com** www.boxes.com
- **Bubble Fast** www.bubblefast.com
- **Go Packaging** www.gopackaging.com
- **Office Depot** www.officedepot.com
- **OfficeMax** www.officemax.com
- **Packaging Supplies** www.packagingsupplies.com
- **PaperMart** www.papermart.com
- **Staples** www.staples.com
- **Uline** www.uline.com
- **ValuDisplay** www.valudisplay.com
- **VeriPack** www.veripack.com

Shipping tips from the post office

The United States Post Office offers the following advice for preparing a package to be shipped.

1. **Choose the right box.** Choose a box with enough room for cushioning material around the contents. If you are reusing a box, cover all previous labels and markings with heavy black marker or adhesive labels.

2. **Provide cushioning.** Place the cushioning all around your items. Close and shake the box to see whether you have enough cushioning. Add more newspaper, Styrofoam, or bubble wrap if you hear items shifting.

3. **Seal the box properly.** Tape the opening of your box and reinforce all seams with 2" wide tape. Use clear or brown packaging tape, reinforced packing tape, or paper tape. Do not use cord, string, or twine.

4. **Use the correct address.** Using a complete and correct address is critical for efficient delivery. Use ZIP Code + 4 when possible.

5. **Add desired additional services.** Delivery confirmation, signature confirmation, return receipt, and insurance, for example, are available for an additional fee from the U.S. Postal Service.

6. **Calculate the correct postage.** See this Web page for current rates and details: http://postcalc.usps.gov.

7. **Drop off the package.** Packages may be handed to your carrier or taken to the Post Office. Packages may also be dropped into a blue collection box. Since the tragedies of 9/11, packages over a certain weight must be brought to the post office in-person, unless you're using a registered postage machine to pay for the shipping (as opposed to traditional stamps.) Contact the post office for shipping guidelines for packages.

Important Information About Copyrights and Trademarks

Respecting copyrights and trademarks you don't own

As you begin planning and creating your website, you might be tempted to "borrow" artwork, text, graphics, audio clips, video clips, animation sequences, or other materials that you don't own. On the Web, hundreds of sites offer royalty-free, public-domain Web-page content you're free to download and use on your page. If any type of content you want to use is copyrighted or trademarked by another individual or organization, however, you should obtain permission to use that content before adding it to your site. Unless the content you want to use specifically states that it's available royalty free and copyright free, assume that the content is copyrighted.

Information about copyrights

According to the Library of Congress Copyright Office, "Copyright" is a form of protection provided by the laws of the United States Title 17 to the authors of "original works of authorship," including literary, dramatic, musical, artistic, and certain other intellectual works. This protection is available to both published and unpublished works. Title 17 of the 1976 Copyright Act generally gives the owner of the copyright the exclusive right to do and to authorize others to do the following:

- To reproduce the copyrighted work in copies or phonorecords
- To prepare derivative works based on the copyrighted work
- To distribute copies or phonorecords of the copyrighted work to the public by sale or other transfer of ownership, or by rental, lease, or lending
- To perform the copyrighted work publicly, in the case of literary, musical, dramatic, and choreographic works; pantomimes; motion pictures; and other audiovisual works
- To display the copyrighted work publicly, in the case of literary, musical, dramatic, and choreographic works; pantomimes; and pictorial, graphic, or sculptural works, including the individual images of a motion picture or other audiovisual work
- In the case of sound recordings, to perform the work publicly by means of a digital audio transmission

It is illegal for anyone to violate any of the rights provided by the copyright code to the owner of the copyright. These rights, however, are not unlimited in scope. Title 17/1-107 through Title 17/1-120 of the 1976 Copyright Act establish limitations on these rights. In some cases, these limitations are specified exemptions from copyright liability. One major limitation is the doctrine of "fair use," which is given a statutory basis in Title 17/1-107 of the 1976 Copyright Act. In other instances, the limitation takes the form of a "compulsory license," under which certain limited uses of copyrighted works are permitted upon payment of specified royalties and compliance with statutory conditions. For further information about the limitations of any of these rights, consult the copyright code or write to the Copyright Office.

Copyright protects "original works of authorship" that are fixed in a tangible form of expression. The fixation need not be directly perceptible as long as it can be communicated with the aid of a machine or device. Copyrightable works include the following categories:

1. Literary works
2. Musical works, including any accompanying words
3. Dramatic works, including any accompanying music
4. Pantomimes and choreographic works
5. Pictorial, graphic, and sculptural works
6. Motion pictures and other audiovisual works
7. Sound recordings
8. Architectural works

These categories should be viewed broadly. For example, computer programs and most "compilations" can be registered as "literary works"; maps and architectural plans can be registered as "pictorial, graphic, and sculptural works."

Several categories of material are generally not eligible for federal copyright protection. These include, among others, the following:

- Works that have not been fixed in a tangible form of expression

- Titles, names, short phrases, and slogans; familiar symbols or designs; mere variations of typographic ornamentation, lettering, or coloring; mere listings of ingredients or contents

- Ideas, procedures, methods, systems, processes, concepts, principles, discoveries, or devices, as distinguished from a description, explanation, or illustration

- Works consisting entirely of information that is common property and containing no original authorship (for example, standard calendars, height and weight charts, tape measures and rulers, and lists or tables taken from public documents or other common sources)

The use of a copyright notice is no longer required under U.S. law, although it is often beneficial. Because prior law did contain such a requirement, however, the use of notice is still relevant to the copyright status of older works.

Notice was required under the 1976 Copyright Act. This requirement was eliminated when the United States adhered to the Berne Convention, effective March 1, 1989. Although works published without notice before that date could have entered the public domain in the United States, the Uruguay Round Agreements Act (URAA) restores copyright in certain foreign works originally published without notice.

The Copyright Office does not take a position on whether copies of works first published without notice before March 1, 1989, which were distributed on or after March 1, 1989, must bear the copyright notice.

Use of the notice might be important because it informs the public that the work is protected by copyright, identifies the copyright owner, and shows the year of first publication. Furthermore, in the event that a work is infringed, if a proper notice of copyright appears on the published copy or copies to which a defendant in a copyright infringement suit had access, then no weight shall be given to such a defendant's interposition of a defense based on innocent infringement in mitigation of actual or statutory damages, except as provided in Title 17/5-504 of the copyright code. Innocent infringement occurs when the infringer did not realize that the work was protected.

The use of the copyright notice is the responsibility of the copyright owner and does not require advance permission from, or registration with, the Copyright Office.

The notice for visually perceptible copies should contain all of the following three elements:

1. The symbol © (the letter in a circle), or the word "Copyright" or the abbreviation "Copr."; and

2. The year of first publication of the work. In the case of compilations or derivative works incorporating previously published material, the year date of first publication of the compilation or derivative work is sufficient. The year date can be omitted where a pictorial, graphic, or sculptural work, with accompanying textual matter, if any, is

reproduced in or on greeting cards, postcards, stationery, jewelry, dolls, toys, or any useful article; and

3. The name of the owner of the copyright. The name of the owner of the copyright in the work, or an abbreviation by which the name can be recognized, or a generally known alternative designation of the owner. Example: © 1998 John Doe.

In general, copyright registration is a legal formality intended to make a public record of the basic facts of a particular copyright. However, registration is not a condition of copyright protection. Even though registration is not a requirement for protection, the copyright law provides several inducements or advantages to encourage copyright owners to make registration. Among these advantages are the following:

- Registration establishes a public record of the copyright claim.

- Before an infringement suit may be filed in court, registration is necessary for works of U.S. origin and for foreign works not originating in a Berne Union country.

- If made before or within five years of publication, registration will establish *prima facie* evidence in court of the validity of the copyright and of the facts stated in the certificate.

- If registration is made within three months after publication of the work or prior to an infringement of the work, statutory damages and attorney's fees will be available to the copyright owner in court actions. Otherwise, only an award of actual damages and profits is available to the copyright owner.

- Registration allows the owner of the copyright to record the registration with the U.S. Customs Service for protection against the importation of infringing copies. For additional information, request Publication No. 563 from www.customs.ustreas.gov/index.htm; ATTN: IPR Branch,

Franklin Court, Ste. 4000, U.S. Customs Service, 1301
Constitution Ave. N.W., Washington, DC 20229.

- Registration may be made at any time within the life of the
  copyright. Unlike the law before 1978, when a work has
  been registered in unpublished form, it is not necessary to
  make another registration when the work becomes published, although the copyright owner may register the published edition, if desired.

To register a work, send the following three elements in the
same envelope or package to

Library of Congress
Copyright Office
Register of Copyrights
101 Independence Ave. S.E.
Washington, DC 20559-6000

- A properly completed application form
- A nonrefundable filing fee of $30 for each application
- A nonreturnable deposit of the work being registered. The
  deposit requirements vary in particular situations.

All copyright application forms can be downloaded from the
Internet and printed for use in registering a claim to copyright.
The forms can be accessed and downloaded by connecting to
the Copyright Office home page on the World Wide Web. The
address is www.loc.gov/copyright.

Trademark information

A trademark is a word, phrase, symbol, or design, or combination of words, phrases, symbols. or designs, that identifies and
distinguishes the source of the goods or services of one party
from those of others. A service mark is the same as a trademark
except that it identifies and distinguishes the source of a service
rather than a product. The terms "trademark" and "mark" are
used to refer to both trademarks and service marks, whether

they are word marks or other types of marks. Normally, a mark for goods appears on the product or on its packaging, whereas a service mark appears in advertising for the services.

A trademark is different from a copyright or a patent. A copyright protects an original artistic or literary work; a patent protects an invention. For copyright information, see the preceding section.

What is a trademark? A trademark includes any word, name, symbol, or device, or any combination, used, or intended to be used, in commerce to identify and distinguish the goods of one manufacturer or seller from goods manufactured or sold by others, and to indicate the source of the goods. In short, a trademark is a brand name.

A service mark is any word, name, symbol, device, or any combination used, or intended to be used, in commerce to identify and distinguish the services of one provider from services provided by others, and to indicate the source of the services.

Trademark rights arise from either (1) actual use of the mark, or (2) the filing of a proper application to register a mark in the Patent and Trademark Office (PTO) stating that the applicant has a *bona fide* intention to use the mark in commerce regulated by the U.S. Congress. Federal registration is not required to establish rights in a mark, nor is it required to begin use of a mark. However, federal registration can secure benefits beyond the rights acquired by merely using a mark. For example, the owner of a federal registration is presumed to be the owner of the mark for the goods and services specified in the registration, and to be entitled to use the mark nationwide.

There are two related but distinct types of rights in a mark: the right to register and the right to use. Generally, the first party who either uses a mark in commerce or files an application in the PTO has the ultimate right to register that mark. The PTO's authority is limited to determining the right to register. The right to use a mark can be more complicated to determine. This is particularly true when two parties have begun use of the same or similar marks without knowledge of one another and neither has a federal registration. Only a court can render a decision about the right to use, such as issuing an injunction or awarding damages for infringement. It should be noted that a federal registration can provide significant advantages to a party involved in a court proceeding. The PTO cannot provide advice concerning rights in a mark. Only a private attorney can provide such advice.

Unlike copyrights or patents, trademark rights can last indefinitely if the owner continues to use the mark to identify its goods or services. The term of a federal trademark registration is 10 years, with 10-year renewal terms. However, between the fifth and sixth year after the date of initial registration, the registrant must file an affidavit setting forth certain information to keep the registration alive. If no affidavit is filed, the registration is canceled.

Anyone who claims rights in a mark may use the TM (trademark) or service mark designation with the mark to alert the public to the claim. It is not necessary to have a registration, or even a pending application, to use these designations. The claim may or may not be valid. The registration symbol, ®, can be used only when the mark is registered in the PTO. It is improper to use this symbol at any point before the registration issues. Please omit all symbols from the mark in the drawing you submit with your application; the symbols are not considered part of the mark.

To learn more about trademarks and trademark law, contact a lawyer or visit the United States Patent and Trademark Office's website at www.uspto.gov. You can search the USPTO's Trademark Database Online at www.uspto.gov./main/sitesearch.htm.

If you need answers to specific trademark questions or want to know more about trademarks in general, contact the Trademark Assistance Center at 800-786-9199. If you live in Northern Virginia, the number is 571-272-1000.

A

B